QUEER FRIENDSHIP

Friendship in the classical world was celebrated as among the highest human achievements: Nothing was more likely to lead to the divine than looking for it in the eyes of a friend. In exploring the complexities of male–male relations beyond the simple labels of sexuality, *Queer Friendship* shows how love between men has a rich and varied history in English literature. The friend could offer a reflection of one's own worth and a celebration of a kind of mutuality that was not connected to family or home. These same-sex friendships are memorable because they give shape to the novels of which they are a part, and they question the assumption that the love between friends is different from the love between lovers. *Queer Friendship* explores English literary friendship in three ways: the elegiac, the erotic, and the platonic, by considering a myriad of works, including Sterne's *Tristram Shandy*, Tennyson's *In Memoriam A.H.H*, and Dickens' *Great Expectations*.

GEORGE E. HAGGERTY is Distinguished Professor and Chair in the Department of English, University of California, Riverside.

QUEER FRIENDSHIP

Male Intimacy in the English Literary Tradition

GEORGE E. HAGGERTY

CAMBRIDGE
UNIVERSITY PRESS

CAMBRIDGE
UNIVERSITY PRESS

University Printing House, Cambridge CB2 8BS, United Kingdom

One Liberty Plaza, 20th Floor, New York, NY 10006, USA

477 Williamstown Road, Port Melbourne, VIC 3207, Australia

314–321, 3rd Floor, Plot 3, Splendor Forum, Jasola District Centre, New Delhi – 110025, India

79 Anson Road, #06-04/06, Singapore 079906

Cambridge University Press is part of the University of Cambridge.

It furthers the University's mission by disseminating knowledge in the pursuit of education, learning, and research at the highest international levels of excellence.

www.cambridge.org
Information on this title: www.cambridge.org/9781108418751
DOI: 10.1017/9781108291385

First published 2018

Printed in the United States of America by Sheridan Books, Inc.

A catalogue record for this publication is available from the British Library.

Library of Congress Cataloging-in-Publication Data
Names: Haggerty, George E. author.
Title: Queer friendship : male intimacy in the English literary tradition / George E. Haggerty.
Description: Cambridge, United Kingdom; New York: Cambridge University Press, 2018. | Includes bibliographical references and index.
Identifiers: LCCN 2017060365 | ISBN 9781108418751 (hardback)
Subjects: LCSH: English fiction – History and criticism. | Gays in literature. | Male friendship in literature.
Classification: LCC PR830.G34H34 2018 | DDC 823.009/352664–dc23
LC record available at https://lccn.loc.gov/2017060365

ISBN 978-1-108-41875-1 Hardback

For my husband Ed O'Bannon
and
in memory of Philip Brett

Contents

Acknowledgments

I would like to thank Rebecca Addicks-Salerno for her tireless research and editing assistance throughout this entire project. Other colleagues and friends who have read and commented on portions of this work include: Heidi Brayman, Joseph Childers, Bea Ganim, John Ganim, Alessa Johns, Katherine Kinney, Jeanette Kohl, Susan L. Lanser, Stephen Orgel, Ruth Smith, and Traise Yamamoto.

I am also grateful to two anonymous readers at Cambridge University Press. Their thoughtful and generous criticism has made this a far better book than it would otherwise have been.

I want to thank the Regents of the University of California for sabbatical leave and research funds that helped me to keep this project alive during a busy academic schedule.

I want to thank family, especially my sister Pat De Camp and my brother Rick Haggerty, and friends, especially Robert Glavin and Davitt Moroney. They all encouraged work on this book and allowed me to talk about it at length. I owe so very much to my husband Ed O'Bannon, who has lived with this project for several years. I dedicate this book to him and to the memory of my first partner, Philip Brett, who died in 2002. Philip taught me the meaning of love and friendship, and I would like to think he would be proud of what I have made of them in this book and in the life I am sharing with Ed.

Introduction
Male Friendship and Greek Love

Friendship is rarely as simple as it sounds. In the classical world, it was celebrated as among the highest human achievements. Nothing was more likely to lead to the divine than looking for it in the eyes of a friend. The friend could offer a reflection of one's own worth and a celebration of a kind of mutuality that was not connected to family or home. As Ivy Schweitzer reminds us, "by the time of Socrates, an ideal of friendship emerged as a primary personal connection that was separate from the exchange relations of marriage and commerce and vitally concerned the moral character and disinterested actions of the partners."[1] Throughout the history of Western culture, this notion of a friend might have held sway, or it might just as easily have been challenged or undermined. Schweitzer's study considers how this ideal changes over time. It is important to emphasize, however, just how central this concept remains to the articulations of friendship throughout the early modern age in England, and indeed still has resonance in the literature of the eighteenth and nineteenth centuries.

If friendship has always held a special place in the English literary imagination, then it is worth looking at a group of literary works to tease out the meaning of this trope in both personal and cultural terms. In drama, fiction, opera, and oratorio, friendship was regularly represented and enthusiastically celebrated throughout the eighteenth and nineteenth centuries. From the celebration of heroic friends in the dramas of the late seventeenth century to the representation of more common friends in novels such as *Great Expectations* or *The Longest Journey*, the concept of friendship offered a means whereby same-sex intimacy could be explored within a context that was culturally idealized. At times, as the novels of Smollett or Wilde suggest, these friendships are openly erotic and potentially transgressive.

---

[1] Ivy Schweitzer, *Perfecting Friendship: Politics and Affiliation in Early American Literature* (Chapel Hill: University of North Carolina Press, 2006), 32.

At others, as in Sterne or Scott, the intensity of friendship is not especially erotic or transgressive, but it can speak for itself.

Friends are physical, emotional, and psychological partners, who love and are loved in ways that culture at large has always preserved for cross-gender relations. What continues to fascinate me, however, is not the transgressive potential of this love, but rather its own seeming normativity.[2] So often in the works I discuss, men turn to each other for emotional support and erotic-seeming expressions of devotion. Friendship models offer writers the opportunity to contain this emotional excess in intimately personal terms.[3] The more closely we look at these models of male friendship, the more clearly they redefine and at times even confound our sense of the normative. Indeed, they repeatedly push in directions that force us to reconsider what friendship actually means when it is invoked as a trope in the literature of the eighteenth and nineteenth centuries.[4]

Male–male relations may have been idealized in the culture as a whole, but these examples challenge that idealization, either with something more than "male bonding" can accommodate, or with an obsessional fixation that belies their seemingly secondary role. These same-sex friendships are memorable because they give shape to the novels of which they are a part; and they have cultural significance because they have been hiding in plain sight throughout the period I examine. Just like Tennyson's *In Memoriam*, which became a widely celebrated poem despite its insistence on male love – or, perhaps because of that love – these works harbor loving relationships that are all too easy to overlook.[5] We often want to assume that the love between friends is different from the love between lovers. As I hope to show, that is rarely an easy distinction.

The works I discuss celebrate male friendships in ways we are only just beginning to understand. I use the overarching rubrics of "Elegiac Friendship," "Erotic Friendship," and "Platonic Friendship" in order to distil the central rationales for intimate relations. By grouping works

---

[2] George E. Haggerty, *Men in Love: Masculinity and Sexuality in the Eighteenth Century* (New York: Columbia University Press, 1999), 26.

[3] George E. Haggerty, *Horace Walpole's Letters* (Lewisburg: Bucknell University Press, 2011), chapter 1.

[4] Laurie Shannon calls Renaissance friendships "homonormative." See *Sovereign Amity: Figures of Friendship in Shakespearean Contexts* (Chicago: University of Chicago Press, 2002), 19. See below, pp. 6–8.

[5] What we mean by "love" has of course tremendous bearing on this argument. As Susan Ackerman argues, in *When Heroes Love: The Ambiguity of Eros in the Stories of Gilgamesh and David* (New York: Columbia University Press, 2005), the meaning of the Hebrew word for love, specifically as used in the Old Testament story of David and Jonathan from 1 and 2 Samuel, has everything to do with how we can interpret that story (170–4).

together in this way, moreover, I can place them in meaningful relation to one another and use them more precisely to expand our understanding of how friendship functions in these seemingly disparate literary texts. The groupings also help to explain significant features of each example.

While I look closely at the concept of friendship, building on the work of Alan Bray and others, in order to show how friends became a touchstone of intimate value in the works of writers from Defoe to Forster, I also try to show how certain friendships defy even our broadest understanding of that term.[6] When friendships become tantamount to a marriage between men, as they do in many of the works I discuss, then even the term friendship itself starts to seem inadequate. I will discuss such configurations at length. It is no accident that friendships are central to the works I discuss, nor is it perplexing that they loom so large in the lives of which they are a part.

In his deeply powerful study of friendship, *Love Undetected: Notes on Friendship, Sex, and Survival,* Andrew Sullivan makes a cogent argument about the place of friendship in the lives of gay men: "For, of all our relationships, friendship is the most common, and the most natural. In its universality, it even trumps family. Many of us fail to marry, and many more have no children … But any human being who has lived for any time has had a friend."[7] Sullivan wants to distinguish friends from lovers. It is an important feature of his argument that erotic desire does not complicate friendships: "[a virtuous man] comes to a friend in exactly the opposite way that a lover comes to a beloved. He comes not out of need, or passion, or longing. He comes out of a radical choice. Friendship, in this way, is a symbol of man's freedom from his emotional needs; love is a symbol of his slavery to them."[8] I think these distinctions between erotic love and friendship are sometimes overly rigid; but even as he celebrates gay friends as a special case, Sullivan is looking for a kind of love that transcends (rather than avoids) the erotic. I am confused that he does not turn to Plato in order to solve his dilemma, but instead he considers friendship's failures and wonders with Cicero, "how can one love another imperfect human being?"[9] Sullivan's friendships are liable to this kind of betrayal, unless they are secured from betrayal in the virtue of Christ. If instead of Christ

---

[6] I am speaking of Alan Bray's study, *The Friend* (Chicago: University of Chicago Press, 2003); another important study is that of Richard Dellamora, *Friendship's Bonds: Democracy and the Novel in Victorian England* (Philadelphia: University of Pennsylvania Press, 2004).

[7] Andrew Sullivan, *Love Undetected: Notes on Friendship, Sex, and Survival* (New York: Vintage, 1999), 176.

[8] Sullivan, *Love Undetected*, 211.

[9] Sullivan, *Love Undetected*, 225.

we imagine a higher power of love in friendship – an ideal, say, of platonic love – then we may be able to understand how friendships became so important in the English literary tradition.

For the purposes of this introduction and a consideration of friendship in these terms, I think the most useful text of Plato's would be the *Lysis*, in which he discusses the nature of friendship and love between young men and their admirers, both young and old. In the dialogue, Socrates advises the young Hippothales, who is infatuated with Lysis, how best to express his love and what he can expect in return for his affection. Lysis is an attractive young man: "He stood out among the boys and older youths, a garland on his head, and deserved to be called not only a beautiful boy but a well-bred young gentleman."[10] While Socrates carries on his conversation with some other young men, Lysis keeps looking over, and finally he joins in the conversation. Socrates engages him in a conversation in which the young man is led point by point to declare, with Socrates' encouragement, that he would choose wisdom over other virtues: "if you become wise, my boy, then everybody will be your friend, everybody will feel close to you because you will be useful and good" (694). Later, Socrates turns to Lysis's friend Menexenus and says:

> So Menexenus, tell me something … You know how it is, everybody is different: one person wants to own horses, another dogs, another wants money, and another fame. Well, I'm pretty lukewarm about those things, but when it comes to having friends, I'm absolutely passionate … and, I swear by Zeus above, that I would rather possess a friend than all Darius' gold, or even than Darius himself. That's how much I value friends and companions. And that's why, when I see you and Lysis together, I'm really amazed; I think it's wonderful that you two have been able to acquire this possession so quickly and easily while you're still so young. (695)

After this flattering opening, Socrates challenges Menexenus to talk about the kind of affection that friends feel. At first Menexenus insists that he and Lysis love each other equally, but then Socrates poses a relation in which one participant may love and the other hate: "Isn't this how men are often treated by the young boys they are in love with? They are deeply in love, but they feel that they are not loved back, or even that they are hated" (696); and he goes on to ask: "then which is the friend of the other? Is the lover the friend of the loved, whether he is loved in return or not, or is even hated? Or is the loved the friend of the lover? Or in a case like

---

[10] Plato, *Lysis*, trans. Stanley Lombardo, in *Plato: Complete Works*, ed. John M. Cooper (Indianapolis: Hackett, 1997), 687–707 (691). Further parenthetical references are to this edition.

this, when the two do not both love each other, is neither the friend of the other?" (696).[11]

Before going further or anticipating where Socrates hopes to lead his interlocutor – and of course the conversation itself is the model of platonic love at work – it is important to notice the role that love, which for Plato clearly includes the concept of sexual desire, plays in this articulation of friendship. That is the assumption with which Socrates starts the entire discussion. Later, when he moves beyond physical love per se to talk about the love of the beautiful, that attachment to beautiful bodies has not been lost:

> Maybe the old proverb is right, and the beautiful is a friend. It bears a resemblance, at any rate, to something soft and smooth and sleek, and maybe that's why it slides and sinks into us so easily, because it's something like that. Now I maintain that the good is beautiful. What do you think? (700)

What is fascinating about Socrates' perspective here is his attachment of the good to this concept of the beautiful. Friendship encompasses the good and the beautiful by means of a physical connection that is unmistakable. I cannot here follow the ups and downs of the *Lysis* any further, but I can say that this concept of friendship, which includes intense personal affection, is something that reappears in the works I am going to discuss, even as the friendships themselves can function also in the public in ways that will become clear as I proceed.

In this context, it is interesting to consider a provocative and often overlooked comment made by Alan Bray in the Introduction to his posthumous study, *The Friend*. In discussing some of the features of this topic, Bray makes the following assertion:

> What I have sought to convey is the conviction at the heart of these cultural practices that the ethics of friendship operated persuasively only in the larger frame of reference that lay *outside* the good of individuals for whom the friendship was made. To pose the historical question in terms of the essential good or ill of sexuality therefore, the question that has come to dominate the corresponding debates, operates necessarily by contrast *within* the friendship. The inability to conceive of relationships in other than sexual terms says something of contemporary poverty; or, to put the point more precisely, the effect of a shaping concern with sexuality is precisely to obscure that larger frame.[12]

---

[11] For a similar assessment of *Lysis*, see Schweitzer, *Perfecting Friendship*, 33–4.
[12] Bray, *The Friend*, 6.

Before I address some questions that emerge from this statement, I want to make clear what a splendid job Bray has done in taking friendship out of the chambers of privacy and into the public staterooms of power. He has made it clear that in early modern culture, in England and elsewhere, friendship, even publicly acknowledged and sworn bonds between two men, most often served a larger cultural purpose of alliance and public recognition. I do not need to rehearse the splendid work Bray has done with Antonio Perez and the accusation of sodomy to make it clear that I find this work valuable and inspiring in many ways.[13]

In this book too, Bray makes the absolutely persuasive point that in early modern culture friendship serves a public function, and that expressions of intimacy are best understood in terms of power relations and jockeying for position among members of the elite class of courtiers and those aspiring to the court. These observations are a wonderful corrective to the impulse among gay and queer scholars to eroticize friendship first and then afterwards look for the possible public implications of the eroticization. I think Bray is right to say that "the inability to conceive of relationships in other than sexual terms says something of contemporary poverty," and I want to start with that comment in the hopes of articulating an alternative thesis.[14]

If we look at those friendships embedded in the literary culture of eighteenth- and nineteenth-century England, a richer and more varied picture emerges. For me, what Bray's stunning study leaves out is the way that emotion, once expressed, can begin to convey a kind of intimacy that the term "friendship" can hardly represent. I am not saying that I want to reintroduce sexuality into these friendships – I see what Bray means by poverty, and I have confronted those limitations in my own work on Walpole and others – but instead I want to think about the kinds of male intimacy that Bray describes and reintroduce private meaning into these public displays. Laurie Shannon makes a similar argument: "Renaissance friendship's intersubjective position founds itself on emphatic principles of sameness; its most consistent impulse is homonormative. Using the word *normative* in this way, I mean to evoke the strange blend of ordinariness, idealization, and ideology entailed in this rhetorical regime. Homonormativity … suggests both an affective regime and a political one" (19). If I am interested

[13] See Alan Bray, "Homosexuality and the Signs of Male Friendship in Elizabethan England," *History Workshop Journal* 29 (Spring 1990): 1–19; reprinted in *Queering the Renaissance*, ed. Jonathan Goldberg (Durham, NC: Duke University Press, 1994), 40–61.
[14] Shannon, *Sovereign Amity*, 19.

more in the affective regime, that is partly as a corrective to the politicizing of Bray and others.

In her own study of friendship, Schweitzer discusses these issues at length, and she makes it clear that her study allows a richer range of reference:

> Aristotle's notion of *philia*, which recurs in various guises with remarkable frequency in early as well as in later and contemporary American texts ... Cicero incorporated ideas from Greek sources that reinforce the classical ideal as a heroic and spiritual connection (although eroticism and sexuality sometimes play central roles) freely entered into by virtuous men of relatively equal and elevated status who mirror each other.

If the heroic and the spiritual are sometimes infused with eroticism and sexuality, then friendship itself can be dynamic and varied in these ways, as this study will show. Schweitzer goes on to talk about the ways in which Cicero's account shifts into the elegiac, and this configuration seems to me as important, if not more important, than the erotic and sexual one. I will of course talk about both.

> Cicero's account, however, is saturated with masculine political melancholia arising from the untimely death of his great friend Scipio and the loss of the Republic and its tradition of military and civic honor figured by that friendship. This compelling linkage of friendship and loss influenced other important contributors to the tradition such as Francesco Petrarch and Michel de Montaigne and set the overriding mood for postmodern conceptions of friendship epitomized by Jacques Derrida's 2001 collection of eulogies on friends entitled *The Work of Mourning*.[15]

The issues raised here almost outline the study I have begun. For if it is useful to describe this range of friendship's possibilities for American culture in the eighteenth and nineteenth centuries, how even more telling for the English literary culture that is at issue here. For now, it is important to remember that Michel de Montaigne articulated the concept of loving-friendship between men for the early modern era, and although he distinguished it from the pederasty of the Greeks, he nevertheless saw it as a "perfect union and congruity." He says: "In the friendship which I am talking about, souls are mingled and confounded in so universal a blending that they efface the seam which joins them together so that it cannot be found. If you press me to say why I loved him, I feel that it cannot be expressed except by replying: 'Because it was him: because it was me.'"

---

[15] Schweitzer, *Perfecting Friendship*, 13.

Although Montaigne distinguishes this model of loving-friendship from pederasty, he connects it to marriage: "For the perfect friendship I am talking about is indivisible: each gives himself so entirely to his friend that he has nothing left to share with another … [I]n this friendship love takes possession of the soul and reigns there with full sovereign sway."[16] This possession, as spiritual and emotional as it is, seems to assume a physical bond as well: this mutual giving is certainly intense, and body and soul seem almost indivisible. It is interesting to note that the most recent translator of Montaigne's essays changes the title of the essay that has long been known as "On Friendship." The new title is "On Affectionate Relationships," and it is a title that comes closer to describing the kinds of friendships I am looking at in this study. If these friendships can be understood as "affectionate relationships" in the way that Montaigne describes, then they will defy attempts to dismiss their emotional significance.

In his discussion of Christopher Marlowe's *Edward II*, Jonathan Goldberg chides Bray for forgetting his own point about the ways in which sodomy and friendship can so easily be misrecognized.[17] If this is true for sodomy – and I will leave Goldberg to make that argument – how much truer might it be for the kind of friendship I am discussing here. For if the conventions of friendship include deeply emotional language, as Bray argues, then where is the place for the expression of emotion? I would argue that it is present even in the conventionality of the language Bray describes. How often are we assaulted by the public convention of a statement such as "I love you": how hackneyed that phrase is, and how devoid of meaning. That is true until, of course, it is reanimated with meaning by two people who love each other. The analogy is not exactly the same, but it does begin to get at the nature of language, which can be public and conventional and still express something deeply private and personal.

As hard as it is to imagine how men in earlier centuries narrated their attachment to one another, one thing that we do understand in the twenty-first century is love, even if our contemporary understanding of love is diluted by popular culture and over-familiarity. Still, when two people say that they love each other, we understand what that means. When those two

---

[16] Michel de Montaigne, "On Affectionate Relationships," in *The Complete Essays*, ed. and trans. M. A. Screech (London: Penguin, 2003), 211–12, 215. For Bray, some of the language of intimacy has a traditional valence that challenges modern interpretations; see Bray, *The Friend*, 140–77.

[17] Jonathan Goldberg, *Sodometries: Renaissance Texts, Modern Sexualities* (Palo Alto: Stanford University Press, 1992).

people are a man and a woman, we are happy to invest the emotion with erotic feeling as well. We are loath to make the same assumption when the two loving participants are male. But why should we, in cases like some of those before us, assume that this friendship serves only a public and political form when the terms are so deeply personal? I would go even further to say that at the beginning of the longer eighteenth century, it was becoming possible to read these outpourings of emotionality as expressions of a love that is none other than the love that we recognize as existing between men and women in love poetry, Restoration comedy, heroic drama, and even the early novel: physical, emotional, lustful, spiritual love. I have talked about such examples, in my earlier study of male love and friendship in the eighteenth century, but I want to return to them in this context to see what we can make of the love that is expressed between men.[18]

In this study, the friendships I will be talking about are exclusively literary representations. I might, in some cases, refer to a writer's life and/or his own friendships, but for the most part my examples will be literary. Another proviso is that I am talking primarily about male friendships and intimate male relations in this study. There are various reasons for this: I have written extensively about women's literary friendships elsewhere;[19] male friendships have a cultural significance that Alan Bray and others have discussed; my interest in the "history of sexuality" dictates this one-sided approach, since male friendships are in so many ways foundational to Western masculinist culture; and finally, I think it is time to reconsider some of the groundbreaking work that was done in this field in the latter part of the twentieth century. I am thinking primarily of the work of Eve Kosofsky Sedgwick, whose *Between Men: English Literature and Male Homosocial Desire* is an indispensable source for thinking about this topic. If I feel that homosociality itself now needs revision, then that is not on account of anything in Sedgwick's work, but rather on account of some of the uses to which it has been put in the last twenty-five years. Interestingly, the notion of homosociality that Sedgwick first articulated – far more culturally complicit than the "male bonding" it has come to mean in critical discussion since its first articulation – would dovetail nicely with the public and very masculinist concept of friendship that Bray describes. I am also indebted to work by writers such as Christopher Craft, Cameron McFarlane, G. S.

---

[18] For this earlier argument, see Haggerty, *Men in Love*, 5–6.

[19] George E. Haggerty, *Unnatural Affections: Women and Fiction in the Later Eighteenth Century* (Bloomington: Indiana University Press, 1998).

Rousseau, Hans Turley, Thomas King, Richard Dellamora, and others, the importance of whose work will emerge in more specific contexts. I am building on this work, I hope, and adding to our understanding of the literary representation of male friendships in the English literary tradition.[20]

I want to introduce the concept of platonic love into this discussion because I think it offers answers in exactly the places where our questions are most perplexing.[21] Plato was perhaps not as huge an influence in the eighteenth century as in the centuries before and after – it probably took Jowett and the great nineteenth-century translations to make Plato fully accessible to undergraduates – but in both the seventeenth and nineteenth centuries, Plato's literary influence was enormous.[22] I hope to examine some of the details of this influence and to show how platonic love, both in its larger cultural and philosophical context and in its more local and popular dissemination, had a profound effect on the history of sexuality as it emerged in the work of sexologists in the later nineteenth and early twentieth centuries. Aristotle too, as Schweitzer reminds us, holds an important place in discussion of friendships:

> Emphasizing two crucial requirements for the achievement of friendship's highest form – voluntary, rational choice and an equality between friends that makes such choice possible – Aristotle offers a definition that has dominated the long philosophical and popular discourse: "a friend is another self" (*philos allos autos*) so that "Equality – and likeness – is friendship, and especially those alike in virtue." Philosophers have taken this to mean that what Aristotle understands as self-love is the best model for love of another.[23]

---

[20] See Eve Kosofsky Sedgwick, *Between Men: English Literature and Male Homosocial Desire* (New York: Columbia University Press, 1985), esp. 21–7; see also: Dellamora, *Friendship's Bonds*; Christopher Craft, *Another Kind of Love: Male Homosexual Desire in English Discourse, 1850–1920* (Berkeley: University of California Press, 1994); Cameron McFarlane, *The Sodomite in Fiction and Satire, 1660–1750* (New York: Columbia University Press, 1997); Thomas King, *The Gendering of Men, 1600–1750*, 2 vols (Madison: University of Wisconsin Press, 2004, 2008); Hans Turley, *Rum, Sodomy, and the Lash: Piracy, Sexuality, and Masculine Identity* (New York: New York University Press, 2001); and G. S. Rousseau, "The Pursuit of Homosexuality in the Eighteenth Century: 'Utterly Confused Category' and/or Rich Repository?" *Eighteenth-Century Life* 9 (1985): 132–68.

[21] Richard Dellamora, the most recent of these friendship commentators, makes the important point, following Bray, that "in Greek and Roman philosophic and literary tradition, perfect friendship between two men is often taken as paradigmatic of the virtues that are necessary in a just polity." He says further that "within the Athenian institution of pederasty, a citizen and an adolescent joined in a mentor-protégé relationship, motivated by erotic attraction." See Dellamora, *Friendship's Bonds*, 21.

[22] Pat Rogers, Introduction to "The Eighteenth Century," in *Platonism and the English Imagination*, ed. Anna Baldwin and Sarah Hutton (Cambridge University Press, 1994), 181–5; see also Linda Dowling, *Hellenism and Homosexuality in Victorian Oxford* (Ithaca: Cornell University Press, 1994).

[23] Schweitzer, *Perfecting Friendship*, 35; quotation from Aristotle, *Nicomachean Ethics*, 9:4, 29: 8:8, 12.

The chapters that follow explore English literary friendship in three distinct ways: the elegiac, the erotic, and the platonic. The result is a new understanding of the role of friendship in the English literary tradition. I think such a reassessment of friendship is long overdue. In Chapter 1, "Elegiac Friendship," I explore the role of friendship, melancholic loss, and remembrance in three classic texts and one modern one: Sterne's *Tristram Shandy*, Tennyson's *In Memoriam*, Scott's *Waverley*, and Woolf's *Jacob's Room*. By beginning with these elegiac expressions of love and loss, I hope to establish the astonishing range and depth of male relations, first in two deeply felt accounts of personal loss – an almost shocking moment in Laurence Sterne's novel, and the decades-long near desperation of Alfred Tennyson – and one evocative reflection of a kind of cultural loss, which is expressed in personal terms in Walter Scott's *Waverley*. Woolf's *Jacob's Room* expresses the loss implicit in World War I, but it also cries out in deeply personal terms as well. These three works mark out a vast emotional canvas that some version of friendship is meant to fill. By starting here, we can begin to understand how this emotionality is constituted in loss, and what that means for the literary tradition I am describing.

In Chapter 2, "Erotic Friendship," I discuss the outright sodomitical friendship in Tobias Smollett's *Roderick Random*; I consider the permutations of friendship in Henry Fielding's novel about marriage, *Amelia*. I also look at the almost Gothic dimensions of friendship as a kind of haunting negativity in Godwin's *Caleb Williams* and in Mary Shelley's *Frankenstein*. The friendships in this chapter are fraught: they are bandied about as the subterfuge for seduction; they are falsely promulgated as a means of deception; and they are elicited only as a pretext for the exertion of class superiority. Erotic friendship suffers by the very contradiction in its articulation, but out of that contradiction some of the most telling distinctions emerge.

Chapter 3, "Platonic Friendship," takes its title from a philosophical tradition that has a vivid second life in the later decades of the nineteenth century. I start with Charles Dickens' remarkably moving novel that places a male relation at its very heart: *Great Expectations*. Then I look at the specific quality of platonic love in Wilde's opening chapter of *The Picture of Dorian Gray*. The special quality of male friendship and love in E. M. Forster's two astonishing novels, *The Longest Journey* and *Maurice*, fill out the final section of this chapter.

In the Epilogue, I consider Christopher Isherwood's novel, *A Single Man*, and its anticipation of contemporary issues in queer theory. This piece helps me to bring to a conclusion this study placing friendship at the center of the English literary tradition, where it belongs. In exploring the complexities of male–male relations beyond the simple labels of sexuality, I will have shown how love between men has a rich and varied history in English literature, and I hope that the examples I offer here help to make clear how very much in need of revaluation that history has been.

CHAPTER I

Elegiac Friendship

Elegiac friendship occupies a central place in the panoply of friendship in the English literary tradition. As Peter M. Sacks reminds us in *The English Elegy*, the elegy is primarily a poetic form, one of "mortal loss and consolation."[1] Sacks further describes the poetic process as "loss and figuration": "What … the poet pursues turns into a sign that carries within itself the reminder of the loss on which it was founded." In the case of Apollo and Daphne, which Sacks uses as an illustration, Daphne is turned first into a laurel, and only later is she represented in a wreath of leaves that Apollo plucks from the tree and wears as a mode of consolation.

> Ovid's narrative invites us to watch the emergence of this arbitrariness and disjunctiveness as an event to reintegrate the sign with the passionate story of its derivation. If there is a necessary distance between the wreath and what it signifies, that distance is the measure of Apollo's loss. Daphne's "turning" into a tree matches Apollo's "turning" from the object of his love to a sign of her. It is this substitutive turn or act of troping that any mourner must perform.[2]

The function of sexual desire in this classical example is clear. For Sacks, Ovid is interested in presenting "the precise moment at which the original loses itself to the substitute" and also in revealing "the very point beyond which the sexual impulse is both continued and deflected." For Apollo and Pan, whose own loss of Syrinx is described in similar terms, with their laurels and reeds, "not only have the forms of their desired objects changed but the form of their desires must, in this moment of recognition and acceptance, change as well … One of the most profound issues to beset any mourner and elegist is his surviving yet painfully altered sexuality."[3]

[1] Peter M. Sacks, *The English Elegy: Studies in the Genre from Spenser to Yeats* (Baltimore: Johns Hopkins University Press, 1985), 3.
[2] Sacks, *The English Elegy*, 5.
[3] Sacks, *The English Elegy*, 7.

Sacks goes on to describe this alteration as a kind of castration:

> The movement from loss to consolation thus requires a deflection of
> desire, with the creation of a trope both for the lost object and for the
> original character of the desire itself. The laurel and the flute must sym-
> bolize not only Daphne and Syrinx but also the thwarted sexual impulse
> of the pursuers. As the texts suggest, that thwarting resembles a castration
> since in each case it is in the father's territories that the pursuer is forced
> to check his desires and since Apollo's sign and Pan's new instrument
> are the pieces of their transformed loves and of their own transformed
> sexual powers, broken or cut, wreathed or sealed. Each is left grasping the
> sign of what he lacks, an elegiac token that one can recognize in the cut
> flowers and the (sometimes broken or resigned pipes of Alexandrian and
> Elizabethan elegies, or in Milton's painful plucking and shattering of ber-
> ries and leaves, no less than in the mounds of broken lilacs in Whitman's
> elegy for Lincoln).[4]

This passage offers an almost breathtakingly rich perspective on the
entire elegiac tradition: loss and figuration, consolation and castration.
This outline begins to suggest both the resonance of the English elegy
and why English poets and, indeed, novelists return to the form again
and again. There is no mistaking the intensity of the emotion that is
represented in the elegy, even from its earliest examples. And when that
emotional energy shifts, as it repeatedly does, from the intensity of sexual longing between a man and a woman – either Aphrodite mourning
the loss of her Adonis or, as just mentioned, Apollo his Daphne – to
one of emotional loss between friends or emotional soulmates – Lycidas,
Adonais, Hallam – the process remains the same: loss and figuration,
consolation and castration. Elegiac friendship emerges from the tradition that Sacks describes, and it is as one with it: the classic elegies are
the laments of friends, after all.

"Alas, poor Yorick!": Elegiac Friendship in *Tristram Shandy*

> A few hours before *Yorick* breath'd his last, *Eugenius* stept in with an intent
> to take his last sight and last farewell of him: Upon his drawing *Yorick's*
> curtain, and asking how he felt himself, *Yorick*, looking up in his face,
> took hold of his hand, – and, after thanking him for the many tokens
> of his friendship to him, for which, he said, if it was their fate to meet
> hereafter, – he would thank him again and again. – He told him, he was

---

[4] Sacks, *The English Elegy*, 7–8.

within a few hours of giving his enemies the slip for ever. – I hope not, answered *Eugenius*, with tears trickling down his cheeks, and with the tenderest tone that ever man spoke, – I hope not, *Yorick*, said he. – *Yorick* replied, with a look up, and a gentle squeeze of *Eugenius's* hand, and that was all, – but it cut *Eugenius* to the heart. – Come, – come, *Yorick*, quoth *Eugenius*, wiping his eyes, and summoning up the man within him, – my dear lad, be comforted, – let not all thy spirits and fortitude forsake thee at this crisis when thou most wants them; – who knows what resourses are in store, and what the power of God may yet do for thee? – *Yorick* laid his hand upon his heart, and gently shook his head; – for my part, continued *Eugenius*, crying bitterly as he uttered the words, – I declare I know not, *Yorick*, how to part with thee, – and would gladly flatter my hopes, added *Eugenius*, chearing up his voice, that there is still enough left of thee to make a bishop, – and that I may live to see it. – I beseech thee, *Eugenius*, quoth *Yorick*, taking off his night-cap as well as he could with his left hand, – his right being still grasped close in that of *Eugenius*, – I beseech thee to take a view of my head. – I see nothing that ails it, replied *Eugenius*. Then, alas! my friend, said *Yorick*, let me tell you, that 'tis so bruised and misshapen'd with the blows which ***** and *****, and some others have so unhandsomely given me in the dark, that I might say with *Sancho Pança*, that should I recover, and "Mitres thereupon be suffer'd to rain down from heaven as thick as hail, not one of 'em would fit it." – *Yorick's* last breath was hanging upon his trembling lips ready to depart as he uttered this; – yet still it was utter'd with something of a *cervantick* tone; – and as he spoke it, *Eugenius* could perceive a stream of lambent fire lighted up for a moment in his eyes; – faint picture of those flashes of his spirit, which (as *Shakespear* said of his ancestor) were wont to set the table in a roar!

Eugenius was convinced from this, that the heart of his friend was broke; he squeezed his hand, – and then walk'd softly out of the room, weeping as he walk'd. *Yorick* followed *Eugenius* with his eyes to the door, – he then closed them, – and never opened them more.

He lies buried in a corner of his church-yard, in the parish of –, under a plain marble slabb, which his friend *Eugenius*, by leave of his executors, laid upon his grave, with no more than these three words of inscription serving both for his epitaph and elegy.

Alas, poor YORICK!

Ten times in a day has *Yorick's* ghost the consolation to hear his monumental inscription read over with such a variety of plaintive tones, as denote a general pity and esteem for him; – a foot-way crossing the church-yard close by the side of his grave, – not a passenger goes by without stopping to cast a look upon it, – and sighing as he walks on,

Alas, poor Y O R I C K!

(*Tristram Shandy* 1.33–6; 1.xii)[5]

Not far into the first volume of Sterne's *Tristram Shandy*, we are presented with the death scene of Yorick, the country parson who plays a central role in the novel. Yorick has barely made his appearance before his death is lamented in one of the novel's most arresting passages. This death scene is unexpected and out of sync with the story as it is being told. Readers are not yet aware that events transpire according to a system all their own; nor do they yet realize that death is implicit in the lives of *Tristram Shandy* as perhaps in no other novel, certainly no other comic novel, of the last half of the eighteenth century. Most readers are aware that Sterne uses the self-effacing parson to represent himself not only in *Tristram Shandy*, but also in *A Sentimental Journey*, which was written right after this novel and has Yorick as its putative hero. Of course, in *Tristram Shandy*, there is no law about when things happen or how they relate to matters around them, except perhaps some supple notion of memory and the association of ideas, as articulated by Locke.[6] Still, Sterne has made no bones about his ill-health and how short a time he has for writing his novel, and in that sense this scene could be placed anywhere and it would be perfectly intelligible. One critic, at least, reads the novel as a direct reflection of Sterne's awareness of his own mortal illness.[7]

For all the more reason, Yorick's death scene resonates powerfully. Like many of his near contemporaries in the age of sensibility, Sterne here manages to dilate on his own death, and he does so in terms that are both

---

[5] Page references are to the Florida edition of *Tristram Shandy*, ed. Melvyn New and Joan New, 3 vols. (Gainesville: University Press of Florida, 1978); further references to this edition are included parenthetically in the text.

[6] Sterne cites Locke's concept more than once, but perhaps nowhere more vividly than he does shortly before this in Volume 1, when he is lamenting the connection his mother made on the first Sunday of the month: "from an unhappy association of ideas which have no connection with nature, it so fell out at length, that my poor mother could never hear the said clock wound up, – but the thoughts of some other things unavoidably popp'd into her head, – *& vice versa*; – which strange combination of ideas, the sagacious *Locke*, who certainly understood the nature of these things better than most men, affirms to have produced more wry actions than all other sources of prejudice whatsoever" (1.7).

[7] A very rich study of time in *Tristram Shandy* is that by Clare Lawlor, who says Sterne "incorporates the idiosyncratic rhythms of his disease into the narrative of *Tristram Shandy*, whether it be done consciously or unconsciously." Clare Lawlor, "Consuming Time: Narrative and Disease in *Tristram Shandy*," in *Laurence Sterne's* Tristram Shandy: *A Casebook*, ed. Thomas Keymer (Oxford: Oxford University Press, 2006), 147–67 (149).

uncannily familiar and new in ways that a reading of this passage may lead us to call Shandean. What results is one of the most beautifully depicted death scenes of the eighteenth century. Like Thomas Gray's representation of his own demise in "An Elegy Written in a Country Churchyard" or Tennyson's fantasies of his own end in commemorating the death of Hallam in *In Memoriam*, this death is self-reflective: it is an attempt to confront mortality directly and to make some sense of the final scene, and it is also meant to tell us something about the life it brings to a close as well as about "life" itself. Sterne does that and more in this amazing passage, both revealing his own feelings and exploring the character of Yorick at the same time that he presents death as an arresting figure in his novel.

Of course, other commentators have noted Sterne's reflection on his own mortality in these pages. Ross King says, "the scarred or diseased body is so ubiquitous in *Tristram Shandy* that, despite the novel's humor, readers may be forgiven for dwelling more on infirm and suffering figures than on Sterne's buffers of mirth."[8] Clare Lawlor goes even further to suggest, "disease time traumatizes the narrative of *Tristram Shandy*; but there is also a teleology to the time of consumption itself that increases its danger to the narrative and its author, who will write as long as he lives."[9] Readers are hardly aware of illness or disease when this death occurs. As I said above, we are just being introduced to Yorick when we learn about his death. It is typical of Tristram to think about death when he is presenting a life, and that is surely one of the most salient features of the novel.

The most important, and less frequently discussed, feature of this death scene is Yorick's having a companion in these final moments. Just before Yorick closes his eyes forever, Eugenius steps into the room to offer friendship and support. Most accounts of this novel, and of *A Sentimental Journey*, identify Eugenius as Sterne's close college and life-long friend John Hall-Stevenson.[10] The death scene begins with these two men clasping hands together: "*Yorick*, looking up in his face, took hold of his hand, – and, after thanking him for the many tokens of his friendship to him, for which, he said, if it was their fate to meet hereafter – he would thank him again and again." These gestures are the expressions of mutual devotion, to be sure, but also they express something more than simple friendship in the

---

[8] Ross King, "*Tristram Shandy* and the Wound of Language," in *Laurence Sterne's* Tristram Shandy: *A Casebook*, ed. Thomas Keymer (Oxford: Oxford University Press, 2006), 123–46 (124).

[9] Lawlor, "Consuming Time," 152.

[10] John Hall-Stevenson was a friend from Yorkshire and Cambridge. Sterne valued him as a friend and always had "high regard for him" (*Tristram Shandy* 3.73–4, nn. 33.4–6, 34.19–22). Also see, Ian Campbell Ross, *Laurence Sterne: A Life* (Oxford: Oxford University Press, 2001), 42.

hope that it might be "their fate to meet hereafter." Yorick tries to push the friendship beyond death in a gesture that reminds us of a different kind of male intimacy. In the hope that they will spend eternity together, Sterne gives Yorick a gift like no other. No one else can share this intimate occasion besides this friend: there is no one as meaningful to him nor as promising of a contented afterlife. This surely gives us an understanding of friendship that challenges any but its most profound assessments. In a moment, I will turn to the language of friendship codified by Montaigne and his classical forebears, but before I do I want to make sure that we understand what Sterne is depicting here. It is nothing less than the language of the elegiac tradition that has emerged here, almost magically, in this early section of the novel.

In invoking the elegiac tradition, Sterne writes his own epitaph, as it were, and suggests that the only form of elegiac mourning he understands is that between men, as the elegiac tradition celebrates. Ross King, in a wonderfully perceptive essay about *Tristram Shandy*, notes that the "procedure of textual compensation for loss testifies to a specific view of the powers and uses of language" (124). And later in the same essay, he adds: "Why the wounded body should seek compensation through performative language had been suggested by Shoshona Felman, who argues that the speech act by its very nature – as *both* speech *and* act – interweaves language and body, pointing to the indissoluble relations between the linguistic and the physical."[11] What is remarkable about these terms of analysis is not merely their perspicuity: in a welter of critical commentary about the novel, no one raises these issues so directly; but even more remarkable is their complete refusal to mention the elegiac tradition into which this attempt for consolation and compensation for loss in language is most deeply rooted. Indeed, the best elegiac writing is performative in the ways that Felman and King suggest. Still, it is stunning that *Tristram Shandy* has not been placed within this tradition, where I think it truly belongs.

When Yorick and Eugenius speak, the emotional valence of their bond and the measure of their impending loss both become even more intense:

> He told him, he was within a few hours of giving his enemies the slip for ever. – I hope not, answered *Eugenius*, with tears trickling down his cheeks, and with the tenderest tone that ever man spoke, – I hope not, *Yorick*, said

---

[11] King, "*Tristram Shandy* and the Wound of Language," 125; internal quotation is to Shoshona Felman, *The Literary Speech Act: Don Juan with J. L. Austin, or Seduction in Two Languages*, trans. Catherine Porter (Ithaca: Cornell University Press, 1983), 92–4.

> he. – *Yorick* replied, with a look up, and a gentle squeeze of *Eugenius's* hand, and that was all, – but it cut *Eugenius* to his heart. (1.33–4; 1.xii)

It is perhaps a commonplace for men of sensibility to cry, but the tears in this case are so clearly the tears of impending loss, that we should be forgiven for taking them more seriously than we might take other tears of sensibility. Here, the tears trickle down Eugenius' cheeks as a mark of the devotion these men feel toward each other. Yorick's jaunty language of giving his enemies the slip only makes Eugenius sadder: it is this indomitable spirit in Yorick that he will miss. His care is a sign of his friendship for Yorick: he values these simple details of his personality, and these are what he knows he will not be able to replace. The tenderness in his voice as he says the three words "I hope not" is answered by Yorick's "gentle squeeze" of Eugenius' hand. This touch, reflecting and yet anticipating an entire elegiac tradition as it does, crosses the boundary between two human beings and offers a kind of consolation that can answer the lack that is always already looming in the language of the elegy. In later elegies, from Whitman to Wilfred Owen, the moment of touch is crucial and offers the hope of reaching beyond the grave.[12] What Tennyson would not have given for such a touch from Hallam: he pleads for it, imagines it, even feels it; but it is never as palpable as it is here: a gift from Yorick as he dies. This is why Eugenius is cut "to his heart."

As this conversation continues, its contours take an even more interesting shape:

> Come, – come, *Yorick*, quoth *Eugenius*, wiping his eyes, and summoning up the man within him, – my dear lad, be comforted, – let not all thy spirits and fortitude forsake thee at this crisis when thou most wants them. (1.34; 1.xii)

Eugenius becomes the man to Yorick's lad in this passage – as if this familiar configuration from portrayals of friendship from Plato and beyond is not enough to remind us why this is a crucial transformation, Sterne's language can help us to do so. Eugenius summons up the man within him; that is, he asserts a manliness that he might not really feel. He does this for the sake of his friend; and as he does so, the friend slips almost automatically into the role of the lad, chided and encouraged as if less manly or ready to face the world. From what we know of Yorick, this may well describe

---

[12] See Michael Moon, "Memorial Rags," in *Professions of Desire*, ed. George E. Haggerty and Bonnie Zimmerman (New York: MLA, 1995), 233–40; and Santanu Das, *Touch and Intimacy in First World War Literature* (New York: Cambridge University Press, 2005).

his personality, and more than once he seems childish in his behaviors and responses, as critics have been happy to point out.[13] Rather than criticizing the man of feeling on those grounds here, we might be tempted to celebrate the configuration of the mode of friendship that enables the older man to instruct and inspire the younger one. Here, the older man (not older in any sense but in spirit) offers the perspective of health to his ailing friend, and ill-health renders Yorick almost a child. This is a beautiful transformation in its way, and because of it Eugenius is able to offer advice and even some hope.

This does not sustain Eugenius for long, however, and soon he once again is dissolved in tears and trying to accommodate his friend's loss:

> who knows what resources are in store, and what the power of God may yet do for thee? – Yorick laid his hand upon his heart, and gently shook his head; – for my part, continued *Eugenius*, crying bitterly as he uttered the words, – I declare I know not, *Yorick*, how to part with thee, – and would gladly flatter my hopes, added *Eugenius,* chearing up his voice, that there is still enough left of thee to make a bishop, – and that I may live to see it. (1.34; 1.xii)

Eugenius tries to offer hope, even the power of God, to assist Yorick in recovery. By invoking God in his desperation, Eugenius does what mourners have done from the time of the classical elegy: they challenge the supernatural to prevent this loss or to redress it.[14] In this case, Eugenius seeks an intervention that would deliver Yorick from his pain and place him in a public position once again. If Yorick gently refuses this hope, he does so in the awareness that he has very few moments to live. More tears are the result, and Eugenius is "crying bitterly," even as he is "chearing up his voice," once more to chide and challenge Yorick. This encounter reaches its climax, however, as Eugenius utters the finally brutal truth, "I know not, *Yorick*, how to part with thee." Who has not said or felt these things at the bedside of a loved one? I say that because it is the love that is implicit in these words that gives them meaning. This is not a statement about knowledge, in other words, it is a statement about intimacy and its devastating loss.

---

[13] See Eve Kosofsky Sedgwick, *Between Men: English Literature and Male Homosocial Desire* (New York: Columbia University Press, 1985), 67–82; John Mullan, *Sentiment and Sociability: The Language of Feeling in the Eighteenth Century* (Oxford: Clarendon, 1988), 147–200; and Robert Markley, "Sentimentality as Performance: Shaftesbury, Sterne, and the Theatrics of Virtue," in *The New Eighteenth Century*, ed. Felicity Nussbaum and Laura Brown (New York: Routledge, 1987), 210–30 (227–8).

[14] For this and other specific features of the elegy form, see Sacks, *The English Elegy*, 1–37.

In his essay on friendship, *"de l'amitié,"* Montaigne describes friendship in this way: "souls are mingled and confounded in so universal a blending that they efface the seam which joins them together so that it cannot be found."[15] If this description defies a common-sense notion of friendship and places it in a realm of intimacy closer to what I have elsewhere called the conjugal, it surely makes sense to connect it to this ideal of elegiac friendship I am talking about here: "For the perfect friendship I am talking about is indivisible: each gives himself so entirely to his friend that he has nothing left to share with another ... In this friendship love takes possession of the soul and reigns there with full sovereign sway" (215).[16] The friendship these men share in Yorick's final moments – expressed in touch and glance – begins to approximate *l'amitié* that Montaigne describes. When Derrida discusses lines like these, he underlines the inaccessibility of the state they describe. He suggests that this language of friendship always requires a projection beyond death. Admittedly he is talking more about Aristotle than he is about Montaigne, when he makes this challenging statement: "If *philia* lives, and if it lives at the extreme limit of its possibility, it therefore *lives*, it stirs, it becomes *psychic* from within [a] resource of survival. This *philia*, this *psukhé* between friends, survives. It cannot survive itself as act, but it can survive its object, it can love the inanimate."[17] If survival is the key, then what Derrida emphasizes is its elegiac quality. He does not say that directly, but he is talking about how impossible it is to fulfill the ideal language of friendship anywhere but in memory. At another point, Derrida says, "Friendship tells the truth – and this is always better left unknown. The protection of this custody guarantees the truth of friendship, its ambiguous truth, that by which friends protect themselves from the error or the illusion on which friendship is founded – more precisely, the bottomless bottom founding a friendship, which enables it to resist its own abyss."[18] Of course this abyss is approached directly and challenged, if not overcome, in the very best poetry of the elegiac tradition. Sterne seems to understand this implicitly, and he makes this commitment ceremony between friends clearly one that is predicated on death.

---

[15] Michel de Montaigne, "On Affectionate Relationships," in *The Complete Essays*, ed. and trans. M. A. Screech (London: Penguin, 2003), 205–19 (211–12, 215).

[16] Montaigne, "On Affectionate Relationships," 215. For Alan Bray, some of the language of intimacy has a traditional valence that challenges modern interpretations; see Bray, *The Friend* (Chicago: University of Chicago Press, 2003), 140–77. See also Charles Lamb, "Sterne's Use of Montaigne," *Clio* 32.1 (Winter 1980): 1–41.

[17] Jacques Derrida, *The Politics of Friendship*, trans. George Collins (New York: Verso, 2005), 13.

[18] Derrida, *The Politics of Friendship*, 53.

This both places this friendship within the elegiac tradition and explains why it flourishes so readily there.

In the little drama that follows, Eugenius tells Yorick that "there is still enough left of thee to make a bishop" (1.34; 1.xii); but Yorick answers, using his left hand (because his right still clings to Eugenius) to take off his cap and exclaim about the blows his poor head has received. He cannot give up, it seems, without his characteristic joking, and Eugenius sees deeply into these words. He compares himself to Don Quixote's sidekick, Sancho Panza, and he quotes from Cervantes at this final moment:

> that I might say with *Sancho Pança*, that should I recover, and "Mitres thereupon be suffer'd to rain down from heaven as thick as hail, not one of 'em would fit it." – *Yorick's* last breath was hanging upon his trembling lips ready to depart as he uttered this; – yet still it was utter'd with something of a *cervantick* tone; – and as he spoke it, *Eugenius* could perceive a stream of lambent fire lighted up for a moment in his eyes; – faint picture of those flashes of his spirit, which (as *Shakespear* said of his ancestor) were wont to set the table in a roar! (1.34; 1.xii)

As he dies, in other words, Yorick calls up Cervantes and employs a cervantic tone to give his sufferings a comic edge. I do not mean to say that Yorick is joking, but rather he invokes a deeply comic vision of death and loss: comic that is in the context of this friend. As he does so, Eugenius can perceive a "stream of lambent fire lighted up for a moment in his eyes." Yorick takes his last breath as he attempts to entertain his friend. The bond between these two men is represented in this lambent light, which illumines the moment of death with the glow of male friendship shining from within.

The passage comes to a conclusion with Eugenius recognizing that the last breath inspired this touching moment, and he sees what it means and walks away:

> *Eugenius* was convinced from this, that the heart of his friend was broke; he squeezed his hand, – and then walk'd softly out of the room, weeping as he walk'd. *Yorick* followed *Eugenius* with his eyes to the door, – he then closed them, – and never opened them more. (1.35; 1.xii)

This final squeeze of the hand expresses the love that these men have shared, and as Eugenius walks away crying, Yorick "followed *Eugenius* with his eyes to the door": it is almost as if their souls communicate in this silent look. It is these eyes that he closes never to open, the eyes that have gazed on Eugenius with the deep love of friendship. This "longing, lingering look," to quote from Gray's *Elegy*, is pregnant with the meaning

[37]

Figure 1.1   "Alas, Poor Yorick!"
Taken from *The Florida Edition of the Works of Laurence Sterne, Vol. 1: The Life and Opinions of Tristram Shandy, Gentleman*, edited by Melvyn and Joan New. Gainesville: University Press of Florida, 1978.

of the devotion between these two men.[19] The passage ends with a description of the simple marble slab that makes his grave, the slab that Eugenius has placed there, with the three words that "serve both for his epitaph and elegy": "Alas, poor Yorick" (1.35; I.xii).

What is so devastatingly beautiful about this passage, the epitaph, and the black page are both their invocation of this elegiac tradition and also their unmistakable place as one of the most moving eighteenth-century articulations of what this tradition can mean. Yorick and Eugenius in this scene fulfill the consolation of mourning after which so much elegiac writing strives. Sterne has established in the first volume of his masterpiece the terms under which we are to proceed. Peter J. de Voogd, in his essay "*Tristram Shandy* as Aesthetic Object," makes the often underappreciated point that this novel can be viewed as a " 'coextential' verbo-visual whole."[20] By that he means that rather than supplementing the text or illustrating it in a typical way, a coextential relation between word and image happens "when the text's verbal and visual elements are so innately interwoven that they form an aesthetic whole. Text and picture cannot be separated from one another without serious loss" (109–10). De Voogd makes this point by considering various pages of the text and how their visual conception contributes to their meaning. Nowhere is this clearer, I would claim, than in the presentation of the black page and the epitaph for Yorick. The black page does not represent the anticipated loss in some way, but it is an expression of that loss, as powerful in its way as, if not more powerful than, the words that surround it. The whole conception is one of staggering complexity in its very simplicity. "Alas, poor Yorick" has never been so deeply felt.

Death and friendship are of course more intimately connected than we like to acknowledge. Jacques Derrida makes the case that the signal friendships that determine the tradition – from Aristotle, from Cicero, and from Montaigne – are all defined by loss. "If friendship projects its hope beyond life – an absolute hope, an incommensurable hope – this is because the friend is ... our own ideal image."[21] Alan Bray is making a similar point when he talks about the joint graves that entomb his early modern loving friends: In his chapter "The Body of a Friend," Bray talks about the

---

[19] Thomas Gray's *Elegy Written in a Country Churchyard*: "For who to dumb Forgetfulness a prey,/ This pleasing anxious being e're resigned,/Left the warm precincts of the cheerful day./Nor cast one longing ling'ring look behind?" (ll. 85–8)

[20] Peter J. de Voogd, "*Tristram Shandy* as Aesthetic Object," in *Laurence Sterne's* Tristram Shandy: A Casebook, ed. Thomas Keymer (Oxford: Oxford University Press, 2006), 108–19 (109).

[21] Derrida, *The Politics of Friendship*, 4.

relationship between John Finch and Thomas Baines, which is represented by a public memorial in the chapel of Christ's College in Cambridge.

Bray describes the monument in this way:

> Sir Thomas Baines died in September 1681 in Constantinople, where John Finch had been ambassador for Charles II; his remains were brought by his friend to England, where Finch was himself to die the following year. The monument signed by the sculptor Joseph Catterns marks their burial together in the vault nearby and is a graphic expression of the nature of their friendship. The two halves of the monument are each surmounted by a portrait of one of the friends; and the monument is linked by the image of a knotted cloth, set between the two tables of the inscription, that corresponds to the single flaming funerary urn set above, in a visual pun on the marriage or love-knot. That same terminology of marriage had already been employed by Finch in the inscription he left to the memory of Baines in Constantinople. In it he had described their friendship as an "Ammorum Connubium": a marriage of souls.[22]

It is hard to look at a memorial such as this, with the inscription insisting on intimacy, without imaging that there is something deeply personal about the relationship that is being described. But Bray insists that similar expressions were used earlier in the seventeenth century to describe friendships between men. "In describing their friendship," Bray suggests, "as a 'marriage of souls,' Finch used the same term employed by Jeremy Taylor, the Caroline divine (and later bishop) in his *Discourse of Friendship*, a work that was reprinted some seven times between 1657 when it first appeared, and 1684, when the monument in Christ's College was completed." Bray goes on to argue that Taylor's celebration of brotherhoods, "like those of David and Jonathan, brotherhoods made social and confederate ... by something more than nature ... [in] Jeremy Taylor's terms are those in which this monument is designed, and it conveys at the end of the seventeenth century in England, that formal and objective character that friendship could evidently still possess, so curiously unfamiliar to the modern eye."[23] That cannot belie the deep emotionality that a shared grave seems to claim, as "Alas, poor Yorick" reminds us.

In an earlier essay, I have talked about the deeply moving expressions of loss that elegies articulate as the precondition for the articulation of same-sex love. What Sterne does is anticipate the elegiac moment by showing the love and imagining its loss.[24] In so many ways extraordinary, here *Tristram*

---

[22] Bray, *The Friend*, 140–1.

[23] Bray, *The Friend*, 142–3.

[24] George E. Haggerty, "Desire and Mourning: The Ideology of the Elegy," in *Ideology and Form*, ed. David Richter (Lubbock: Texas Tech University Press, 1999), 184–206.

Shandy invokes the elegiac tradition only to rewrite it in terms that make the emotions of loss even more powerful because they are founded in physical intimacy, not the intimacy between a lover and a wounded corpse as in the classical elegies of Bion or Moschus, but rather with the living friend who offers companionship at the moment of death and in the hereafter. What could be more consoling?

This consolation answers the loss that is such a constant in the novel. If loss is the precondition for everything that transpires in the novel's nine volumes, the consolation that friendship offers puts that loss in a context and gives it positive meaning. As a result, I would raise the black page from an extraordinary feature of the novel's form to an expression of the terms through which all life transpires. "Et in Arcadia Ego" says the image of mortality in the pastoral setting. Sterne's black page says as much if not more: it reminds of death and it asserts death as the condition of life and love and humor. But it commemorates death as an act of remembrance that defies mortality at the same time that it celebrates it. But death is death, and Sterne's black page could be considered the rock of the real in the novel: a dark glimpse of an un-symbolizable condition, the very condition that gives coherence to everything around it.[25] Thus, the novel functions on the knife edge of the cultural symbolic on the one hand – family, friendship, society, and love – and on the other confronts the hideous reality of human experience that a scene like this one, so often taken for granted, heightens and transforms.

"The last Vich Ian Vohr": History as Loss in *Waverley*

Sir Walter Scott's *Waverley, or Sixty Years Since*, published in 1814, recreates for its readers the 1745 Jacobite Rebellion. The eponymous hero of this ambitious novel, Edward Waverley, is a gentleman from northern England, whose family is riven by the conflict between the staunch Whiggish politics of his father and the Jacobite leanings of his uncle. As a child, he is shifted from house to house in the division of his guardianship (because of his father's serving as a minister in London), and Edward finds himself

---

[25] Of course I am alluding here to the work of Slavoj Žižek, whose *The Sublime Object of Ideology* (New York: Verso, 1989) outlines in detail how such a Lacanian construct comes to be almost inevitable. See pp. 74–5: "This, then, is symptom: a particular, 'pathological', signifying formation, a binding of enjoyment, an inert stain resisting communication and interpretation, a stain which cannot be included in the circuit of discourse, of social bond network, but is at the same time a positive condition of it" (75).

attracted, in spite of his paternal logic, to the romance of Highland life and the cause to which so many Scots had devoted themselves.[26]

Waverley-Honour is the home of his uncle, and when there Edward's imagination is given free reign:

> The library at Waverley-Honour, a large Gothic room, with double arches and a gallery, contained such a miscellaneous and extensive collection of volumes as had been assembled together, during the course of two hundred years, by a family which had been always wealthy, and inclined, of course, as a mark of splendour, to furnish their shelves with the current literature of the day, without much scrutiny, or nicety of discrimination. Throughout this ample realm Edward was permitted to roam at large.[27]

Edward's ability to roam in this Gothic room and range among his uncle's volumes awakens him to romantic possibilities. And romance in this context concerns most centrally the cause of the Pretender and the Stuart line, which in the Scottish Highlands is something of a cause célèbre.[28]

Unsure how to handle his future, Waverley enters the military, and once stationed in the north, he asks for a leave to travel and visit a friend of his uncle's. The implicit romance of this venture is heightened when Edward encounters this family friend, the almost caricatured version of a Jacobite, the Baron of Bradwardine. The Baron's estate is in some disarray, but his instincts are nonetheless generous and welcoming to his friend's nephew. There are other inhabitants at this estate, and most important among them is Rose Bradwardine, a shy and self-effacing young girl who is attracted to Edward Waverley but cannot express herself in any way that is more than fraternally engaging to the young man. As Waverley tells himself, Rose is "too frank, too confiding, too kind; amiable qualities, undoubtedly, but destructive of the marvellous, with which a youth of imagination delights to address the empress of his affections" (121). Edward spends a great deal of time with Rose, sometimes in her evocative Gothic chambers, and when she tells him about their Highland neighbors, Vich Ian Vohr – son of John

[26] On the historical character of this novel, and on historical fiction in general, see Andrew Hook, "Introduction," in *Waverley; Or Sixty Years Since* (London: Penguin, 1988), 9–27; see also Ina Ferris, *The Achievement of Literary Authority: Gender, History, and the Waverley Novels* (Ithaca: Cornell University Press, 1991), 195–236; and Walter Brown, *Walter Scott and the Historical Imagination* (London: Routledge & Kegan Paul, 1979), 6–30.

[27] Sir Walter Scott, *Waverley; Or Sixty Years Since* (London: Penguin, 1988 [1814]), 47. Further page references are to this edition.

[28] One critic who sees the Scott hero as passive and theorizes such passivity at length is Alexander Welsh, *The Hero of the Waverley Novels, with New Essays on Scott* (Princeton: Princeton University Press, 1992), 21–31. See also, Judith Wilt, *Secret Leaves: The Novels of Sir Walter Scott* (Chicago: University of Chicago Press, 1985), 26–37.

the Great – and his sister Flora, "Waverley could not help staring at a story which bore so much resemblance to one of his own day-dreams. Here was a girl scarce seventeen, the gentlest of her sex, both in temper and appearance, who had witnessed with her own eyes such a scene as he had used to conjure up in his imagination, as only occurring in ancient times, and spoke of it coolly, as one very likely to occur" (129).

Shortly after these daydreams, a skirmish with local Highlanders, who have absconded with some of the Baron's cattle, brings Waverley into direct confrontation with the world of the Highlands. An emissary from Vich Ian Vohr, their Highland protector, arrives to give them an account of what has passed. The appearance of this emissary and the nature of his speech are two things that impress Waverley deeply. Evan Dhu is "a stout, dark, young man of low stature, the ample folds of whose plaid added to the appearance of strength which his person exhibited. The short kilt, or petticoat, showed his sinewy and clean-made limbs; the goat-skin purse, flanked by the usual defences, a dirk and steel-wrought pistol, hung before him" (131). At his very first appearance, this Highlander shows signs of strength and aggression, and the Highland dress reveals "sinewy and clean-made limbs" that become a signal for Highland strength and beauty, and also a symbol for something that has been lost in the modern world of the eighteenth century.

Evan leads Waverley into the hills – he accepts the challenge to go up to meet Vich Ian Vohr – and across an impressive landscape for many miles, until they cross a lake and enter a cave. There Waverley encounters a figure, "totally different in appearance and manner from what his imagination had anticipated." These descriptions are so much like set-pieces – like the blazons of courtly love – that they deserve extended quotation:

> David Bean Lean was ... thin in person and low in stature, with light sandy-coloured hair, and small pale features, from which he derived his agnomen of *Bean*, or white; and although his form was light, well-proportioned and active, he appeared, on the whole, rather a diminutive and insignificant figure. He had ... put on an old blue and red uniform, and a feathered hat, in which he was far from showing to advantage. (141)

This incongruous figure plays a large part in the story, and it is interesting to see the male interaction that becomes so crucial for the remainder of the novel. Waverley is presented to David Bean Lean (pronounced "Bane Lane," the note tells us)[29] as if he were a foreign dignitary. The narrator

---

[29] See *Waverley*, 137n.

calls his figure insignificant, but he is a thief and a scoundrel, performing a role that neither suits him nor presents him as intimidating. As Bean Lean questions him, about his background and his politics, in a Highland language that challenges Waverley:

> Waverley felt an involuntary shudder creep over him at the mysterious language held by this outlawed and lawless bandit, which, in despite of his attempts to master it, deprived him of the power to ask the meaning of his insinuations. A heath pallet, with the flowers stuck uppermost, had been prepared for him in a recess of the cave, and here, covered with such spare plaids as could be mustered, he lay for some time watching the motions of the other inhabitants of the cavern. (143)

The geographical movement of the novel is also a temporal movement into an age that is lost to those south of the Scottish border. Scott performs this act of recall as his own kind of elegy, and each of these figures, lovingly presented, takes his place in an elegiac panoply that builds to a crescendo around the figure of Bonnie Prince Charlie.

While Waverley is with David Bean Lean, he learns the history of the Sidier Dhu, or the black soldiers, so-called because of the black-watch tartans they wear, and he is told that Vich Ian Vohr commanded one of these regiments. Later, with the help of Evan Dhu, he makes his way to the residence of this figure, Fergus Vich Ian Vohr, who is presented as follows:

> When Fergus and Waverley met, the latter was struck with the peculiar grace and dignity of the Chieftain's figure. Above the middle size, and finely proportioned, the Highland dress, which he wore in its simplest mode, set off his person to great advantage. He wore the trews, or close trowsers, made of tartan, chequed scarlet and white; in other particulars, his dress strictly resembled Evan's excepting that he had no weapon saving a dirk, very richly mounted with silver ... His countenance was decidedly Scottish, with all the peculiarities of northern physiognomy, but yet had so little of its hardness and exaggeration, that it would have been pronounced in any country extremely handsome. (153–4)

Fergus steps out of the world of elegiac romance to dazzle Waverley with his dignity, his dress, his handsomeness: the impression is charged with an emotional intensity that Waverley's hours in the library have only increased. Edward is ready to like Fergus, as much on account of his position in the Highlands as anything else; but his appearance helps create this initial impression. And even if it is quickly made more complicated, it continues to impress: "Even his courtesy, though open, frank, and unconstrained, seemed to indicate a sense of personal importance; and, upon any check or accidental excitation, a sudden, though transient, lour of the eye, showed a hasty, haughty, and vindictive temper, not less to be dreaded because it seemed so much under the owner's command" (154).

What this detailed description emphasizes is something about the power of the figure. Now we see "peremptory command and decisive superiority," but we have no reason to think that Waverley will not be attracted as much to this demeanor as he is to the handsomeness of dress or coloring. Moreover, when the narrator turns to the "hasty, haughty, and vindictive temper," this might be just as impressive to the young hero as the other details in the description of this elegant chieftain. Andrew Hook makes the point that Edward is overwhelmed with his romantic welcome: "For most of the novel ... Waverley finds himself in a romantic country surrounded by romantic people. His response, as we would expect, is uninhibited."[30] What is the meaning of this romance? It seems to me to serve the function of creating a bond that will need to be broken as the novel proceeds. Loss can be articulated only when the bond is most intense. And in scenes like this, Scott makes the bond to the historical past primarily a personal one. To do so makes the lament all that more powerful when it is finally articulated.

Fergus' position in Highland politics is quickly summarized: "From his infancy upward, he had devoted himself to the cause of the exiled family [of the Pretender], and had persuaded himself, not only that their restoration to the crown of Britain would be speedy, but that those who assisted them would be raised to honour and rank" (158). What is recorded here is nothing less than belief in a probable future, which is also an act of faith in the justness of their cause. For this devotion, Fergus and his family are richly rewarded:

> This zeal on their behalf the House of Stuart repaid with a considerable share of their confidence, an occasional supply of louis d'or, abundance of fair words, and a parchment, with a huge waxen seal appended, purporting to be an Earl's patent, granted by no less a person than James the Third King of England, and Eighth King of Scotland, to his right leal, trusty, and well-loved Fergus Mac-Ivor of Glennaquoich, in the county of Perth, and kingdom of Scotland. (159)

From this perspective, Fergus seems almost like a hireling of the House of Stuart, but it also makes clear that he is recognized and can look forward to ultimate awards in the form of position and money in the not-too-distant future. The future, that is, of Jacobite ascendancy.

---

[30] Hook, "Introduction," 21.

In this context of Highland politics and almost feudal rewards, the narrator introduces the figure of Flora Mac-Ivor, Fergus' sister. Her room is plainly decorated,

> But there was no evidence of this parsimony in the dress of the lady herself, which was in texture elegant, and even rich, and arranged in a manner which partook partly of the Parisian fashion, and partly of the more simple dress of the Highlands, blended together with great taste. Her hair was not disfigured by the art of the friseur, but fell in jetty ringlets on her neck, confined only by a circlet, richly set with diamonds. (167)

Flora seems in some ways a female version of Fergus, dignified and haughty, at the same time that she is open and friendly. Her beauty is emphasized, and it is depicted as richly appointed and deeply elegant. Waverley is attracted to the woman at once. Her own politics seem almost more intense than her brother's:

> In Flora's bosom, on the contrary [to Fergus], the zeal of loyalty burnt pure and unmixed with any selfish feeling ... Such instances of devotion were not uncommon among the followers of the unhappy race of Stuart ... But peculiar attention on the part of the Chevalier de St. George and his princess to the parents of Fergus and his sister, and to themselves when orphans, had riveted their faith. (169)

Flora very quickly becomes the object of Waverley's attention, not least of all because of her zealous faith in the Stuart cause. Even more crucial to her appeal, however, is her exotic Highland breeding and her unfailing devotion to her brother and his prospects. Waverley is caught in the magic of the Mac-Ivors, brother and sister both, as models from a romantic world that he does not fully understand. When Fergus bedecks his sister with diamonds, he is only partly showing off his own rich position. Rather, he takes pleasure in Flora as a sibling who takes his cause as her own. In that sense, he sees her as a comrade who can help him to fulfill his destiny. Waverley, on the other hand, sees her as a beautiful woman whom he would love to pursue. When he makes these intentions clear to her, she dissuades him in terms that emphasize her own version of the fraternal bond. Her answer brings Waverley pain:

> "I dare hardly," she said, "tell you the situation of my feelings, they are so different from those usually ascribed to young women at my period of life; and I dare hardly touch upon what I conjecture to be the nature of yours, lest I should give offence where I would willingly administer consolation. For myself, from my infancy till this day, I have had but one wish – the restoration of my royal benefactors to their rightful throne. It is impossible to

express to you the devotion of my feelings to this single subject; and I will
frankly confess, that it has so occupied my mind as to exclude every thought
respecting what is called my own settlement in life. Let me but live to see
the day of that happy restoration, and a Highland cottage, a French con-
vent, or an English palace, will be alike indifferent to me." (214)

It would be hard for any hero to argue with such clear purpose, and Waverley
does not press his suit further. Flora has but one romantic goal, and there
is room for no others in her imagination. Waverley is disappointed, but he
also admires her commitment. Once she places love beyond his reach, he
can do little but acquiesce. In doing so, of course, she establishes his relation to this world as a relation of loss. Her devotion to a cause can only be
measured as loss for Edward. Flora predicts a different kind of woman for
Waverley – "The woman whom you marry ought to have affections and
opinions moulded upon yours. Her studies ought to be your studies; – her
wishes, her feelings, her hopes, her fears, should all mingle with yours. She
should enhance your pleasures, share your sorrows, and cheer your melancholy" (215) – but he is not yet ready to forsake his romantic ideal. Instead,
chastened and not quite ready to rethink his position, he heads back south
with the strong encouragement of Fergus and the benign approval of his
sister. Moreover, he is not yet persuaded of the Stuart cause: "he was aware
that unless he meant at once to embrace the proposal of Fergus Mac-Ivor,
it would deeply concern him to leave the suspicious neighbourhood without delay … Upon this he the rather determined, as Flora's advice favoured
his doing so, and because he felt inexpressible repugnance at the idea of
being accessory to the plague of civil war" (221–2).

The high point of Waverley's visit to Fergus and his family is his participation in a Highland hunt that Fergus insists Edward attend. The hunt is
a complicated event, and Waverley does not seem to understand what the
ritual involves. At a specified moment the stags turn and charge the hunt-
ers, who have all lowered themselves behind bushes for safety. Waverley
does not manage this movement quickly enough, and he is injured by
a stag. This misunderstanding betokens an even larger misunderstanding: Waverley only slowly begins to recognize that the hunt is in fact a
meeting of clans for the purpose of planning Bonnie Prince Charlie's invasion. Alison Lumsden says that Waverley's inability to understand that the
hunt is serving this double purpose reflects his larger inability to take in
the specific cultural context in which he is trying to function.[31] Waverley

---

[31] See Alison Lumsden, *Sir Walter Scott and the Limits of Language* (Edinburgh: Edinburgh University
Press, 2010), 89.

thought he was going on a hunt with a friend, and instead he finds himself catapulted into history. Suddenly Fergus is nowhere to be seen, while Waverley is lost in a crowd he does not understand and wounded in a sudden charge of deer that he did not expect. Nature, in other words, overwhelms him. If it were necessary to do more to suggest that romance has led his hero astray, Scott merely has Waverley attended to by a surgeon who insists on treatments that Waverley classes as mere superstition. "Edward observed, with some surprise, that even Fergus, notwithstanding his knowledge and education, seemed to fall in with the superstitious ideas of his countrymen" (191): Waverley begins to wonder what he is doing in this exotic locale. If his wounding at a hunt recalls the wound of Adonis in the originary elegy of Bion, then we might mark this hunt as the beginning of Waverley's own elegiac relation to a past that he does not yet understand. He feels the pain of loss in direct relation to Highland plotting – the hunt was actually an attempt to bring the clans together for a council of war – and from this point in the novel he is reeling in reaction to events that are overwhelming.

The mood of elegy already looms large here, not only because Waverley is caught up in this romantic encounter with a past that is always already lost, but also on account of the passage of time and history themselves. As I mentioned above, Alan Bray makes the crucial points that friendship serves a public function, and that expressions of intimacy are best understood in terms of power relations and jockeying for position among members of the elite class of courtiers and those aspiring to the court.[32] This move from private to public also embodies a loss, as Bray understands, focusing his study, as he does, on gravestones and memorials. *Waverley* itself could be said to be a memorial, and scenes like this remind us that Waverley's own relation to the past is melancholy and debilitating.

In this mood, Waverley heads south, but he finds that he is already under suspicion for having emerged from the Highlands, and before long he has been taken into custody by Major Melville of Cairnvreckan who has a warrant for his arrest. Waverley's cavalier attitude toward his military appointment has led to this warrant, and the gentleman who has apprehended him is ready to hand him over to the authorities. But Major Melville is kindly, and he is persuaded to leniency by means of the reasoning of his clergyman, Mr. Morton, who not only preaches forgiveness but also offers to meet with Waverley to hear his story. This gesture provides a touching scene between Waverley and Mr. Morton, as Waverley seems to

---

[32] Bray, *The Friend*, 6.

be reconsidering his own decisions. Waverley sees "fighting ... for love, for loyalty, and for fame" to be preferable to any kind of incarceration, and this romantic spirit of independence makes him susceptible to the charms of the representative of the Stuarts. As he is being taken from the control of Major Melville to his next magistrate, he is captured, not without receiving a serious wound, and he is taken once more into the Highlands. His captor, David Bean Lean, reappears here and deposits him in a well-secreted hovel, where there are a group of females to nurse him back to health. After a period spent in this strange place, where he copes with a fever and becomes increasingly intrigued by the mysterious females who are attending him, he finds himself carried to the very heart of the Jacobite revolt:

> On the opposite bank of the river, and partly surrounded by a winding of its stream, stood a large and massive castle, the half-ruined turrets of which were already glittering in the first rays of the sun. It was in form an oblong square, of size sufficient to contain a large court in the centre. The towers at each angle of the square rose higher than the walls of the building, and were in their turn surmounted by turrets, differing in height, and irregular in shape. Upon one of these a sentinel watched, whose bonnet and plaid streaming in the wind declared him to be a Highlander, as a broad white ensign, which floated from another tower, announced that the garrison was held by the insurgent adherents of the House of Stuart. (283)

This is a scene to capture Waverley's imagination, and as he ponders the grandeur of the scene, he is also caught up in the tartan colors and the "broad white ensign" that announces the presence of Charles Edward.

As Waverley enters the castle, its sublime features greet him immediately: "Waverley found himself in front of the gloomy yet picturesque structure which he had admired at a distance. A huge iron-grated door, which formed the exterior defence of the gateway, was already thrown back to receive them; and a second, heavily constructed of oak, and studded thickly with iron nails, being next opened, admitted them into the interior court-yard" (283–4). He seems to be entering an inner-sanctum of some kind, the very chamber in a Gothic novel where one would encounter a ghost. Is not Charles Edward Stuart a kind of ghost? Such Gothic conventions work to deepen the mood of emotional uneasiness, a loss already experienced even as Waverley first meets the already doomed prince. Loss is figured even in the grace of their first meeting.

When shortly after this, Waverley is presented to Prince Charles Edward, he is suitably impressed:

> A young man, wearing his own fair hair, distinguished by the dignity of his mien and the noble expression of his well-formed and regular features,

advanced out of a circle of military gentlemen and Highland Chiefs, by whom he was surrounded. In his easy and graceful manners Waverley afterwards thought he could have discovered his high birth and rank, although the star in his breast, and the embroidered garter at his knee, had not appeared as its indications.

"Let me present to your Royal Highness," said Fergus, bowing profoundly –

"The descendant of one of the most ancient and loyal families in England," said the young Chevalier, interrupting him, "I beg your pardon for interrupting you, my dear Mac-Ivor; but no master of ceremonies is necessary to present a Waverley to a Stuart."

Thus saying, he extended his hand to Edward, with the utmost courtesy, who could not, had he desired it, have avoided rendering him the homage which seemed due to his rank, and was certainly the right of his birth. (293–4)

Waverley is almost caught off guard, but he also seems ready to pay his homage where it is due. This is an important scene, because it shows the prince recognizing Waverley first, and it marks the moment when Waverley becomes swept up in the Jacobite cause. He has moments of resistance after this, to be sure, but this encounter with handsomeness and politeness does a great deal to win Waverley over. This is the romance of the Highlands that we have been waiting for. Waverley has met a prince, and he is almost immediately ready to embrace this figure out of romance and to make him his own prince. Waverley is seduced by the charm of this historical figure, only partially aware of the ghostly impossibility of this bond.

When Charles Edward makes his case more directly, he does so in a way that makes it almost impossible for Waverley to resist:

"But I desire to gain no adherents save from affection and conviction; and if Mr. Waverley inclines to prosecute his journey to the south, or to join the forces of the Elector, he shall have my passport and free permission to do so.... But," continued Charles Edward, after another short pause, "if Mr. Waverley should, like his ancestor, Sir Nigel, determine to embrace a cause which has little to recommend it but its justice, and follow a prince who throws himself upon the affections of his people, to recover the throne of his ancestors or perish in the attempt, I can only say, that among these nobles and gentlemen he will find worthy associates in a gallant enterprise, and will follow a master who may be unfortunate, but, I trust, will never be ungrateful." (294)

The generous invitation and studied rhetoric of this speech suggests a speaker so inured to the political that it colors his every word. Nevertheless, it is very welcoming to the young hero, and the narrator tells us that Waverley is utterly overcome:

> Unaccustomed to the address and manners of a polished court, in which Charles was eminently skilful, his words and his kindness penetrated the heart of our hero, and easily outweighed all prudential motives. To be thus personally solicited for assistance by a Prince, whose form and manners, as well as the spirit which he displayed in this singular enterprise, answered his ideas of a hero of romance; to be courted by him in the ancient halls of his paternal palace, recovered by the sword which he was already bending towards other conquests, gave Edward, in his own eyes, the dignity and importance which he had ceased to consider as his attributes. Rejected, slandered, and threatened upon the one side, he was irresistibly attracted to the cause which the prejudices of education, and the political principles of his family, had already recommended as the most just. These thoughts rushed through his mind like a torrent, sweeping before them every consideration of an opposite tendency, – the time, besides, admitted no deliberation, – and Waverley, kneeling to Charles Edward, devoted his heart and sword to the vindication of his rights! (294–5)

If this is an act of seduction on Charles Edward's part, Waverley is "penetrated" with affection and finds himself devoted heart and sword to this suddenly engaging cause. If this is the moment to which all the narrative has been tending, then all the romantic aspirations of the hero are here fulfilled in this moment of friendship and obeisance: Waverley now resigns himself to this greater cause. As the narrator tells us further:

> This Fergus had foreseen from the beginning. He really loved Waverley, because their feelings and projects never thwarted each other; he hoped to see him united with Flora, and he rejoiced that they were effectually engaged in the same cause. But, as we before hinted, he also exulted as a politician in beholding secured to his party a partisan of such consequence; and he was far from being insensible to the personal importance which he himself gained with the Prince, from having so materially assisted in making the acquisition. (295–6)

Waverley's commitment to Charles Edward is in a sense an act of devotion to Fergus as well. Friendship is what makes this bond so vivid, and it is friendship in and through politics, as it often can be. Jacques Derrida reminds us, in *The Politics of Friendship*, "Friendship tells the truth – and this is always better left unknown. The protection of this custody guarantees the truth of friendship, its ambiguous truth, that by which friends protect themselves from the error or the illusion on which friendship is founded – more precisely, the bottomless bottom founding a friendship, which enables it to resist its own abyss."[33] Fergus' notion of friendship barely hides this truth of an overriding political agenda, and until Edward Waverley recognizes that and acts accordingly, he will find himself the victim of political expediency. For Waverley, though, it is a deeply emotional bond, and that makes the eventual loss even more devastating.

As if to highlight the political implications of this transaction, Fergus asks his assistant to aid him in fitting out Waverley as a Highland officer:

> "Get a plaid of Mac-Ivor tartan, and sash," continued the Chieftain, "and a blue bonnet of the Prince's pattern, at Mr. Monat's in the Crames. My short green coat, with silver lace and silver buttons, will fit him exactly, and I have never worn it. Tell Ensign Maccombich to pick out a handsome target from among mine. The prince has given Mr. Waverley broadsword and pistols, I will furnish him with a dirk and purse; add but a pair of low-heeled shoes, and then my dear Edward (turning to him) you will be a complete son of Ivor." (300)

Fergus makes Waverley a brother by dressing him in this way, and in his attention to detail, he might even be fitting out a wedding dress for our hero. It almost seems like that kind of an alliance of aristocratic households. Indeed, Fergus' desire that Waverley marry his sister, who herself has no intention of marrying, is almost a transposed quasi-incestuous desire for Waverley himself. This scene gives that desire an almost lurid substance: now he is a "complete son of Mac Ivor."

The scenes that involve the increasingly self-assured invading forces also emphasize the domestic affairs of the household of Charles Edward. What is most interesting from the perspective of friendship is Fergus' deepening interest in Rose Bardwardine, which is coupled with his self-assurance that Edward Waverley will be able to win the heart of his sister. He so persuades himself that this is an accomplished fact that he is taken aback when the Prince tells him that he is certain Rose's heart is already spoken for. The Prince was really speaking out of turn, but it has put the two friends in agonizing conflict, and that is precisely where Scott wants the action to go.

It is hard to explain how this transition has taken place, but Waverley has been noticing Rose and comparing her favorably to his former love, Flora. Rose's sense and her caring nature make these attractions tenable, but Waverley has not acted on them at all at the time when Fergus makes his claim:

> Rose Bradwardine gradually rose in Waverley's opinion. He had several opportunities of remarking, that, as her extreme timidity wore off, her

[33] Derrida, *The Politics of Friendship*, 53.

manners received a higher character; that the agitating circumstances of the
stormy time seemed to call forth a certain dignity of feeling and expression,
which he had not formerly observed; and that she omitted no opportunity
within her reach to extend her knowledge and refine her taste. (367)

When Fergus attacks Waverley about Rose, he does it by insisting that
Waverley take up his sister. When Waverley refuses, because of Flora's own
attitudes, Fergus takes offense, but his own sense of honor restrains him:

the modern code of honour will not permit you to found a quarrel upon
your right of compelling a man to continue his addresses to a female relative, which the fair lady has already refused. So that Fergus was compelled
to stomach this supposed affront, until the whirligig of time, whose motion
he promised he would watch most sedulously, should bring about an opportunity of revenge. (393)

This all comes to a head just as battle approaches. Fergus, almost crip-
pled with anger, disciplines his own soldiers mercilessly. Later it seems that
this brooding anger is more properly directed at Waverley: "Your affected
ignorance shall not save you, sir. The Prince – the Prince himself, has
acquainted me with your manoeuvers. I little thought that your engage-
ments with Miss Bradwardine were the reason of your breaking off your
intended match with my sister" (397–8); and he proceeds, as he draws his
sword, to demand that Waverley give up Rose "for ever" (398). Waverley
responds in kind: " 'What title have you,' cried Waverley, utterly losing
command of himself, – 'What title have you, or any man living, to dictate
such terms to me?' And he also drew his sword" (398). It takes Charles
Edward to separate the men here and to remind them of the grander purpose for which they are fighting. But this rivalry is crucially important: for
all the brooding tension between these friends is suddenly exposed. This
is the hidden truth of friendship: the knowledge of a deep-seated enmity
simmers just beneath the surface of this friendship, and as Charles Edward
recognizes, quarrels such as these will destroy his hopes of achieving vic-
tory in his risky invasion.

The loss of the friendship – first in this emotional alienation and soon
in Fergus' execution – begins to make the elegiac features of this novel
more vivid. Waverley's relation to the past, to the friendship that was
rooted in the past, and to the romance of a Stuart claim on the English
throne is a relation of loss; and like the loss in an elegy, it needs to be
refigured and commemorated in some way that does not drag Waverley
into an abyss of melancholy. That is what transpires in the last chapters
of the novel.

A rapprochement of sorts is achieved, however, when the forces of Charles Edward are retreating and Fergus confronts a ghost that harkens his own demise. Waverley approaches Fergus first: "Waverley, who was really much affected by the deep tone of melancholy with which Fergus spoke, affectionately entreated him to banish from his remembrance any unkindness which had arisen between them, and they once more shook hands, but now with sincere cordiality" (404). Fergus tells the story of the "Grey Spectre" that predicts his death, and he says that he "would not willingly fall until I am in charity with a wronged friend" (407). These friends face each other on the eve of defeat, and they seem to find in each other the meaning of the battle for them. This ghost story shimmers between them as a monument to their friendship and also as a measure of all they are about to lose.

After the defeat of the invading forces and the loss of everything the Highlanders were fighting for, Waverley again confronts Fergus, but now the latter is in prison awaiting execution, and their intimacy can do very little to sustain them. Still they reconnect:

> "You are rich," [Fergus] said, "Waverley, and you are generous. When you hear of these poor Mac-Ivors being distressed about their miserable possessions by some harsh overseer or agent of the government, remember you have worn their tartan and are an adopted son of their race. The Baron ... will apprize you of the time and means to be their protector. Will you promise this to the last Vich Ian Vohr?"
>
> Edward, as may well be believed, pledged his word; which he afterwards so amply redeemed, that his memory still lives in these glens by the name of the Friend of the Sons of Ivor.
>
> "Would to God," continued the Chieftain, "I could bequeath to you my rights to the love and obedience of this primitive and brave race: – or, at least, as I have striven to do, persuade poor Evan to accept of his life on those terms, and be to you what he has been to me, the kindest – the bravest – the most devoted" –
>
> The tears which his own fate could not draw forth, fell fast for that of his foster-brother. (472)

This final scene between these friends underlines the depth of their feelings and the world they tried to create. Fergus tries to make Waverley one of his own clan and to offer him his servant as a sign of the love they share. These are gestures of intimacy that Waverley understands and values. Their parting on the eve of Fergus' trial is the parting of true friends: it is as emotionally powerful as any of the more understandably emotional bonds.

The loss of Fergus is the loss of this heroic history, and Waverley must turn from it and rediscover a life in the present. This he does through long passages in which he reconnects with Rose and with her aid manages to aid the Baron in rebuilding the home that the invading forces had destroyed. As Andrew Hook observes:

> Before the end of the novel Waverley learns of the collapse of the Jacobite uprising and sees something of the inevitable retribution that follows. In particular he returns to the mansion house at Tully-Veolan to find it a scene of savage devastation and desolation. This scene of wanton destruction is the book's most powerful image of the true meaning of civil war – the anarchy, the senseless violence and ruin it produces. Yet Scott cannot leave the matter there.[34]

In fact, this situation is rectified when Waverley, with the help of his friend Talbot, salvages the house and restores it to its former grandeur before returning it to the Baron and his daughter. This offers the prospect of a happy ending between Edward and Rose; but this never feels fully satisfactory. Claire Lamont suggests that there is a clash between "the story of Edward Waverley and the history which it was the novel's other aim to present."[35] But the real story seems to be the tragic one of the friendship between Edward and Fergus, who has been a victim of historical change. Here friendship has to be sacrificed to politics, but in the end, it emerges as the only value that can sustain this historical romance into a recognizable present. The value of the story is in the friendship between Waverley and his Highland friend. That is the purpose of the tale and that is what gives it meaning.

That meaning is constituted in loss, and in that sense *Waverley* can be considered Scott's elegy for a lost age and the romance that age represents. Waverley's loss is refigured in the world he creates around him at the end of the novel. For Scott, the novel itself is the elegiac refiguration of the loss that he feels for the romantic aspirations of a past age. He creates the friendships he does as a way of giving that loss a personal complexity and emotional depth. The very act of creating that world and then destroying it is what allows him to place it aesthetically and give it an almost Gothic power. That is why it continues to resonate as powerfully as it does.

---

[34] Hook, "Introduction," 25.
[35] Claire Lamont, "Introduction," in Sir Walter Scott, *Waverley* (Oxford: Oxford University Press, 1998 [1986]), vi–xx (xiv). Julian Meldon D'Arcy pushes this "dissonance" even further to suggest a subversive political agenda in the novel: see *Subversive Scott: The Waverley Novels and Scottish Nationalism* (Reykjavik: University of Iceland Press, 2005), 55–74.

"O Sorrow, wilt thou live with me": Love and Loss in Tennyson's *In Memoriam*

> O Sorrow, wilt thou live with me
> No casual mistress, but a wife,
> My bosom-friend and half of life;
> As I confess it needs must be. (*In Memoriam* LIX, 1–4)[36]

Alfred Tennyson's *In Memoriam* is one of the great elegies in the English language. It is addressed to Tennyson's friend Arthur Hallam, who died in 1833. As Sacks notes, "Refusing to submit the idiosyncrasy of his grief to the shape of conventional ceremony, the poet is concerned rather to accentuate each moment and nuance, each erratic fluctuation of response … [Elegiac] elements are thoroughly dispersed among details of personal narrative and reflection."[37] Sacks goes on to say that certain formal features of the poem – "the slow and lengthy accretiveness, the stress on disjointed, self-enclosed fragments, the resistance to time or narrative – reflect an attitude that we recognize as melancholia."[38] Melancholia, of course, helps to shape every elegy. *In Memoriam* displays the features that Sacks describes, and it does what every elegy attempts to do: it invokes loss as the only way to recreate the love that the poem works so hard to declaim in every way possible.

The unmistakable love that Tennyson expresses for Hallam is what gives the poem its power; and as Tennyson struggles with what this love means in a world of change and loss, he also comes to understand his love in a new way and to celebrate its transcendent power in such moving terms that critics have been afraid to face the implications of the poem or to give it the place it so clearly deserves in the history of platonic friendship. Critics have not been hesitant to talk about the implicit homoerotics of the poem. Christopher Ricks tried to stave off possibly homosexual readings by pointing out the biographical conundrum that the poem poses. After a lengthy discussion of whether or not Tennyson can be labeled "homosexual," Ricks asks, "But why does it matter?" (179).[39] This demand for proof, one way or the other, would seem reasonable enough, if it were not that it undermines many otherwise rich readings of the poem. Ricks elsewhere

---

[36] Alfred, Lord Tennyson, *In Memoriam*, the Norton Critical Edition, ed. Erik Gray (New York: Norton, 2004), 43. Further references to this edition of the poem are included in parentheses.

[37] See Sacks, *The English Elegy*, 168.

[38] Sacks, *The English Elegy*, 169.

[39] Christopher Ricks, "*In Memoriam*, 1850," in *Tennyson*, 2nd ed. (London and Berkeley: Macmillan and University of California Press, 1989), 201–18.

quotes George Elliot's remark that "the deepest significance of the poem is the sanctification of human love as a religion," and it would seem to me to be possible to contemplate Tennyson's sanctifying love for his friend and come up with something richer and perhaps more revealing than any twentieth-century label for sexual identity.[40] What Tennyson's love invokes is the love first articulated in the writings of Plato and revisited throughout the elegy tradition, from classical times through the writings of Shelley and Byron.

Christopher Craft places *In Memoriam* in the context of later nineteenth-century sexologists who saw the poem as an example of exalted love that could help displace the insistent and at the time mostly unwanted promptings of desire. Craft sees this as a kind of duplicity in the poem, which for him points to the question of "whether *In Memoriam* 'can properly be termed homosexual.'"[41] For Craft, Hallam's centrality to the poem creates a problem for Tennyson, and

> the elegy negotiates its problematic desire less by a centering of its warmth than by the dispersal of its bliss, less by acts of specific definition than by strategies of deferral, truncation, and displacement, strategies that everywhere work to "refine and spiritualize" what otherwise would be "the wish too strong for words to name" [93]. But *In Memoriam* is more than a machine for the sublimation, management, or transformation of male homosexual desire; it is, rather, the site of a continuing problematization: the problem not merely of desire between men, but also the desire (very urgent in the elegy) to speak it.[42]

I am sympathetic with Craft's position here, but I think he misunderstands the emotional valence of the poem and its place within an elegiac tradition.

All elegies have an urgent desire to speak of the emotional attachment to the figure who is lost and who represents loss. The project of the elegy is perhaps to find some mode of sublimation that can lead one from the paralysis of grief to the kind of transformation that poetry makes possible. Tennyson writes sooner, as it were, than other elegists do, still working through the very process of mourning. As a result, the expression of desire in the poem is vivid and unmistakable. I see the awkwardness that Craft

[40] Ricks, "*In Memoriam,* 1850," 180; no reference is given for the Elliot quotation.
[41] Christopher Craft, "'Descend, Touch, and Enter': Tennyson's Strange Manner of Address," in *Another Kind of Love, Male Homosexual Desire in English Discourse 1850–1920* (Berkeley: University of California Press, 1994), 44–70 (46); the internal quote is from: Havelock Ellis, *Sexual Inversion,* 3rd ed. (Philadelphia: F. A. Davis, 1931), 339; Ellis questions "whether or not such [exalted and passionate] friendship can properly be termed homosexual."
[42] Craft, "Descend, Touch, and Enter," 47; internal reference is to section XCIII of *In Memoriam,* from which his title also comes.

does, but I would ascribe it to the complexity and immensity of the emotion that Tennyson can hardly find the language for. Whatever sublimation the poem achieves is a triumph of emotional will rather than a failure to self-identify. It seems to me that Tennyson would be more than ready to identify his love for Hallam in sexual terms if that would bring him back. The truth of the poem is that he is lost: sexuality is spiritualized precisely because in the elegy there is no other form for it to take.[43]

What all such readings do is demonstrate how sometimes in the late twentieth century the urge to "out" writers and define works by their sexuality has somehow distorted the very love that has always already been present in the poem. None of the queer readings say as elegantly as Eric Gray does, in his introduction to the poem, what such readings might achieve: "Queer criticism helps remind us that *In Memoriam* is not only an elegy but one of the most beautiful love poems in English."[44] If elegies are really love poems, then they express a very special kind of love: lost, idealized, and transformed or refigured in poetic form.

As Christopher Ricks points out in a footnote, "Arthur Hallam had discussed Plato's 'frequent commendation of a more lively sentiment than has existed in other times between man and man, the misunderstanding of which has repelled several from the deep tenderness and splendid imaginations of the Phaedrus and the Symposium.'"[45] I would love to know what Hallam meant by "misunderstanding," but for "deep tenderness" and "splendid imaginations," we need go no further than Tennyson's poem.

If I am going to argue *In Memoriam* is a love poem, you might ask, how is that different from talking about its sexuality? But if we see love as a kind of religion, as Ricks suggests that we might, and if we understand the desperate need of the elegiac tradition to establish a bond with the lost loved one, then we can start to imagine a kind of love that is physical and meaningful but does not circumscribe emotion in terms of sexuality. The poem is about a kind of love that is rarely achieved in human relations. It is, to my mind, a unique expression of love and loss. It does not fail to express that love; but in fact it so dazzlingly succeeds that critics are afraid to take that love seriously. That is what I intend to do here.

---

[43] See also Jeff Nunokawa: "*In Memoriam* proposes a developmental model of male sexuality which establishes the homoerotic as an early phase that enables and defines the heterosexual"; and he says further that the poem is an "elegy for the homosexual" in that it moves toward marriage while "matured male love leaves behind no mark"; Jeff Nunokawa, "*In Memoriam* and the Extinction of the Homosexual," *English Literary History* 58.2 (1991): 427–38.

[44] Erik Gray, "Introduction," in *In Memoriam* (New York: Norton, 2004), xi–xxvii (xxv).

[45] Arthur Hallam, "Essay on Cicero," quoted in Ricks, "*In Memoriam*, 1850," 178n 2.

For me, the figuration that Sacks describes actually takes place at the end
of the poem, in the Epithalamium with which it closes. As the end of the
poem approaches, the mood of the elegy has changed. When he returns
to places, like Hallam's street, that earlier tormented him with paralyzing
memories and gloomy loss, now he finds a new kind of consolation, which
might almost be labeled as hope:

> Doors, where my heart was used to beat
>   So quickly, not as one that weeps
>   I come once more; the city sleeps;
> I smell the meadow in the street;
>
> I hear a chirp of birds; I see
>   Betwixt the black of fronts long-withdrawn
>   A light-blue lane of early dawn,
> And think of early days and thee,
>
> And bless thee, for thy lips are bland,
>   And bright the friendship of thine eye;
>   And in my thoughts with scarce a sigh
> I take the pressure of thy hand. (CXIX, p. 89)

The poet returns to Hallam's street, to his house, a source of such incon-
solable torment earlier in the poem (VII, pp. 10–11). Now he comes "not
as one that weeps." His senses seem alive again, as he notes "the chirp of
birds" and the "light-blue lane of early dawn." This is not a consolation,
however, that moves the poet beyond his sense of loss or in spite of his
beloved. Tennyson can "think on early days and thee" because he has a
new certainty about the bond between the living and the dead. In the
last stanza, Hallam is his companion: "bright the friendship of thine eye."
They are together here, and Tennyson ends the poem with an image that
would have been entirely impossible but a few sections earlier: "And in my
thoughts with scarce a sigh / I take the pressure of thy hand." This pressure
of the hand is the touch that the poet asked for in section XCIII: the poet
and his lost friend are now one. This is the love he has been searching for.
    A final poem from the sequence expresses this well:

> Love is and was my Lord and King,
>   And in his presence I attend
>   To hear the tidings of my friend,
> Which every hour his couriers bring.
>
> Love is and was my King and Lord,
>   And will be, tho' as yet I keep
>   Within his court on earth, and sleep
> Encompass'd by his faithful guard,

> And hear at times a sentinel
>> Who moves about from place to place,
>> And whispers to the worlds of space,
> In the deep night, that all is well. (CXXVI, p. 93)

Tennyson personifies love as a god here, as God in fact, and as he does so, he makes this god a personal means of communication with his lost friend. This friend is not so lost because he is found in the Lord and King of Love, where of course he has resided all along. When the poet recognizes the god of love as the spirit of his friend, he hears the sentinel who "whispers to the worlds of space, / In the deep night, that all is well." This sentinel calls him to another world, but it is a world he has already realized in this poem. This is the world of Love.

That is why the poem can end with an Epithalamium. Of course he is celebrating his sister's marriage to Edward Lushington, but even so, it becomes a celebration of the bond with Hallam that he has discovered in the course of writing this poem:

> No longer caring to embalm
>> In dying songs a dead regret
>> But like a statue solid set,
> And moulded in colossal calm.
>
> Regret is dead, but love is more
>> But in the summers that are flown,
>> For I myself with these have grown
> To something greater than before. (ll. 13–20, p. 97)

Here the poet introduces death into his Epithalamium, not to mock the married couple nor to hide his love in heteronormativity. Rather he resists the deathly regret and desperation that he earlier felt: "Regret is dead," he says, "but love is more." That love – unearthly and transcendent – emerges in the poem as a kind of hope. And the hope here is a kind of growing out of oneself. Later in the poem he uses the image of God to pursue this even further.

> No longer half-akin to brute
>> For all we thought and loved and did,
>> And hoped and suffer'd, is but seed
> Of what in them is flower and fruit;
>
> Whereof the man, that with me trod
>> This planet, was a noble type
>> Appearing ere the times were ripe
> That friend of mine who lives in God.

> That God, which ever lives and loves,
>   One God, one law, one element
>   And one far-off divine event
> In which the whole creation moves. (ll. 133–44, pp. 100–1)

At first it seems as if he subsumes "all we thought and loved and did, / And hoped and suffer'd" into some version of the union his sister and Lushington realize in marriage. But then he places his friend Hallam in the same trajectory: "Appearing ere the times were ripe / That friend of mine who lives in God." Tennyson does not present Hallam as a potential bridegroom for his sister, but he presents him as his friend. That he lives in God is what the earlier poems have taught: God is love, and love is Hallam too. "That God which ever lives and loves" is the God that Tennyson has found to answer his loss. In God he finds the spirit of Hallam, not for divine belief but for human love. If there is any meaning to platonic love it is here: "One God, one law, one element / And one far-off divine event." Tennyson imagines a union with his beloved, Spirit to Spirit, Ghost to Ghost in this element of transcendence that has meaning only in these personal terms. "The whole creation moves" in this element of love that Tennyson has discovered in Hallam and commemorated in this poem.

As Eric Gray argues in his introduction, "Hallam seems to have become many different selves: Hallam the memory, the corpse, the dream, the angel. Wishing to address his friend but at a loss where to direct his speech, Tennyson turns to the yew tree in the graveyard."[46] Elegiac writing finds consolation in nature, but early in the poem, the image of the yew tree confronts the poet with its ability to grasp the bones of the dead and make them its own. Tennyson wants to imitate this process, as the last line ("grow incorporate into thee") suggests, but the grasping and incorporation is still far beyond him. This bleak poem is a poem of recognition: a failure. But Tennyson knows that by knocking his head against the reality of nature, he may find a way back to Hallam. Sacks calls this poem an "anti-pastoral, cutting against the grain of conventional elegy"; but of course this anti-pastoral uses specific imagery from the elegy – the yew, the grave, the bleakness of nature – to create what Sacks calls a "fibrous knot" of grief.[47] The imagery of the knot – the grasping mentioned above – suggests the desperate need to cling to whatever shred of memory the poem can recreate.

When in the first poem of the series Tennyson says famously, "Let Love clasp Grief lest both be drown'd" (p. 7), he initiates his elegy in terms

---

[46] Gray, "Introduction," xix–xx.
[47] Sacks, *The English Elegy*, 173.

almost antithetical to any notion of "working through" his grief. He wants to experience it directly as a way of discovering the love that has been lost to him. The poem repeatedly recreates the intimacy Tennyson shared with Hallam and recounts the immensity of loss. In remembering their time together in the landscape they shared, Tennyson invokes the imagery of elegy in order to place himself in the natural world as well. When he imagines Hallam in the shadow of death, the best that Tennyson can do is to imagine that he will someday die too. There is little consolation in this image, but it heightens the sense of the absolute quality of this loss and the distance that Tennyson must still cover before he can find any means of consolation.

"Be near me," the poet says in section L with an almost desperate plea:

> Be near me when my light is low,
>   When the blood creeps, and the nerves prick
>   And tingle; and the heart is sick,
> And all the wheels of Being slow.
>
> Be near me when the sensuous frame
>   Is rack'd with pains that conquer trust;
>   And Time, a maniac scattering dust,
> And Life, a Fury slinging flame.
>
> Be near me when my faith is dry,
>   And men the flies of latter spring
>   That lay their eggs, and sting and sing
> And weave their petty cells and die.
>
> Be near me when I fade away,
>   To point the term of human strife,
>   And on the low dark verge of life
> The twilight of eternal day. (L; pp. 37–8)

The poem begins in an almost Gothic dark night of the soul, and through it Tennyson reaches into the beyond to call his dear friend as an answer to the prick and tingle of his nerves. Time is his enemy here, because it enforces the madness of separation, and Life a torment because it consumes him in absence and loss. He loses faith in human value in the course of the poem precisely because the nearness he craves cannot immediately be achieved. The most moving stanza, though, is the last. Here he imagines his own demise and his entry into the eternal day of paradise: at this "low dark verge of life" he can imagine his friend with him at last. For if he does not meet him in this glorious and ghostly twilight, where will he or can he?

This understanding gives away again to grief, as it necessarily must, and
in but a few sections the poet is again lamenting and giving in to the melancholia that the lament represents:

> O Sorrow, wilt thou live with me
>   No casual mistress, but a wife,
>   My bosom-friend and half of life;
> As I confess it needs must be;
>
> O Sorrow, wilt thou rule my blood,
>   Be sometimes lovely like a bride,
>   And put thy harsher moods aside,
> If thou wilt have me wise and good.
>
> My centered passion cannot move,
>   Nor will it lessen from to-day;
>   But I'll have leave at times to play
> As with the creature of my love;
>
> And set thee forth, for thou are mine,
>   With so much hope for years to come,
>   That, howsoe'er I know thee, some
> Could hardly tell what name were thine. (LIX, p. 43)

Gray offers the following gloss on these lines: "My love for Hallam will never
waver (lines 9–10), but my sorrow, the result or 'creature' of that love (line
12) will take different forms, to the point that others may scarcely recognize it
as sorrow at all."[48] That is a helpful gloss, but it underestimates the confusion
of the poem by which sorrow and Hallam are sometimes seen as one. When
the poet invites sorrow to cohabit as his wife, he is admitting how impossible
it will be to move beyond the sorrow of loss he feels. Still, he puts that sorrow in terms that he might offer to his friend: "wilt thou sometimes rule my
blood, / Be sometimes like a lovely bride" or "But I'll have leave at times to
play / As with the creature of my love." Tennyson seems to search within sorrow for the happiness he shared with Hallam, and in that sense sorrow comes
to represent the love he has lost. That is why "howsoe'er I know thee, some
/ Could hardly tell what name was thine": Hallam becomes the sorrow that
Tennyson can imagine as a wife. It is the bond he has been seeking: instead of
moving through his grief, he moves into it even more deeply.

Soon after this, the poet admits how hard it is to see the features of
his beloved and how impassible seems the gulf between life and death,

---

[48] Tennyson, *In Memoriam*, 43, n. 2.

but then suddenly that changes and something completely different emerges:

> I cannot see the features right,
>> When on the gloom I strive to paint
>> The face I know; the hues are faint
> And mix with hollow masks of night;
>
> Cloud-towers by ghostly masons wrought,
>> A gulf that ever shuts and gapes,
>> A hand that points, and palled shapes
> In shadowy thoroughfares of thought;
>
> And crowds that stream from yawning doors,
>> And shoals of pucker'd faces drive;
>> Dark bulks that tumble half alive,
> And lazy lengths on boundless shores;
>
> Till all at once beyond the will
>> I hear a wizard music roll,
>> And thro' a lattice in the soul
> Looks thy fair face and makes it still. (LXX, p. 49)

This startlingly vivid poem talks more directly about communion with the dead – not hope for a touch or confusion about a feeling – but direct visual communication. Twelve of the fifteen lines tell about the obstructions and confusions that barricade the living from the dead: "cloud-towers by ghostly masons wrought." The "shadowy thoroughfares of thought" are crowded with "pucker'd faces" and "dark bulks," but the image he hopes to conjure lies beyond imagining. Or at least it seems that way. But then, suddenly, there is a breakthrough both sudden and magical. Its suddenness is also a feature of its being impossible to control: "all at once beyond the will"; and its magic engages sound as well as sight: "I hear a wizard music roll." The final vision is partial at the same time it is playful: "thro' a lattice in the soul"; but suddenly rather than looking the poet is being looked at. For through this lattice, "Looked thy fair face and makes it still." What Hallam's fair face makes still is of course the poet's soul. If I pause for a minute over the image of "a lattice in the soul," that is because the soul becomes a kind of window. In traditional poetry the eyes are a window to the soul, but in this poem, the soul offers a window to the eyes of the lost lover. When the poet stops looking actively, that is, the lover comes into focus as a desiring and protective force beyond the will. What more beautiful love poem to a lost love could there be?

One more beautiful poem follows some twenty sections later, as time persuades him only that he feels his loss even more (LXXXI, p. 55) and he begins to doubt that his vision could be anything other than a form of madness. This builds to a crescendo in section XCIII:

> I shall not see thee. Dare I say
>   No spirit ever brake the band
>   That stays him from the native land
> Where first he walk'd when claspt in clay?
>
> No visual shade of some one lost,
>   But he, the Spirit himself, may come
>   Where all the nerve of sense is numb
> Spirit to Spirit, Ghost to Ghost.
>
> O, therefore from thy sightless range
>   With gods in unconjectured bliss,
>   O, from the distance of the abyss
> Of tenfold-complicated change,
>
> Descend, and touch, and enter; hear
>   The wish too strong for words to name;
>   That in this blindness of the frame
> My Ghost may feel that thine is near. (XCIII, pp. 67–8)

At first this seems like a setback from the poem just quoted. "I shall not see thee" is as clear and direct as any statement in the poem. The poet seems resigned to the distance between the living and the dead. But no sooner has he given up sight, than a different possibility presents itself: "he, the Spirit himself, may come." If in section LXX the poet had to give up willing to see Hallam for a vision to be possible, then here "all the nerve of sense" must be "numb" for the encounter to take place. Is it more or less than a vision to meet Hallam "Spirit to Spirit, Ghost to Ghost"? I would have to say that this is more because it exists in a realm that cannot be accommodated by the senses. In this realm, the "distance of the abyss" between life and death, the "tenfold-complicated change" becomes the space of spiritual communion. Eric Gray calls this the culmination of the entire poem, and how could it not be?[49] "Descend, and touch, and enter": it certainly sounds more than spiritual, and surely Tennyson meant that it should. He embraces the spirit of his lost friend and expresses this union in physical terms so as not to be euphemistic or ashamed of this love in some way. He

---

[49] Tennyson, *In Memoriam*, 68, n. 1; see also Craft, "Descend, Touch, and Enter." For Craft, this section is also a kind of culmination.

does so because the physical intimacy he describes is what comes closest to expressing the spiritual bond he feels. His love is platonic in the sense that its physicality leads to something even more profound.

These spirits engage on a higher plane, to be sure, but they can only do so because they were bounded by love in their physical selves. As Diotima remarks in Plato's *Symposium*, "You see, the man who has been thus far guided in matters of Love, who has beheld beautiful things in the right order and correctly, is coming now to the goal of Loving; all of a sudden he will catch sight of something wonderfully beautiful in its nature; that, Socrates, is the reason for all his earlier labors."[50] This encounter with the beautiful occurs in and through an encounter with physical beauty in the world. In this remarkable section by Tennyson as these spirits mingle at last, that transformative encounter has to be assumed.

Once the possibility of this encounter can be articulated in the poem, it can move toward the conclusion I discussed above. An Epithalamium is appropriate in the terms that Plato provides. Platonic love is not the answer to the enormity of loss articulated in the poem unless it can be realized in the process that Tennyson dramatizes. As I have described it, I think Tennyson does realize what love means in Platonic terms. That leaves him at the end of the poem not castrated by the deflection of his desire that Sacks has described. Instead, he is fulfilled by loss in a way that could almost be called transcendent. Tennyson does not find substitutes for his love in the poem, but he finds Love itself.

"Jacob! Jacob!": The Culture of Loss in *Jacob's Room*

Virginia Woolf's novel, *Jacob's Room*, was published in 1922 at the Hogarth Press in Richmond, the press that she and Leonard Woolf had recently established. Its position as her first Hogarth Press book, the first book, that is, about which she took full control, is important to its deeply elegiac significance. *Jacob's Room* is a novel about loss, and it places loss so centrally in its fictive universe that it could almost be said to be about nothing else, for the Jacob of the title is already doomed. He is marked with the death that will overtake him at the end of the novel, and everything that happens in the novel leads to that death and gives it cultural meaning. "Jacob! Jacob!" Bonamy laments on the last page, calling out, as it were, to his absent friend and marking the enormity of loss as well as its inevitability.

---

[50] Plato, *Symposium*, trans. Alexander Nehamas and Paul Woodruff, in *Plato: Complete Works*, ed. John M. Cooper (Indianapolis: Hackett, 1997), 457–505 (493).

Some critics have complained that we do not get to know Jacob well or that he is the absence at the center of the novel. But Jacob slips out of our grasp because death separates him from us and makes it impossible to know him intimately. Every time we might feel that we get close to him, he slips away.

The novel starts with tragic acknowledgment of loss – Mrs. Flanders has to clear the tears from her eyes as she tries to write home from Cornwall where she is on holiday with her boys – and even the world seems askew as she looks up from the tear-stained page:

> "So of course," wrote Betty Flanders, pressing her heels rather deeper in the sand, "there was nothing for it but to leave."
>
> Slowly welling from the point of her gold nib, pale blue ink dissolved the full stop; for there the pen stuck; her eyes fixed, and tears slowly filled them. The entire bay quivered; the lighthouse wobbled; and she had the illusion that the mast of Mr. Connor's little yacht was bending like a wax candle in the sun. She winked quickly. Accidents were awful things. She winked again. The mast was straight; the saves were regular; the lighthouse was upright; but the blot spread.[51]

This simple visual cue – "the entire bay quivered" – begins the novel in an elegiac tone that it never loses. The blot that spreads on her page is the blot of experience marked by loss, and it is the visual sign that this novel will proceed like a literary requiem for the title character.

After a few more lines describing her situation and the friend she is writing to in Scarborough, the narrative is interrupted with a shout: " 'Ja – cob! Ja – cob!' Archer shouted" (5). The novel begins with this shrill call as if to remind us what is the real source of grief in this novel. When Jacob shortly after this appears, carrying a sheep's skull as if it were a memento mori, Woolf has set her agenda clearly and directly:

> There he stood. His face composed itself. He was about to roar when, lying among the black sticks and straw under the cliff, he saw a whole skull, perhaps, with the teeth in it. Sobbing, but absent-mindedly, he ran farther and farther away until he held the skull in his arms. (7)

Jacob feels drawn to the mystery of this skull, which is of course the mystery of life and death. Mrs. Flanders is disgusted – "What has he got hold of? Put it down, Jacob! Drop it this moment!" (8) – but Jacob cannot resist – "But he ducked down and picked up the sheep's jaw, which was

---

[51] Virginia Woolf, *Jacob's Room* (Oxford: Oxford University Press, 2008 [1922]), 3. Further parenthetical page references refer to this edition.

loose" – and instead he carries the memento home with him. It may seem a little heavy-handed, but Woolf does not want us to miss her central concern.

In his own study of the elegy W. David Shaw tells us, "The classical elegist is always trying to break through the barrier of mere descriptive naming in quest of the vocative of direct address. To speak to the dead is already to have made a breech in the wall, to have battered down a boundary or divide."[52] Woolf does not herself address Jacob directly, but she intones his name through a character like Archer, Jacob's older brother, who shouts it more to the lucid skies of the seaside than to the person invoked. It is almost as if he were keening the name of someone lost, which indeed he is, even if he does not know he is.

The novel proceeds to lead us through Jacob's life, always reminding us that this procedure is as much a funeral for Jacob as it is his biography. A few pages after this, for instance, we hear about Jacob's butterfly collection: it is another story of death:

> The stag-beetle dies slowly (it was John who collected the beetles). Even on the second day its legs were supple. But the butterflies were dead. A whiff of rotten eggs had vanquished the pale clouded yellows which came pelting across the orchard and up Dods Hill and away on to the moor, now lost behind a furze bush, then off again helter skelter in a broiling sun. (25)

This "whiff of rotten eggs" carries with it a sense of death. Woolf insists on the smell so that we are not mistaken: this is a scene of death. Jacob and the pale clouded yellows represent a deathly confrontation.

Like an elegy as well is the repeated reference to flowers and the floral tribute that is so central to the process of elegy. This description of a sunny afternoon in Cornwall, as bright and lively as it seems, can also be imagined to invoke the floral tribute of an elegy:

> The whole city was pink and gold; domed; mist-wreathed; resonant; strident. Banjoes strummed; the parade smelt of tar, which stuck to the heels; goats suddenly cantered their carriages through crowds. It was observed how well the Corporation had laid out the flower-beds. Sometimes a straw hat was blown away. Tulips burnt in the sun. Numbers of sponge-bag trousers were stretched in rows. Purple bonnets fringed soft, pink, querulous faces on pillows in bath chairs. Triangular hoardings were wheeled along by men in white coats. (18)

---

[52] W. David Shaw, *Elegy and Paradox: Testing the Conventions* (Baltimore: Johns Hopkins University Press, 1994), 15.

The image is intensely visual, but it does more than simply create a sense of the scene at the Cornish seaside. It has almost performative value, as does the strewing of the hearse in Milton's *Lycidas* or the flowers on the corpse of Shelly's *Adonais*. Here the colors, flowers, sound, and smell combine to celebrate the loss in terms that are familiar.

A similar note is struck when Jacob and his friend Timmy Durrant are punting during a lazy Cambridge afternoon:

> Now there was a shiver of wind – instantly an edge of sky; and as Durrant ate cherries he dropped the stunted yellow through the green wedge of leaves, their stalks twinkling as they wriggled in and out, and sometimes one half-bitten cherry would go down red into the green. The meadow was on a level with Jacob's eyes as he lay back; gilt with buttercups, but the grass did not run like the thin green water of graveyard grass about to overflow the tombstones, but stood juicy and thick. Looking backwards, he saw the legs of children deep in the grass, and the legs of cows. Munch, munch he heard; then a short step through the grass; then again munch, munch, munch, as they tore the grass short at the roots. In front of them two white butterflies circled higher and higher round the elm tree. (45–6)

This passage narrates a Cambridge afternoon even as it performs an elegiac function. The wriggling, stunted cherries are sometimes dropped almost bloodied into the water. Jacob is adorned with the gilt of buttercups, and the grass is compared to graveyard grass. The munch, munch of the cows is almost a natural commentary on physicality and mortality. Woolf creates an elegiac moment in the midst of a quiet Cambridge afternoon.

A Cambridge evening scene teases us with another elegiac moment. This the hint of the kind of friendship that animates elegies from Bion to Tennyson and beyond: that is, of course, deeply loving male friendship.

> There were young men who read, lying in shallow armchairs, holding their books as if they had hold in their hands of something that would see them through; they being all in a torment, coming from midland towns, clergymen's sons. Others read Keats. And those long histories in many volumes – surely someone was now beginning at the beginning in order to understand the Holy Roman Empire, as one must. That was part of the concentration, though it would be dangerous on a hot spring night – dangerous, perhaps, to concentrate too much upon single books, actual chapters, when at any moment the door opened and Jacob appeared; or Richard Bonamy, reading Keats no longer, began making long pink spills from an old newspaper, bending forward, and looking eager and contented no more, but almost fierce. Why? Only perhaps that Keats died young – one wants to write poetry too and to love – oh, the brutes! It's damnably difficult. (54–5)

This evening scene is also punctuated by death – if only Keats' early death – and desire, as Bonamy looks up fiercely at Jacob's entrance. "Oh, the brutes!" the narrator records: the brutes who look at experience and fail to see its pain and its ever deeper loss. It is "damnably difficult."

Alex Zwerdling notes the elegiac impulse in *Jacob's Room*, but he calls it a satiric elegy. Woolf cannot be serious, he suggests, about this meaningless life: "By its very nature, such a stage cannot be a record of triumphs, and those who are going through it often seem simply confused and self-indulgent to their elders, particularly those with short memories. Furthermore, a person in this position remains in some sense a blank, indefinable, unknowable – and therefore not an easy subject for fiction."[53] I would argue that scenes such as this one remind how absolutely serious Woolf is both about the pain of experience and the enormity of loss that is the real subject here. She can be serious about a "meaningless" life such as this, and the novel demonstrates how very serious she is.

Almost in defiance of Zwerdling, Woolf makes this observation, later when Jacob is in London:

> The proximity of omnibuses gave the outside passengers an opportunity to stare into each other's faces. Yet few took advantage of it. Each had his own business to think of. Each had his past shut in him like the leaves of a book known to him by heart; and his friends could only read the title, James Spalding, or Charles Budgeon, and the passengers going the other way could read nothing at all – save "a man with a red moustache", "a young man in grey smoking a pipe." (85)

Of course no one can know another: these blank exteriors are what Zwerdling worries about, but this is Woolf's diagnosis of experience in the modern world. We are shut off from each other, and there is no way to get past the external details, even in the experience of intimacy, as Jacob's extended and utterly unfocused relations with Florinda seem to suggest. That is why the narrative is broken and unsuccessful at penetrating Jacob's interior. That interior is impossible to penetrate, and we are left with silence and speculation.

Shaw makes this point about modern elegies:

> The hallmark of truth-saying [Griemas's veridiction] in pastoral elegies is a quasi-magical performative use of words that allows the elegist to achieve maximum cathartic effect with minimum material ... Modern elegies take [Wordsworth's] reticence one step further. The slight impediments to speech become more pronounced and audible. They become open sites of fracture

---

[53] Alex Zwerdling, "*Jacob's Room:* Woolf's Satiric Elegy," *ELH* 48 (1981): 894–913; reprinted in the Norton Critical Edition of *Jacob's Room*, ed. Suzanne Raitt (New York: Norton, 2007), 244–63 (250).

and breakdown ... Breakup itself becomes a sign of veridiction whenever the hesitations or ambivalence of a self-divided mind are interpreted as a positive quality, as a mark of superior alertness or discernment. If one axiom of modernism is that there are no truths outside the creative power of our own subjective lenses, then to succeed in saying so is also to fail. For if it is true that no marks of veridiction in modern elegies are really true, then something is true after all.[54]

Woolf uses hesitations and breakdowns, to be sure, but here she also puts her faith in the language's ability to perform the elegy even if the process could be mistaken as "mere description" or "poetic language": Woolf knows that language can perform its elegiac function just as she knows that the grieving process is neither simple nor direct.

Later, when the narrative jumps from point to point in Jacob's young life, and when the narrative thread seems lost, then we can remember Shaw's words about the modern elegy, in which "breakup itself becomes a sign of veridiction whenever the hesitations or ambivalence of a self-divided mind are interpreted as a positive quality." For Woolf any sign of "breakup" is the measure of what it takes to write an elegy in this form. As the narrator remarks when considering the solemnity of St. Paul's Cathedral:

> Dim it is, haunted by ghosts of white marble, to whom the organ forever chaunts. If a boot creaks, it's awful; then the order; the discipline. The verger with his rod has life ironed out beneath him. Sweet and holy are the angelic choristers. And for ever round the marble shoulders, in and out of the folds of the fingers, go the thin high sounds of voice and organ. For ever requiem – repose. (86)

Even in this "sweet and holy" moment, Woolf evokes the elegy: "For ever requiem." The ghostly indirection of the narrative asks us almost to gaze into the grave: "ghosts of white marble" haunt this scene, as do the "thin high sounds of voice and organ." These descriptions certainly perform the truth of the narrative no matter what they actually say.

In her essay on "Significant Form" in *Jacob's Room*, Kathleen Wall makes the point, "While one must, of necessity, speak of modernism's multiple and often contradictory poetic, its often aestheticized repose to the chaos, fragmentation, discontinuity, and alimentation of modernity (particularly after the great War) was to create a formal order that was meant both to reveal and transcend the particularities of individual experience."[55] This is another

---

[54] Shaw, *Elegy and Paradox*, 147.

[55] Kathleen Wall, "Significant Form in *Jacob's Room*: Ekphrasis and the Elegy," *Texas Studies in Literature and Language* 44.3 (2002): 302–23; reprinted in the Norton Critical Edition of *Jacob's Room*, ed. Suzanne Raitt (New York: Norton, 2007), 281–302 (283).

way of expressing what Shaw expresses above. The elegy finds its own mode of expression, performs its own grief, in terms that the fragmented culture would understand. Wall goes even further: "If we situate the autobiographical sources of *Jacob's Room* in the context of this change of form and character in the elegy, we can see the way in which the novel is emblematic of this conflict between the work of mourning and the social rites that provide a vehicle for that work and the elegy's response to that conflict."[56]

The work of mourning that Wall mentions, the process of creating a response to loss that also helps the poet cope with that loss, is everywhere apparent in this novel. All the passages I have quoted, and many I have not, attempt to accommodate loss without becoming its victim. Wall claims that Woolf is "transforming her elegy for her brother into an elegy for a generation of young men, for an age, and for its worldview."[57] The work of that kind of elegy is the work that this novel form provides.

The city almost seems funereal as Woolf uses her narrative lens to capture this image of the late urban afternoon commute:

> Beneath the pavement, sunk in the earth, hollow drains lined with yellow light for ever conveyed them this way and that, and large letters upon enamel plates represented in the underworld the parks, squares, and circuses of the upper ... Home they went. The grey church spires received then, the hoary city, old, sinful, majestic. One behind another, round or pointed, piercing the sky or massing themselves, like sailing ships, like granite cliffs, spires and offices, wharves and factories crowd the bank; eternally pilgrims trudge; barges rest in mid stream, heavy laden; as some believe, the city loves her prostitutes. (88–9)

This extended image feels graveyard-like, as if the city itself commemorates loss. "Hollow drains lined with yellow light" almost sounds like an image from science fiction. This is not science fiction, however, it is the hollow truth of experience itself. Shaw tells us about a primal loss basic to human experience: "According to Kristeva, all the signs and symbols in our language are made accessible by a negation of a fundamental loss – the loss of a primal object, the mother or thing."[58] Woolf could almost be channeling Kritseva here, as she does elsewhere in *Jacob's Room*: the gloom of this description seems to recognize the loss of a primal object, and only loss makes the description itself possible. For Kristeva it is not so much that the

[56] Wall, "Significant Form," 284.
[57] Wall, "Significant Form," 285.
[58] Shaw, *Elegy and Paradox*, 218. See Julia Kristeva, *Black Sun: Depression and Melancholia*, trans. Leon S. Roudiez (New York: Columbia University Press, 1989).

loss is negated; but rather language itself emerges as a result of that loss and
carries its mark.

A little later, the narrator offers something like a footnote to these reflec-
tions. Betty Flanders is thinking about her sons Jacob and Archer, but she
recognizes the activity as futile:

> In any case life is but a procession of shadows, and God knows why it is
> that we embrace them so eagerly, and see them depart with such anguish,
> being shadows. And why, if this and much more than this is true, why are
> we yet surprised in the window corner by a sudden vision that the young
> man in the chair is of all things in the world the most real, the most solid,
> the best known to us – why indeed? For the moment after we know noth-
> ing about him.
>   Such is the manner of our seeing. Such the conditions of our love. (96)

Jacob is real in his mere physicality, but he remains nonetheless a
shadow: "such is the manner of our seeing." If the mother cannot see her
son as anything more than a shadow, then how can the novelist pry behind
the surface or into the shadow. "Such the conditions of our love": how can
this be anything but an indictment of human emotion when love is already
a form of loss.

The narrator says the same thing in another way just a few pages down.
Here there is more anxiety about the lack of knowledge described above, as
the narrator describes a conversation between Jacob and Bonamy:

> But though all this may very well be true – so Jacob thought and spoke – so
> he crossed his legs – filled his pipe – sipped his whiskey, and once looked at
> his pocket-book, rumpling his hair as he did so, there remains over some-
> thing which can never be conveyed to a second person save by Jacob him-
> self. Moreover, part of this is not Jacob but Richard Bonamy – the room;
> the market carts; the hour; the very moment of history. Then consider the
> effect of sex – how between man and woman it hangs wavy, tremulous, so
> that here's a valley, there's a peak, when in truth, perhaps all's as flat as my
> hand. Even the exact words get the wrong accent on them. But something
> is always impelling one to hum vibrating, like the hawk moth, at the mouth
> of the cavern of mystery, endowing Jacob Flanders with all sorts of qualities
> he had not at all – for though, certainly, he sat talking to Bonamy, half of
> what he said was too dull to repeat; much unintelligible (about unknown
> people and Parliament); what remains is mostly a matter of guess work. Yet
> over him we hang vibrating. (97–8)

This remarkable description of two men talking leaves the narrator humming "like the hawk moth at the mouth of the cavern." This is a chilling
image. The hawk moth – or perhaps it is the hummingbird hawk moth
that the hum and the moth are meant to suggest – hovers over the cavern

of floral openings with a long proboscis. It is thought to be a smart feeder that learns colors.[59] But it feeds nonetheless, and the humming, hovering figure at the mouth of the cavern is devouring its nectar. The novelist here flutters, hums, probes: but none of this activity can be called successful. "What remains is mostly a matter of guess work." That is because Jacob is always already lost to those who love him.

As Shaw proposes, "An elegy that excludes us from intimacies of consciousness may intimate distresses that are more poignantly felt than any sensations of empathy we prove on our pulses. Though we value elegies that have more tragic catharsis than lyric angst, we recognize that melancholia has its own power and that grief therapy is a dangerous basis for a theory of art."[60] The work of mourning, Shaw suggests, even when incomplete, can result in the powerful artistic expression of loss. Woolf seems to measure the degree of her exclusion from the intimacy that mourning implies, and instead she is exploring the power of melancholia that feels powerless against the power of loss.

She tells the story of Jacob's life, to be sure. We hear about his loves, his ideas, his friendships, and most of all we see him in one context after another, which Woolf provides as she helps us to come to terms with what this young man represents. Here for instance, the narrator recounts a sexual experience between Jacob and Florinda:

> The sitting room neither knew nor cared. The door was shut, and to suppose that wood, when it creaks, transmits anything save that rats are busy and wood dry is childish ... But if the pale blue envelope lying by the biscuit-box had the feelings of a mother, the heart was torn by the little creak, the sudden stir. Behind the door was the obscene thing, the alarming presence, and terror would come over her at death, or the birth of a child ... My son, my son – such would be her cry, uttered to hide her vision of him stretched with Florinda, inexcusable, irrational, in a woman with three children living at Scarborough. And the fault lay with Florinda. Indeed when the door opened and the couple came out, Mrs. Flanders would have flounced upon her. (124)

At the beginning of the passage we are asked to share with Jacob's mother a horror at the reality of his physical experience; and indeed, the creaks of the house and the sudden stir all suggest "that obscene thing." What could be more significant of life than this energetic sexual encounter, but instead Betty Flanders, in the form of the blue envelope that has come from

---

[59] See Wikipedia, c.v "Hummingbird hawk-moth."
[60] Shaw, *Elegy and Paradox*, 180.

Scarborough, feels terror at the prospect of her child's death. That is the obscure obscenity, and Betty Flanders wants to blame someone, of course. This is the anger that is so familiar in traditional elegies. But the anger is diffused by the physical presence of Jacob himself, "in his dressing gown, amiable, authoritative, beautifully healthy, like a baby after an airing, with an eye clear as running water." No, no this image says, Jacob is alive, baby-like, authoritative. Just like a moment in Tennyson's *In Memoriam*, this scene brings a kind of momentary consolation, a glimpse of memory, that will be the only form that consolation takes in the end.

Soon after this, the narrator describes a winter night as follows:

> The snow, which had been falling all night, lay at three o'clock in the afternoon over the fields and the hill. Clumps of withered grass stood out upon the hill-top; the furze bushes were black, and now and then a black shiver crossed the snow as the wind drove flurries of frozen particles before it. The sound was that of a broom sweeping – sweeping ... Spaces of complete immobility separated each of these movements. The land seemed to lie dead ... Then the old shepherd returned stiffly across the field. Stiffly and painfully the frozen earth was trodden under and gave beneath pressure like a treadmill. The worn voices of clocks repeated the fact of the hour all night long. (134–5)

The scene, now almost literally, is cast in the language of the pastoral elegy, both visually and emotionally. Wall would call this an ekphrastic moment: and it is not simply visual, but feeling, smell, sound, and emotion are interweaved as well with the language of description. The most important image, though, is this one: "the land seemed to lie dead." The hints of political decisions and the imminent war have already appeared in the novel, and this passage gives them a pastoral reading, familiar from as far back as Spenser's *The Shepheardes Calendar*. As Sacks claims about that earlier work: "Colin's inability to assume a satisfactory manner of grieving is one of the very themes of 'January.' The immediate cause of Colin's wintry light is neither the season itself, which merely reflects his woe, nor yet his unrequited love as much as it is his sorrowful expressions themselves."[61] Here though, the wintry image does more than just reflect the narrator's woe; instead it casts the pall that forces us to acknowledge this as an elegiac moment. The cold and tired sadness of the passage reminds us that there is no hope for a young man like Jacob Archer. He hears the clocks, rakes the fire and goes to bed, but his sleep will soon be eternal.

---

[61] Sacks, *The English Elegy*, 45; see 38–63.

Fanny Elmer finds herself thinking about something very much like this when she gazes at Jacob:

> And for ever the beauty of young men seems to be set in smoke, however lustily they chase footballs, or drive cricket balls, dance, run, or stride along roads. Possibly they are soon to lose it. Possibly they look into the eyes of far-away heroes, and take their station among us half contemptuously, she thought (vibrating like a fiddle-string, to be played on and snapped). Anyhow, they love silence, and speak beautifully, each word falling like a disc new cut, not a hubble-bubble of small smooth coins such as girls use; and they move decidedly, as if they knew how long to stay and when to go – oh, but Mr. Flanders was only going to get a programme. (160–1)

In this memorial passage, Fanny seems to recognize all that will be lost. She sees the distinction of these young men, but she also sees how they look beyond the present moment "into the eyes of faraway heroes." This sudden recognition is also the undoing of these young men, as Woolf makes clear in an isolated passage:

> The battleships ray out over the North Sea, keeping their stations accurately apart. At a given signal all their guns are trained on a target which (the master gunner counts the seconds, watch in hand – at the sixth he looks up) flames into splinters. With equal nonchalance a dozen young men in the prime of life descend with composed faces into the depths of the sea; and there impassively (though with perfect mastery of machinery) suffocate uncomplainingly together. (216)

This is the closest the narrative comes to describing warfare directly, but it does make a suitable complement to the statement that Fanny Elmer was just expressing. "With equal nonchalance a dozen young men in the prime of life descend with composed faces into the depths of the sea": this is surely a response to Fanny Elmer's notion that Jacob looks beyond the present moment. The nonchalance of these destroyed young lives is a measure of their inability to comprehend what is happening to them, and that is exactly what we might also say about Jacob.

As the novel reaches its conclusion, Jacob travels to Greece and attempts to experience the classical world for himself. The narrator makes it clear that this action demonstrates an utter lack of self-knowledge. Earlier, indeed, she had said:

> A strange thing – when you came to think of it – this love of Greek, flourishing in such obscurity, distorted, discouraged, yet leaping out, all of a sudden, especially on leaving crowded rooms, or after a surfeit of print, or when the moon floats among the waves of the hills, or in hollow, sallow, fruitless London days, like a specific; a clean blade; always a miracle. Jacob knew no

more Greek than served him to stumble through a play. Of ancient history
he knew nothing. (102)

And while in Greece, Jacob seems almost too self-conscious really to be
able to experience his surroundings. Still, the place itself moves him:

> Although the beauty is sufficiently humane to weaken us, to stir the deep
> deposit of mud – memories, abandonments, regrets, sentimental devo-
> tions – the Parthenon is separate from all that; and if you consider how
> it has stood out all night, for centuries, you begin to connect the blaze (at
> midday the glare is dazzling and the frieze almost invisible) with the idea
> that perhaps it is beauty alone that is immortal. (205)

As beautiful as it is, it still contains these memories, abandonments, regrets
and sentimental devotions that are what constitute human experience. Here
in the elegiac process, this is a kind of talismanic encounter: the Parthenon
brings together all the emotion that has been building in the poem, and it is
almost as if this is the real battle that Jacob is fighting. He thinks of Bonamy
in Greece and wants to see him. As if caught in a platonic moment, he writes
him inanities about his love of Greek culture. What is key here is that Jacob
really has discovered something about himself and his love of this heroic culture. It is of course what destroys him, but Woolf seems to be saying here that
the young man recognized his young manhood in Greece long enough before
the war and that his loss is not the utterly meaningless loss it might have been.

At the end, Betty Flanders and Bonamy go into Jacob's room after he
has died:

> Listless is the air in an empty room, just swelling the curtain; the flowers
> in the jar shift. One fibre in the wicker arm-chair creaks, though no one
> sits there.
>
> Bonamy crossed to the window. Pickford's van swung down the street.
> The omnibuses were locked together at Mudie's corner. Engines throbbed,
> and carters, jamming the brakes down, pulled their horses sharp up. A harsh
> and unhappy voice cried something unintelligible. And then suddenly all
> the leaves seemed to raise themselves.
>
> "Jacob! Jacob!" cried Bonamy, standing by the window. The leaves sank
> down again,
>
> "Such confusion everywhere!" exclaimed Betty Flanders, bursting open
> the bedroom door.
>
> Bonamy turned away from the window.
>
> "What am I to do with these, Mr. Bonamy?"
>
> She held out a pair of Jacob's old shoes. (247)

The pain here is palpable – in the listless air of the room, in Bonamy's cry,
which we recall from Archer's similar call in the early pages of the novel,

and in Betty Flanders' plea. The confusion she recognizes is a cultural confusion as much as personal confusion, but it is also the confusion of loss: the loss that both she and Bonamy feel. Yeats finds a way to transform the death of Major Gregory in a kind of ritual rebirth in poetry.[62] Woolf is not so much interested in rebirth as she is in expressing the power of death itself. The empty shoes – weren't shoes often sent back to families of dead soldiers? – are an emblem of emptiness and loss. Betty Flanders turns with them to Bonamy because she seems to understand what friendship means for her son. Woolf wants us to experience the enormity of this loss. Once she has done that, then it is possible that some process of reconciliation can begin. Her elegy does not accomplish this but it puts us in a position to be able to begin that process. For how often we have begun without seeing the loss for what it was. This novel helps us to do that.

[62] See Sacks, *The English Elegy*, 281.

CHAPTER 2

Erotic Friendship

Erotic friendship is as central as elegiac friendship to the literature of the long eighteenth century. If we attempt to revise Sedgwick's notion of homosocial relations in erotic terms, we are not really violating the spirit of her analysis. As she famously outlined in that volume, "in any male dominated society, there is a special relationship between male homosocial (*including* homosexual) desire and the structures for maintaining and transmitting patriarchal power."[1] I want to reduce the complexity of this argument because it now seems unnecessary. It does not surprise us to hear that male relationships can be erotically charged even when they are not the direct result of sexual desire. Sedgwick in fact taught us that, and if I retire the notion of homosociality here, I do so only with great respect for what her study achieved thirty years ago. The erotic friendships I describe here range from the outright and outrageously eroticized male relationships in Smollett's first novel, *Roderick Random*, to the gloomy and obsessively haunted relationship between Frankenstein and his creature in Mary Shelley's *Frankenstein*. The notion of the homosocial is not really useful in these circumstances, for reasons that I hope will become obvious, any more than it is useful in either Fielding's *Amelia* or Godwin's *Caleb Williams*. In each of these works male relationships are eroticized, for reasons of obsession, or competition or rivalry, in ways that animate the text and give it emotional power. Just as elegiac relations can take the form of a process of mourning, so here erotic relations take the shape of an obsessive process that is as destructive as it is exhilarating.

Male friendship figures centrally in the drama and fiction of the eighteenth century, from the heroic friendships of Restoration drama to the friendship bonds that are celebrated in novels throughout the century. Various accounts of male–male devotion challenge the status quo and invoke classical models as a means of bringing men of different ranks into

---

[1] Eve Kosofsky Sedgwick, *Between Men: English Literature and Male Homosocial Desire* (New York: Columbia University Press, 1985), 25.

meaningful relation with each other. This tradition continues into the nineteenth century and beyond, but for important reasons, with this topic as with so many, the eighteenth century witnesses key developments in the meaning of friendship in an increasingly modernized culture.

Smollett's World of Masculine Desire in *The Adventures of Roderick Random*

In his landmark essay, "Forgetting Foucault," David M. Halperin has argued that "before the nineteenth century ... sexual acts could be interpreted as representative components of an individual's sexual morphology ... Sexual acts could [also] be interpreted as representative expressions of an individual's sexual subjectivity." In that same essay, he goes on to explain that "neither ... sexual morphology ... nor sexual subjectivity ... should be understood as a sexual identity, or a sexual orientation in the modern sense – much less as equivalent to the modern formation known as homosexuality."[2] Halperin's comments are useful for those working in the field of the literary history of sexuality, to be sure. He is talking here about the Greek figure of the kinaidos (morphology) and the sodomitical central character of Boccaccio's story of Pietro di Vinciolo of Perugia, the Tenth Story of the Fifth Day of the *Decameron* (subjectivity). Halperin says further that he hopes "to encourage us to inquire into the construction of sexual identities before the emergence of sexual orientation and to do this *without* recurring necessarily to modern notions of 'sexuality' or sexual orientation."[3] I am heartened by Halperin's reassessment of the misuse of Foucault in the study of the history of sexuality, and I am also ready to accept his challenge to look at the construction of sexual identities in literary works that are key in their own way to this history.

For scholars writing about the history of sexuality, or of male–male relations especially, in the eighteenth century, the famous chapters in Tobias Smollett's *The Adventures of Roderick Random* (1748), in which the characters Captain Whiffle and his surgeon Simper are described, can serve as a touchstone. Take, for instance, this lengthy passage in which we are introduced to the first of these characters:

> [O]ur new commander came on board, in a ten-oar'd barge, overshadowed with a vast umbrella, and appeared in everything quite the reverse

---

[2] David M. Halperin, *How to do the History of Homosexuality* (Chicago: University of Chicago Press, 2002), 41–2.
[3] Halperin, *How to do the History of Homosexuality*, 43.

of Oakhum, being a tall, thin, young man, dressed in this manner; a white hat garnished with a red feather, adorned his head, from whence his hair flowed down upon his shoulders, in ringlets tied behind with a ribbon. – His coat, consisting of pink-coloured silk, lined with white, by the elegance of the cut retired backward, as it were, to discover a white sattin waistcoat embroidered with gold, unbuttoned at the upper part, to display a broch set with garnets, that glittered in the breast of his shirt, which was of the finest cambrick, edged with right mechlin.[4]

As this passage continues with its description of breeches and stockings and a "steel-hilted sword, inlaid with figure of gold," Captain Whiffle takes his place as a descendent of Restoration fops like Sir Fopling Flutter from Sir George Etherege's *The Man of Mode* (1676) or Colley Cibber's Sir Novelty Fashion from *Love's Last Shift* (1696). But all those simple examples of gender confusion that expose earlier fops are here more pointed, more significant. As the description continues, it begins to outline a type of behavior and to mark an entire group of men in similar terms:

But the most remarkable parts of his furniture were, a mask on his face, and white gloves on his hands, which did not seem to be put on with an intention to be pulled off occasionally, but were fixed with a ring set with a ruby on the little finger of one hand, and by one set with a topaz on that of the other. – In this garb, captain Whiffle, for that was his name, took possession of the ship, surrounded with a crowd of attendants, all of whom, in their different degrees, seemed to be of their patron's disposition; and the air was so impregnated with perfumes, that one may venture to affirm the clime of Arabia Fœlix was not half so sweet-scented. (195)

Smollett spares no pains in this description, as if he relishes the opportunity to spin out this portrait at greater than usual length. Of course there is nothing yet to insist on a specific reading of the fop. As many have argued, to describe an excess in dress is not tantamount to making any claims about sexuality.[5] Cameron McFarlane, for instance, says that "Whiffle's clothes function seemingly as unequivocal signifiers," but I would insist that their signification itself is overdetermined in this scene. This dress becomes unequivocal precisely because of the exact context that Smollett

---

[4] Tobias Smollett, *The Adventures of Roderick Random*, ed. Paul-Gabriel Boucé (Oxford: Oxford University Press, 1981 [1749]), 194–5 [Chapter xxxiv; further page references are included in the text.

[5] George E. Haggerty, *Men in Love: Masculinity and Sexuality in the Eighteenth Century* (New York: Columbia University Press, 1999), 44–80; see also Cameron McFarlane, *The Sodomite in Fiction and Satire, 1660–1750* (New York: Columbia University Press, 1997), 134–5; Lee Edelman, *Homographisis: Essays in Gay Literary and Cultural Theory* (New York: Routledge, 1994), 174–5; and Susan Staves, "Kind Words for the Fop," *Studies in English Literature* 22 (1982): 413–28.

describes: he gives the captain a partner. Even before that, however, in this first description, Smollett cannot resist mentioning "a crowd of attendants, all of whom, in their different degrees, seemed to be of their patron's disposition." Further mention of perfumes and hints of Arabia start to give a certain valence to this "disposition," a defining function, as it were, which emerges more specifically as the scene continues.

When Roderick enters Whiffle's cabin in order to bleed him, this is what he encounters:

> While I prepared for this important evacuation, there came into the cabbin, a young man, gayly dressed, of a very delicate complexion, with a kind of languid smile on his face, which seemed to have been rendered habitual, by a long course of affectation. – The captain no sooner perceived him, than rising hastily, he flew into his arms, crying, "O! my dear Simper! I am excessively disordered!" – Simper, who by this time, I found, was obliged to art for the clearness of his complexion, assumed an air of softness and sympathy, and lamented with many tender expressions of sorrow, the sad accident that had thrown him into that condition; then feeling his patient's pulse on the outside of his glove, gave it as his opinion, that his disorder was entirely nervous, and that some drops of tincture of castor and liquid laudanum, would be of more service to him than bleeding. (197–8)

Simper is clearly the sympathetic surgeon that Captain Whiffle requires, and in diagnosing the captain's complaint, in addition to soothing him and lamenting with him over the brutality of those around him, feeling his pulse (if he can feel it through the glove Whiffle wears) Simper offers us an implicitly phobic eighteenth-century diagnosis of Whiffle's condition. First he says that the "disorder was entirely nervous." Of course readers, at Smollett's urging, might think the condition in question is some version of eighteenth-century hypochondria.[6] Historians of sexuality have been loath to talk about this clear representation of same-sex desire as a nervous condition in the eighteenth century. Smollett might indeed be the first to make this specific connection, because as Simper grasps his hand – even through the glove – and shows his deep concern, Smollett is suggesting an intimacy "not fit to be named," as he says below. If this language calls to mind the legal understanding of sodomy, then it seems that Smollett is taking it upon himself to diagnose this case of excess and misdirected masculinity. Further, he says that castor and laudanum will work "by bridling the inordinate sallies of his spirits"; again, this is a diagnosis that

---

[6] See George Cheyne, *The English Malady*, ed. Eric Carlson (Delmar: Scholar's Facsimiles and Reprints, 1976 [1733]), 10–17.

reveals an understanding of Whiffle's desires as pathological in specifically neurological ways. Smollett almost seems to be conducting a sexological experiment.

As Smollett continues this description, these terms are more nearly explicit:

> While the captain enjoyed his repose, the doctor watched over him and indeed became so necessary, that a cabin was made for him contiguous to the state-room, where Whiffle slept; that he might be at hand in case of accidents in the night. – Next day, our commander being happily recovered, gave orders, that none of the lieutenants should appear upon deck, without a wig, sword, and ruffles; nor any midshipman, or other petty officer, be seen with a check shirt or dirty linen. – He also prohibited any person whatever, except Simper and his own servants, from coming into the great cabbin, without first sending in to obtain leave. – These singular regulations did not prepossess the ship's company in his favour; but on the contrary, gave scandal an opportunity to be very busy with his character, and accuse him of maintaining a correspondence with his surgeon, not fit to be named. (198–9)

This paragraph has been justly celebrated as "an enduring male homosexual stereotype in modern culture," or "the modern gay man," the "first gay couple," and so on.[7] More important than making such continuist claims, however, we might try to figure out what Smollett is describing here. In the first place, he makes the connection between affected effeminacy and sexual desire. In this he echoes Hester Lynch Thrale Piozzi, who said about Horace Mann, Horace Walpole's friend and correspondent, who was envoy in Florence, "I call these Fellows 'Finger-twirlers,' meaning a decent word for Sodomites; old Sir Horace Mann and Mr. James the Painter had such an odd way of twirling their fingers in Discourse – I see Seutonius tells us the same thing of one of the Roman emperors."[8] Whether or not Piozzi is basing her observation on anything more than hearsay or superficial mannerisms, we can hardly avoid the connection between "morphology" and sexual "propensity," as Piozzi calls Beckford's pederasty.[9] The same is true here. Morphology and sexual propensity come together here as well.

---

[7] McFarlane, *The Sodomite in Fiction and Satire*, 134–5; see also G. S. Rousseau, "The Pursuit of Homosexuality in the Eighteenth-Century: 'Utterly Confused Category' and/or Rich Repository?" *Eighteenth-Century Life* 9 (1985): 132–68. An interesting perspective on Smollett and scatology is offered by Robert Adams Day, "Sex, Scatology, Smollett," in *Sexuality in Eighteenth-Century Britain*, ed. Paul-Gabriel Boucé (Manchester: Manchester University Press, 1982), 225–43.

[8] Brian Fothergill, *The Strawberry Hill Set: Horace Walpole and his Circle* (London: Faber, 1983), 50; see also Timothy Mowl, *Horace Walpole: The Great Outsider* (London: John Murray, 1996), 58.

[9] On the implications of "sexual morphology," see Halperin, *How to do the History of Homosexuality*, 32–8 and 104–37.

Moreover, the members of the crew all notice what's going on. The captain and his surgeon together form a type that can be recognized, and Random calls this a "correspondence ... not fit to be named." Notice, though, that it is the correspondence and not the person that is "not fit to be named." Smollett, or Roderick, does not label an identity; he labels a behavior.

What does it mean, though, to have two chapters on the question of male–male eroticism right in the middle of this quasi-picaresque tale? Cameron McFarlane, who has written the best account of Smollett and sodomy, suggests that Whiffle is marked "as the sodomitical 'other,'" and that the entire episode displays a "comfortable certainty and stability."[10] But Smollett places these characters here in this central position – these scenes occur in chapters 34 and 35 of a sixty-nine-chapter novel – as if he sees them as somehow at the heart of male–male relations. What happens here – so grotesquely and so obviously – is not so clearly "other" as it is an extension of what occurs between men in all the chapters before and all those after this scene. McFarlane says as much, I think, in his extensive analysis, but he does not explain so specifically what that means. For me, it is a precise explanation of the mode of Smollett's phobia, or panic, around the issue of male–male relations. If a captain and his surgeon can cause the ship's crew to imagine a "correspondence ... not fit to be named"; if, that is, two men at the heart of the masculine culture that Smollett has been celebrating in the novel can behave this way, then what defense is there for men who love each other in other contexts and situations, as the men in this novel clearly do?

Various friends and intimates of Roderick – Strap, his servant, Morgan, his shipmate, Bolton, his uncle – are described in intimate terms, and all express their love for Random physically and emotionally. How are these relations to be distinguished from the Whiffle–Simple relation, or can they be distinguished at all? McFarlane reminds us that shortly after this scene, Roderick is dolling himself up in fancy aristocratic clothes in order to cut the right figure in his fortune-hunting expedition. "Roderick has become aware," McFarlane says, "of 'his own attractions,' – indeed, he plans to use them to get ahead in the world. What Roderick is not yet aware of, though, are the 'troublesome consequences to himself' that will ensue."[11]

[10] McFarlane, *The Sodomite in Fiction and Satire*, 135–6. On the question of "vignettes" in Smollett, see Pamela Cantrell, "Writing the Picture: Fielding, Smollett, and Hogarthian Pictorialism," *Studies in Eighteenth-Century Culture* 24 (1995): 68–89.

[11] McFarlane, *The Sodomite in Fiction and Satire*, 138.

The consequences that Smollett (and McFarlane) have in mind have to do with Roderick's encounter with Lord Strutwell. Roderick meets Strutwell through some new-found aristocratic friends, and he is immediately taken with Strutwell's looks, his behavior, and his seeming interest in helping him, a much younger man, get on in the world. As McFarlane says, "this episode completely undermines the certainty about the self and the 'other' which structured the Whiffle scene."[12] I agree that Strutwell is not the grotesque and excessive figure that Whiffle is. In fact, he is an attractive aristocrat for whom Roderick feels admiration and a kind of kinship. This episode makes explicit what previous chapters have only suggested: male relations are always liable to harbor secrets that render them more complex than the mere concept of "friendship" allows. Roderick's attraction to Strutwell, his hope of a fruitful relation, is almost a parody of the other friendships he has formed:

> his lordship ... took me by the hand, assured me he would do me all the service he could, and desired to see me often. – I was charmed with my reception, and although I had heard that a courtier's promise is not to be depended upon, I thought I discovered so much sweetness of temper and candour in this Earl's countenance, that I did not doubt of profiting by his protection. – I resolved therefore, to avail myself of his permission, and waited on him next audience day, when I was favoured with a particular smile, squeeze of the hand, and a whisper, signifying that he wanted half an hour's conversation with me *tête a tête*, when he should be disengaged, and for that purpose desired me to come and drink a dish of chocolate with him to-morrow morning. (307)

The joke, of course, is on Roderick here, and an astute reader may already have picked up the clues of Strutwell's behavior that the hero misses as he flatters himself that this aristocratic attention will be useful to him. Smollett seems to be saying that Roderick has set himself up for this in some way, and of course he does so by making himself available to aristocratic desires. As Sedgwick said in her discussion of William Beckford, in *Between Men*, "An important, recurrent, wishful gesture of this ideological construction [of the aristocracy] was the feminization of the aristocracy as a whole, by which not only aristocratic women ... but the abstract image of the entire class, came to be seen as ethereal, decorative, and otiose in relation to the vigorous and productive values of the middle class."[13] Even more telling, though, are the ways in which Roderick's politic scheming

[12] McFarlane, *The Sodomite in Fiction and Satire*, 139.
[13] Sedgwick, *Between Men*, 93.

has led him directly into the hands of this predatory Earl. What follows when the Earl begins his celebration of male–male love is not so much a crisis of identification, as McFarlane argues, but an attempt at seduction that causes a phobic response. When after a couple of meetings the Earl promises Roderick a position, he launches into a discussion of Petronius Arbiter in these terms:

> I own … that his taste in love is generally decried, and indeed condemned by our laws; but perhaps that may be more owing to prejudice and misapprehension, than to true reason and deliberation. – The best man among the ancients is said to have entertained that passion; one of the wisest of their legislators has permitted the indulgence of it in his commonwealth; the most celebrated poets have not scrupled to avow it at this day; it prevails not only over all the east, but in most parts of Europe; in our own country it gains ground apace; and in all probability will become in a short time a more fashionable vice than simple fornication. – Indeed there is something to be said in vindication of it, for notwithstanding the severity of the law against offenders in this way, it must be confessed that the practice of this passion is unattended with that curse and burthen upon society, which proceeds from a race of miserable deserted bastards, who are either murdered by their parents, deserted to the utmost want and wretchedness, or bred up to prey upon the commonwealth … Nay, I have been told, that there is another motive perhaps more powerful than all these, that induces people to cultivate this inclination; namely, the exquisite pleasure attending its success. (310)

It is truly fascinating that this unique defense of same-sex desire occurs here toward the climax of Smollett's first novel. However violently Roderick reacts to this argument, it is articulated here with such force and clarity that it is hard to resist. Roderick does resist it, of course, but what are readers to make of this lucid account? Once the question is stated in these terms, it has an ontological presence that the Whiffle scene barely suggested. The terms are changed, and every male–male relationship now must come under the scrutiny of a phobic gaze. If Sedgwick says, "there is a special relationship between male homosocial (including homosexual) desire and the structures of maintaining and transmitting patriarchal power," she seems to imply that there is something almost threatening about the ways in which the structures of patriarchal power can also serve a sodomitical purpose.[14] Even if we want to resist the anachronistic "homosocial" and "homosexual," we might still note that a "sodomitical purpose" among male relations of various kinds is exactly what Smollett finds so threatening in *Roderick Random*. Strutwell makes it clear that the line of demarcation is

[14] Sedgwick, *Between Men*, 25.

moveable and the consequences serious for someone like Roderick who is on the make and ready to put himself into anyone's protection.

Roderick's reaction is automatic and unequivocal:

> From this discourse, I began to be apprehensive that his lordship finding I had travelled, was afraid I might have been infected with this spurious and sordid desire abroad, and took this method of sounding my sentiments on the subject. – Fired at this supposed suspicion, I argued against it with great warmth, as an appetite unnatural, absurd, and of pernicious consequence; and declared my utter detestation and abhorrence of it. (310)

Roderick's response is significant in that he talks about being "infected with this spurious and sordid desire abroad." If male–male desire can be caught like a disease, then it is not a feature of identity any more than smallpox or consumption would be. The desire, moreover, "spurious and sordid," is what is discussed. It is not a condition or an identity, or anything more than a behavior that one might fall into, especially when traveling. In what sense is this at all like what was in the later twentieth century called "gay" identity? Gay men did not see themselves in these terms. Indeed, they spoke of gay identity as something innate. The way Roderick talks about this infection suggests, to me at least, a completely different understanding of sodomy, one closer to various phobic responses that have been articulated in hate speech of the twenty-first century. It is something that can be caught, and spread, like a disease.

If we return here to the Halperin essay, we can note that Captain Whiffle, in all his effeminate extravagance, is like the *kinaedos* of ancient Greece, and that Earl Strutwell, in his easily disguised but unmistakable desire for other men, is like the figure of Pietro di Vinciolo of Perugia in Boccaccio. The former is too obvious to miss and easy to mock; the second, easily disguised in aristocratic masculinity and bonhomie, is more dangerous because less discernible and even, it would seem, almost reasonable in his claims. As Cameron McFarlane argues, "Roderick obviously cannot 'read' Strutwell in the same way that he 'read' Whiffle."[15] With Strutwell, in a sense, Roderick has met someone to admire and emulate until he finds himself appalled. How is it possible, the novel seems to ask, that sodomy could be disguised in the figure of a gentleman?

Roderick's response bespeaks an understanding, however, that would more than explain Smollett's use of sodomy in this novel (and indeed in

---

[15] McFarlane, *The Sodomite in Fiction and Satire*, 139.

at least one of his later ones). Sodomy circulates in the world of masculine desire, almost precisely as Sedgwick suggests – eliciting fear that at once yields phobic responses and implies the ever-present danger of male–male seductive power. Earlier Smollett scholars have implied as much in their analyses, McFarlane especially; but consider more closely what a free-floating notion of a threat of sodomy does to other male–male relations in the novel.

Take the relationship between Roderick and his friend/servant Strap. The young and entertaining sidekick to Roderick, so amusingly named, is a given in the novel, as if male relations must be clearly established before any courting of female characters can even be considered. Indeed, it is a commonplace in Smollett criticism to say that whatever courting does take place, whatever articulation of male–female desire, is secondary in this rollicking picaresque world of male–male interaction of various kinds. Smollett, that is, takes a world of masculine desire and plays out its drama in a world almost exclusively male.

When Roderick first sets out on his journey, he meets up with his "old school-fellow" (31) Strap in a barber's shop on the road, and from this moment Strap becomes a devoted companion for Roderick. When they meet, Strap has just started shaving Roderick, and as he asks where Random is from, he becomes more and more agitated, spreading suds all over his face, and finally asks him his name:

> But when I declared my name was Random he exclaimed in a rapture, "How! Rory Random?" The same, I replied, looking at him with astonishment; "What," cried he, "don't you know your old school-fellow, Hugh Strap?" At that instant recollecting his face, I flew into his arms, and in the transport of my joy, gave him back one half of the suds he had so lavishly bestowed on my countenance; so that we made a very ludicrous appearance, and furnished a great deal of mirth to his master and shop-mates, who were witnesses of this scene. – When our mutual caresses were over, I sat down again to be shaved, but the poor fellow's nerves were so discomposed by this unexpected meeting, that his hand could scarcely hold the razor, with which (nevertheless) he found means to cut me in three places, in as many strokes. (32)

Smollett makes sure that we can feel a kind of emotional intensity within the comedy of the scene; but the comedy itself – with the caressing, the mutual effusion of suds, the excitement, the blood – has all the makings of intense physicality. Strap indeed functions throughout *Roderick Random* as an avatar of erotic physicality that can sometimes be taken for the object of desire himself.

Roderick and Strap are separated for some time while Roderick works as a surgeon's mate in the Navy and then as a soldier in Flanders, but when he finds himself in Rheims, there he meets his friend again, described to him as Monsieur D'Estrapes, who works as valet-de-chambre for an English gentleman there. When Roderick reveals himself to Strap, we have a scene of similar intensity to the one quoted above. Roderick speaks in his Scottish-inflected English, and Strap recognizes him:

> When he heard me pronounce these words in our own language, he leaped upon me in a transport of joy, hung about my neck, kissed me from ear to ear, and blubbered like a great school-boy who has been whipt. – Then observing my dress, he set up his throat, crying "O L – d! O L – d! that ever I should live to see my dearest friend reduced to the condition of a foot soldier in the French service!" (252)

Strap is upset that they had parted in some disagreement, and he makes up for it here with this outpouring of emotion and clear articulation of a personal attachment. Roderick makes certain the encounter has a physical component as well. After they make up their differences and Strap invites Roderick home for a meal, Roderick begs his friend for some clothing as well:

> I thanked him for his invitation, which, I observed, could not be unwelcome to a person who had not eaten a comfortable meal these seven months; but I had another request to make, which I begged he would grant before dinner, and that was the loan of a shirt … He stared in my face, with a woeful countenance, at this declaration, which he would scarce believe, until I explained it, by unbuttoning my coat, and disclosing my naked body; a circumstance that shocked the tender-hearted Strap, who, with tears in his eyes, ran to a chest of drawers, and taking out some linen, presented to me a very fine ruffled holland shirt, and cambrick neckcloth, assuring me, he had three dozen of the same kind at my service. – I was ravished at this piece of good news, and having accommodated myself in a moment, hugged my benefactor for his generous offer, saying, I was overjoyed to find him undebauched by prosperity, which seldom fails of corrupting the heart. (252–3)

Roderick seems all too ready to expose his naked flesh to Strap in this scene, and he is "ravished" when Strap offers him clean linen. Then he talks not of Strap's generosity directly, but of his being "undebauched by prosperity." All this language is more than suggestive, I would claim, of the degree of erotic play at work in the union between these two men. The blubbering and ejaculating of the first scene (O L – d! O L – d!) gives way to a play of physicality in a continuum, of sorts, with the earlier scenes I have discussed. Further scenes with Strap can serve to deepen this perception, and I will look at one such scene before moving on to talk about other robust male–male relationships in this novel.

The last important scene with Strap is one in which Roderick takes out his jealousy over a nobleman's attentions to the elusive Narcissa by abusing his faithful valet. Smollett describes the scene this way:

> I went home in the condition of a frantic Bedlamite; and finding the fire in my apartment almost extinguished, vented my fury upon poor Strap, whose ear I pinched with such violence, that he roared hideously with pain, and when I quitted my hold looked so foolishly aghast, that no unconcerned spectator could have seen him, without being seized with an immoderate fit of laughter … [H]e could not help shedding some tears at my unkindness. I felt unspeakable remorse for what I had done, cursed my own ingratitude, and considered his tears as a reproach that my soul, in her present disturbance, could not bear. – It set all my passions into a new ferment, I swore horrible oaths without meaning or application, I foamed at the mouth, kicked the chairs about the room, and play'd abundance of mad pranks that frightened my friend almost out of his senses. – At length my transport subsided, I become melancholy, and wept insensibly. (356–7)

Roderick Random is already upset, but after he abuses Strap and then sees the anguish he has caused, he then feels "unspeakable remorse" and lapses into even more intensely passionate ravings and destruction. It is fitting that Strap is the immediate occasion of this transport of emotion; and it is Strap who gives rise to this "unspeakable remorse." Roderick's debilitating melancholy, that is, does not concern only Narcissa and the jealousy she engenders, but it also concerns Strap and the ways in which he has abused his friend.

Other characters who fall into this male–male economy include Morgan, Roderick's shipmate and fellow victim of the autocratic Captain Oakhum. Morgan, the foul-mouthed and outspoken Welsh surgeon, becomes a friend in difficult circumstances – they are both held for treason on Oakhum's ship, the *Thunder* – and they fight together (and deal with the wounded) in the ill-considered battle of Cartagena. When Random is himself struck low with a fever, Morgan nurses him. After his fever breaks and he is sleeping comfortably, Morgan laments over his enfeebled body:

> "Ay,… he sleeps so sound, (look you) that he will never waken till the great trump plows. – Got be merciful to his soul. He has paid his debt, like an honest man. – Ay, and moreover, he is at rest from all persecutions, and troubles, and afflictions, of which, Got knows, and I know, he had his own share. – Ochree! Ochree! he was a promising youth indeed!" So saying, he groaned grievously, and began to whine in such a manner, as persuaded me he had a real friendship for me. (193)

It might be considered at least odd that Roderick needs this bedside con-
firmation of his mate's affection. Odder still is his decision to counterfeit
death so that he can have an even more extensive display of Morgan's over-
weening emotion:

> The serjeant, alarmed at his words, came into the birth, and while he looked
> upon me, I smiled, and tipt him the wink; he immediately guessed my
> meaning, and remained silent, which confirmed Morgan in his opinion of
> my being dead; whereupon he approached with tears in his eyes, in order
> to indulge his grief with a sight of the object: And I counterfeited death so
> well, by fixing my eyes, and dropping my under-jaw, that he said, "There
> he lies, no petter than a lump of clay, Got help me." And observed by the
> distortion of my face, that I must have had a strong struggle. I should not
> have been able to contain myself much longer, when he began to perform
> the last duty of a friend, in closing my eyes and my mouth; upon which,
> I suddenly snapped at his fingers, and discomposed him so much, that he
> started back, turned pale as ashes, and stared like the picture of horror! (193)

This amusing scene, which emerges as a tantalizing reminder of elegiac
moments of loss, challenges the reader in various ways. What kind of joke
is it to pretend to be dead in order to shake up the emotions of a friend?
Because he has been so convincing as a corpse, Morgan must reach out to
touch him in a deeply felt and intensely intimate way. Roderick uses that
moment to snap at Morgan's fingers, a gesture which turns the kindness
of deep friendship into a kind of proto-Gothic horror. What better way
to represent the workings of homophobia in the text. Intimate gestures
become sites of horror, and male–male intimacy, however deeply felt, is
also the source of blood-curdling distress.

As if to italicize these observations and mark them out in bold,
Roderick's infamous reunion with his father, near the end of the novel,
becomes an orgy of male–male affection that seems more intense than
any other relationship presented in the novel. In discussing this scene, or
series of scenes, McFarlane says that "this conclusion – meant, I would
maintain, to be read in opposition to the Strutwell episode – represents the
achievement of the homosocial ideal, a pure bond between men, cleansed
of the 'sordid and vicious disposition' that characterized other relationships
in the novel." But McFarlane cannot help but add that "the comparison
between the scenes can move in both directions, and this ecstasy of homosocial bonding contains within it the suggestion of an evasive fulfillment
of the more libidinal bonding denounced earlier in the novel."[16] I agree,

---

[16] McFarlane, *The Sodomite in Fiction and Satire*, 143.

but would go even further to say that the scenes with Don Rodriguez that later dissolve in the tears of familial recognition are meant even more vividly to resolve the novel's earlier tensions around sodomy and to offer a transformed quasi-sodomitical model of male love and affection.

Roderick meets Don Rodriguez when he has, because of involvement with the slave trade, landed in Rio de la Plata, to unload a cargo of African slaves and prepare to return across the Atlantic. He enjoys Don Rodriguez, the English gentleman he meets there, and finds himself deeply attracted to his commanding presence:

> He was a tall man, remarkably well-shaped, of a fine mien and appearance commanding respect, and seemed to be turned of forty; the features of his face were saddened with a reserve and gravity ... Understanding from Don Antonio, that we were his countrymen, he saluted us all round very complaisantly, and fixing his eyes attentively on me, uttered a deep sigh. – I had been struck with a profound veneration for him at his first coming into the room; and no sooner observed this expression of his sorrow, directed, as it were, in a particular manner to me, than my heart took part in his grief, I sympathized involuntarily, and sighed in my turn. (411)

This initial encounter is suggestive of an attraction between the two men, and given the context of this moment of male–male intimacy, any reader might connect it to the encounter with Strutwell from some fifteen chapters before. Here, however, the male–male attraction is safely placed in the configuration of father–son love. But like other domestic love that is represented in novels by women in the later part of the eighteenth century – love between sisters, and between mothers and daughters – this love is vividly eroticized, both to fill out the domestic space with the erotic, with which it can at times be rife, and to explain the ways in which erotic relationships are ideally modeled on these family relationships themselves.[17] Here is an example of father–son love performing the same function. After frustrating and unfulfilling male encounters, Roderick falls into the arms of his father as if he were the lover he has been looking for all along.

The moment of recognition is intense: "O bounteous heaven! (exclaimed Don Rodriguez, springing across the table, and clasping me in his arms) my son! my son! have I found thee again? do I hold thee in my embrace, after having lost and despaired of seeing thee, so long?"

> (H)e kneeled upon the floor, lifted up his eyes and hands to heaven, and remained some minutes in a silent exstacy of devotion: I put myself in the

---

[17] See George E. Haggerty, *Unnatural Affections: Women and Fiction in the Later Eighteenth Century* (Bloomington: University of Indiana Press, 1998), for countless examples of this kind of relationship.

same posture, adored the all-good Disposer in a prayer of mental thanks-
giving; and when his ejaculation was ended, did homage to my father, and
craved his parental blessing. He hugged me again with unutterable fond-
ness, and having implored the protection of heaven upon my head, raised
me from the ground, and presented me as his son to the company, who
wept in concert over this affecting scene ... "Dear son, I am transported
with unspeakable joy! – This day is a jubilee – my friends and servants shall
share my satisfaction." (413)

Critics are right to say that there is no more intense personal encounter in the novel, but then how could there be? As McFarlane points out,
"Unutterable. Unspeakable. Unnamable? Manly passion in this scene
finds its (non)articulation in the same terms regularly applied to the sodomite; the ideal and the transgressive collapse into similar representational
structures."[18] What this collapse means – what the representational similar-
ity insists upon – is the recognition of the erotics of the father–son relationship. Why should not this male–male intensity remind the reader of
the potentially sodomitical encounters? Smollett has offered those scenes
in order to make this encounter even more affecting. Love between men is
possible, Smollett seems to say, as long as it is contained in these familiar
structures. Roderick has been looking for a father all along – he has been
trying to seduce various older men who might be able to support and sustain him – and in Don Rodriguez he finds the perfect father at last. Here
is the generous older gentleman who will turn his life around, make him
wealthy, and give him the chance he has always seemed, at least to himself,
to deserve.

The Adventures of Roderick Random is an astonishing novel from this perspective. A "robust adventure story," as it is sometimes called, it puts male–
male relations at the center of the world it describes.[19] Some relationships are
predatory and therefore off-putting, but the closest relationships between
men can only be expressed in erotic terms. This means that the friendships
between Roderick and Strap or Morgan constantly slip into intense physicality, and his relation with his father is almost indistinguishable from a bond
like that which Strutwell is proposing. Early in the century and in the later
seventeenth century, loving relations between men were often represented in
these terms.[20] Smollett has revived this tradition even as he tries to cordon

---

[18] See McFarlane, *The Sodomite in Fiction and Satire*, 143.
[19] See, for instance, Jerry Phillips, "Narrative, Adventure, and Schizophrenia: From Smollett's *Roderick
Random* to Melville's *Omoo*," *Journal of Narrative Theory* 25.2 (1995): 177–201.
[20] Haggerty, *Men in Love*, 23–43.

off actual sodomitical desire. But that cannot work. Love is love, and the love he represents in the scenes I have outlined cannot be distinguished from any other kind of male–male love. They invest each other with significance, as Smollett's novel suggests, with the result that male relations are given an intensity that they rarely have in other fiction of the period. Smollett's fear of giving in to male desire – his almost startling homophobia – means that he only gives in to it more intensely than ever. That is what makes *Roderick Random*'s world of masculine desire so truly robust.

We might return to Halperin at this stage and ask what kind of inquiry "into the construction of sexual identities before the emergence of sexual orientations" this has been;[21] then we could say that we have two different examples that offer very different angles on what would some 150 years later be called homosexuality. In the first place, we have the extravagantly effeminate Captain Whiffle, with his clothes, his neuroses, and his private surgeon. Even Roderick mocks him and labels him, suggesting that he is "maintaining a correspondence with his surgeon, not fit to be named" (199). In accordance with Halperin's notion of sexual morphology, that is, this effeminate type is demarcated and classed as clearly as Smollett dare in a fiction such as this. Second, there is Strutwell, with his apology for same-sex love: later he would have been recognized by sexologists and defined in ways that Smollett's phobic presentation only begins to hint at. Beyond these two clear markers of sexual identity, there are countless other male–male relations that Smollett cannot help but color with the language of emotion, physicality, and same-sex passion. In other words, the Whiffle and Strutwell passages create a context in which all male relations can seem dangerously intimate. It almost seems that it is in that danger that their intensity lies. But that is the fascinating story about masculinity that Smollett has to tell.

Adultery and Friendship in *Amelia*

Henry Fielding's last novel, *Amelia* (1751) is a deeply personal and reflective, if not to say valedictory, novel. Written when Fielding was wracked with ill-health and pressured by the demands of his position as local magistrate, it has neither the delight of discovery that is to be found in *Joseph Andrews* nor the comic majesty of *Tom Jones*. For some, it is badly written and overly sentimental.[22] What it offers in place of Fielding's earlier

---

[21] Halperin, *How to do the History of Homosexuality*, 43.
[22] Peter Sabor, "*Amelia*," in *The Cambridge Companion to Henry Fielding*, ed. Claude Rawson (Cambridge: Cambridge University Press, 2007), 94–108.

achievement, however, is a deeply felt account of the complexities of contemporary life and the burdens to be borne by a young married couple of limited means. While in his earlier novels, topics like friendship or marriage might have been discussed or even represented, in *Amelia*, the terms of representation are more serious and the concepts themselves are subjected to the exigencies of the lived experience of the author. *Amelia* offers a new way of understanding Fielding and a useful perspective from which to view his earlier work.[23]

Friendship in *Amelia* is often celebrated, but it is also shown to be less than ideal. For one thing, it is almost always measured in mercenary terms: a friend is considered more or less stalwart according to how much money he can lend. This happens so often in the novel as to seem like a solid tenet. For another, male friendship almost always founders because of rivalry over a woman. In her description of "homosocial" relationships in English literature, Sedgwick talks about such rivalries: male bonds are charged with emotion, even if that emotion emerges from such negative forces as jealousy or hatred.[24] *Amelia* gives us several examples of friendship that founders on erotic rivalry. But then it almost seems that the erotic rivalry becomes an end in itself: its own kind of emotional bond. Even when Booth and James recognize the bitter rivalry between them, they still, almost inexplicably, remain friends.

Marriage too, although central to Fielding's plan here, never shows itself to be the flawless and consoling structure he sometimes describes. Marriage offers a spectacle of debility for Fielding's hero: Captain Booth rarely has enough money to support his wife and growing family; he squanders what little money he has through silly investments or loses it in gambling; he has sex outside of marriage and puts his wife Amelia in one untenable situation after another; and he is jealous to a fault. There are innumerable pressures and tensions associated with keeping food on the table for a growing family – Amelia herself is seen preparing meals more than once – and at times it seems that no family so constituted can ever survive in a world that undermines marriage in all its basic assumptions about masculinity and power. Despite all these gargantuan pressures and overwhelming tensions, however, marriage emerges intact in *Amelia*. Often labeled a weak character or even a caricature of Fielding's first wife, Amelia emerges as the one character who understands what it means to hold a marriage together in the middle years of the eighteenth century. In *Amelia*, then,

[23] For an account of the reception and publication history of *Amelia*, see Sabor, "*Amelia*."
[24] Sedgwick, *Between Men*, 20–1.

Fielding is trying to show that friendship and marriage are flawed and self-defeating in variously frustrating ways. But Fielding also finds a way of taking strength from the very structures he deconstructs in this way.

Marriage as an ideal is undermined in the novel's earliest scenes. While incarcerated in Newgate, Booth meets the charming Miss Mathews, another prisoner, who tells him the long saga of her family life and unhappy love affair. This account culminates in her stabbing her unfaithful lover with a penknife. Booth is sympathetic and soothing to the teller of this sad tale, and before long it seems that they are becoming almost too intimate. After telling his own long story of his life with Amelia, Booth tries to articulate an ideal of married life, which Miss Mathews can only mock with worldly disdain as "the dullest of all Ideas":

> "I know," said he, "it must appear dull in Description; for who can describe the Pleasures which the Morning Air gives to one in perfect Health; the Flow of Spirits which springs up from Exercise; the Delights which Parents feel from the Prattle, and innocent Follies of their Children; the Joy with which the tender Smile of a Wife inspires a husband; or lastly, the cheerful, solid Comfort which a fond Couple enjoy in each other's Conversation. – All these Pleasures, and every other of which our situation was capable, we tasted in the highest Degree." (147)[25]

This is a beautiful description of a happy marriage; indeed it expresses the ideal of married life rather than any specific lived experience. No sooner has Booth articulated this ideal than he is undermining it: exchanging expressive and increasingly sexually charged looks with his interlocutor; and as Fielding's narrator draws the curtain, he does so with something close to embarrassment, making it clear that if the prison governor has left these two to their own devices, "we will lock up likewise a Scene which we do not think proper to expose to the Eyes of the Public" (153).

The "criminal Conversation" (154), which this scene introduces, gives way to repentance and melancholy for Booth, and jealousy for Miss Mathews, who is exonerated when it turns out her paramour has not died. She receives her discharge and decides to take Booth along with her. But just at this moment Amelia arrives in the prison: "a faint Voice was heard to cry out hastily, 'where is he?' – and presently a female Spectre, all pale and breathless, rushed into the Room, and fell into Mr. *Booth's* Arms, where she immediately fainted away" (159). Fielding puts his hero in the awkward position of holding his loving wife in his arms as his mistress stares at them

[25] Henry Fielding, *Amelia*, ed. Martin C. Battestin (Middletown: Wesleyan University Press, 1983 [1753]); all parenthetical references are to this edition.

with anger in her eyes. The women react to each other with coolness, and the narrator wonders why Miss Mathews would be cool to Amelia when she has designs on her husband, but "there is," he says, "something so outrageously suspicious in the Nature of all Vice, especially when joined with any great Degree of Pride, that the Eyes of those whom we imagine privy to our Failings, are intolerable to us, and we are apt to aggravate their Opinion to our Disadvantage far beyond the Reality" (161). Whatever else is true, however, is this fact of adultery that Fielding has forced on us before giving us the tender scene of Booth and Amelia together. He almost insists, that is, that we see this threat to their marriage first, and only understand the bond with the proviso of this lack of faith.

The topic of adultery is thus established before the wheels of the plot have even started to turn. Indeed, the very basis of action and reaction in the early phases of the novel can be traced to Booth's early transgression. Not only does he seem nervous and distracted around Amelia and his children when they are again together in their London lodging, but he also finds himself monitoring the mail, worrying about visitors, lying, and in many ways undermining his so-called happy marriage. Fielding makes it clear that adultery, or rather the guilt over adultery that the hero feels, comes close to poisoning his marriage. Booth finds himself having to lie to Amelia when a letter from Miss Mathews arrives, and even in the ease with which he deceives his wife, Booth feels the sting of deception:

> *Booth* was overjoyed at this Escape which poor *Amelia's* total Want of Jealousy and Suspicion, made it very easy for him to accomplish: but his Pleasure was considerably abated, when upon opening the Letter, he found it to contain, mixed with several strong Expressions of Love, some pretty warm ones of the upbraiding Kind ... She had already sent Chairman to his Lodgings, with a positive Command not to return without an Answer to her Letter. This might itself have possibly occasioned a Discovery; and he thought he had great Reason to fear, if she did not carry Matters so far as purposely and avowedly to reveal the Secret to *Amelia*, her indiscretion would at least effect the Discovery of that which he would at any Price have concealed. Under these Terrours he might, I believe, be considered the most wretched of human Beings. (171)

It is almost as if the ease of deception makes the fear of exposure even worse. This careful delineation of Booth's response in situations like these gives the novel a compelling sense of the consequences of deception in marriage. Fielding is not content to leave this to the reader's imagination, for he proceeds immediately to say:

> O Innocence, how glorious and happy a Portion art thou to the Breast that possesses thee! Thou fearest neither the Eyes nor the Tongues of

Men. Truth, the most powerful of all things, is thy strongest Friend; and the brighter, the Light in which thou are displayed, the more it discovers thy transcendent Beauties. Guilt, on the contrary, like a base Thief, suspects every eye that beholds him to be privy to his Transgression, and every Tongue that mentions his Name, to be proclaiming them. Fraud and Falsehood are his weak and treacherous Allies, and he lurks trembling in the Dark, dreading every Ray of Light, lest it should discover him, and give him up to Shame and Punishment. (171–2)

What a remarkable apostrophe this is. Fielding almost seems to be speaking through his narrator here in order to make a point about guilt and deception that he has experienced first-hand. This signals the special quality of this novel as personal or valedictory: Fielding is working out complex feelings about the experience of marriage and the complexities of deception and self-contempt within that ultimately sustaining bond. If the narrative voice seems strained at this moment, that may be because the narrator gives way to the author here, as he reflects on the reality of lived experience and the pain of remembrance.

Later, in hopes of disburdening himself to his friend Colonel James, Booth meets this friend and tells him the trouble he has had with Miss Mathews:

After some little Conversation, *Booth* said, "my dear Colonel, I am sure I must be the most insensible of Men, if I did not look on you as the best and truest Friend: I will therefore without Scruple repose a Confidence in you of the highest Kind. I have often made you privy to my Necessities, I will now acquaint you with my Shame." (172)

Booth then acquaints this friend with his embarrassment with Miss Mathews and asks his assistance in dealing with that woman. James responds agreeably enough – "Well … and whatever Light I may appear to you in, if you are really tired of the Lady, and if she be really what you have represented her, I'll endeavour to take her off your Hands" (173) – but no sooner does James go off to accommodate his friend than Booth hears from Miss Mathews that James was the very rival she had told Booth about in prison. That, along with other things like his "forgetting" to return Booth thirty pounds he has borrowed and his making Amelia immediately uncomfortable, makes it clear that this friendship is anything but "the best and truest" as Booth has described it.

Again then Fielding has articulated an ideal only to undermine it. It is almost as if he is insisting that all ideals – marriage, friendship, honor – need to be exposed as false, even as he shows that all attempts at honesty are doomed to failure. Fielding puts it this way:

> To say the Truth, there are Jilts in Friendship as well as in Love; and by the Behaviour of some Men in Both, one might imagine that they industriously sought to gain the Affections of others, with a View to making the Parties miserable.
>
> This was the Consequence of the Colonel's Behaviour to *Booth*. Former calamities had afflicted him; but this almost distracted him; and the more so, as he was not able well to account for such Conduct, nor to conceive the Reason for it. (174)

Booth's very sense of values is challenged here. He treasures friendship, but he finds that his friend is fickle and hard to understand. The reader knows that this situation results from Colonel James' own attraction to Amelia, but it takes a long time before Booth understands this fully.

If it seems as if no one is the person he seems to be and everyone wears a mask of some kind or other, then that might be why the most iconic scene in this novel is the scene at the masquerade. The masquerade, indeed, hangs over the entire novel as a threat of deception and duplicity. So few characters are exactly what they seem – so many disguise behaviors in order to mislead, misinform, or even seduce – that the masquerade takes on added complexity.

Critics have often noted that it is the figure of the masquerade that represents metonymically everything that Fielding thinks is wrong about contemporary culture, and this includes friendship and marriage as well. Linda Bree writes, for instance:

> The centerpiece of *Tom Jones* had been at the inn at Upton, a location embodying temporariness and transition, arrivals and departures, where most of the main characters came together, misunderstood each other, and separated again. It is hugely significant that the equivalent scene in *Amelia* takes place at the much less neutral, much more duplicitous, location of a masquerade.[26]

The masquerade, revealing what Bree calls the heart of "deception" in the novel, offers an opportunity, she says, for "genteel men and women to throw off the ceremonies and formalities of their society and act in transgressive ways."[27] For the novelist, moreover, it offers the chance to show how friendship and marriage function under extraordinary duress. The masquerade is at first threatened when Amelia's (false) friend Mrs.

---

[26] Linda Bree, "Introduction," in *Amelia* (Peterborough, ONT: Broadview Press, 2010), 9–30 (15).
[27] Bree, "Introduction," 15.

Ellison offers tickets to the Masquerade at Ranelagh, which are "a present from My Lord to us" (247). Booth suspects the intentions of the so-called Noble Lord, and he insists that Amelia not accept these tickets. When Mrs. Bennet hears of this offer, she tells Amelia a long and horrifying tale of her own entrapment by the same Mrs. Ellison and the Noble Lord. The masquerade can therefore be seen to function as a snare for unaware young women, married or unmarried, and it becomes almost immediately clear that Amelia is the intended victim of just such a scheme. She has been made aware of the ways in which the traps inherent in the masquerade can destroy a woman and ruin her marriage.[28]

Amelia's integrity is continuously under attack. If the Noble Lord befriends her and offers trinkets to her children, warming her heart but placing her in more danger than she realizes, then Amelia has to learn that even kindness can be barbed. Later, though, when Colonel James, her husband's dear friend, has been over-friendly and attempts everything in his power to bring Amelia under his control, Booth remains ignorant of his designs. He even tries to get Booth a posting abroad so that he can offer to bring Amelia and her children to reside with him and his increasingly dishonest wife. Finally he presses two tickets to the masquerade onto Booth. When he does so, Amelia recognizes that she is in real danger. She dare not let on about James' assiduities to her husband because she fears a duel will bring him harm. As Amelia gets an ever-clearer sense of Colonel James' designs, she turns to their good friend Dr. Harrison to seek advice:

> *Amelia* now informed her Friend of all she knew, all she had seen and heard, and all that she suspected of the Colonel. The good Man seemed greatly shocked at the Relation, and remained in a silent Astonishment. – Upon which, *Amelia* said, "Is Villiany so rare a Thing, Sir, that it should so much surprize you?" "No, Child," cries he, "but I am shocked at seeing it so artfully disguised under the Appearance of so much Virtue ... O Nature, Nature, why are thou so dishonest, as ever to send Men with these false Recommendations into the *World!*"
>
> "Indeed, my dear Sir, I begin to grow entirely sick of it," cries *Amelia*. "For sure all Mankind almost are Villains in their Hearts." (374)

Amelia's exclamation puts succinctly what the novel seems to be arguing at this point. Dr. Harrison offers a powerful corrective – "The Nature of Man is far from being in itself Evil" – but that does not really offer her consolation. He goes on to rail against adultery and argue: "the Community in

---

[28] Terry Castle, *Masquerade and Civilization: The Carnvalesque in Eighteenth-Century English Culture and Fiction* (Stanford: Stanford University Press, 1987), see esp. 219–22.

general treat this monstrous Crime as Matter of Jest" (374–5). What here seems an expostulation to help Amelia in her distress, very soon becomes a formal sermon on the topic, which is read at the masquerade.

Because Amelia has already caught on to James' ploys, and because she fears to tell her husband about his attempts at seduction, when James offers Booth and Amelia masquerade tickets, she realizes the trap and asks Dr. Harrison what to do. He offers his own objections: "I do not like the Diversion itself, as I have heard it described to me: Not that I am such a Prude to suspect every Woman who goes there of any evil Intentions; but it is a Pleasure of too loose and disorderly a Kind for the Recreation of a sober Mind" (406).

Mrs. Atkinson (the former Mrs. Bennet) offers to help Amelia make a plan, and as they take matters into their own hands, the doctor wishes them well. Then, unknown to the reader, Amelia switches places with Mrs. Atkinson, who attends the masquerade in her place. Afterward Amelia reassures her husband who thinks he has seen her in her mask conversing with the noble lord, and Mrs. Atkinson admits that in her disguise as Amelia, she has even procured some advancement for her husband. In this way, both women have defeated the power that the masquerade has held over them.

What is even more remarkable about the masquerade, however, is the public reading of a pointed sermon on adultery that entertains a gang of young bucks at the masquerade itself. The sermon, meant it seems for the ears of Colonel James, has been penned by none other than Booth's and Amelia's dear friend Dr. Harrison, who hovers as a force of beneficence over most of the novel. The adultery sermon stands out as an anomaly in eighteenth-century fiction, and for that reason, it is worth considering more closely.

The adultery sermon addresses topics of friendship and marriage from another perspective: it points out the deficiencies of friendship and the ways in which it undermines the very meaning of marriage. Dr. Harrison begins by reminding his listeners of the punishments promised in scripture, but then he goes on to detail the outline of the sin itself:

> And for what will you submit yourself to this Punishment? Or for what Reward will you inflict all this Misery on another? I will add on your Friend? For the Possession of a Woman, for the Pleasure of a Moment? But if neither Virtue nor Religion can restrain your inordinate Appetites, are there not many Women as handsome as your Friend's Wife, whom, though not with Innocence, you may possess with much less Degree of Guilt? What Motive can thus hurry you on to the Destruction of yourself and your Friend? (415)

By posing the question in this way, Dr. Harrison articulates one of the main concerns of the novel: friendship fails whenever sexual desire for a woman intervenes. Adultery seems to be more concerned with friendship than it does with a woman and her reputation. The rivalry of friends is central to this notion of adultery, as if it were something one friend does to another.[29] This makes the transgression central to all the most deeply held values of the novel: friendship and marriage, to be sure, and their place in the nets of social relation that offer a struggling couple like Booth and Amelia something like hope.

This tension between friends happens twice in the novel, first when it turns out that Miss Mathews, the woman with whom Booth had a brief affair while in prison, much to his later chagrin, is also the object of Colonel James' long-standing desire. This means that when Booth tries, by confiding in James, to shirk off the responsibility he feels toward Miss Mathews, the senior officer is only too happy to take this woman off his hands. Whatever generosity James shows to Booth – and as I mentioned above, this novel most often evaluates friendship by the willingness with which funds are exchanged – is therefore always already tempered by sexual jealousy and a sense of libertine rivalry.

While Booth might seem above such rivalry in certain ways, Amelia knows that he would fight a duel with James if he were ever to discover the truth. And when, later in the novel, James actually sends Booth a challenge, Amelia intercepts it. What ensues is one of her darkest moments:

> It is not easy to describe the Agitation of *Amelia's* Mind when she read this Letter. She threw herself into her Chair, turned pale as Death, began to tremble all over, and had just Power enough to tap the Bottle of Wine, which she hitherto preserved entire for her Husband, and to drink off a large Bumper. (490)

Her panic here is all for the danger Booth is in. James' letter was challenging him because he spent an evening with Miss Mathews, but Amelia ignores this transgression because it pales next to the mortal threat of a duel. Later she reads Booth's letter to her, in which he confesses his marital transgression and laments that he is in the bailiff's house once more. This calms her slightly, and she passes a "miserable and sleepless Night" (493).

---

[29] Adam Potkay makes an important distinction between religious feeling in the novel and the power of "necessity" that Fielding struggles with in the novel. See "Liberty and Necessity in Fielding's *Amelia*," *The Eighteenth-Century Novel* 6–7 (2009): 335–58. See also Amy Wolf, "Bernard Mandeville, Henry Fielding's *Amelia*, and the Necessities of Plot," *The Eighteenth-Century Novel* 6–7 (2009): 73–102.

Amelia understands the power of this masculine rivalry, and she also understands that it can destroy her marriage if she does not take care.

Booth thinks of James as a friend who can sustain him in any adversity. The language of celebration of this kind of friendship is almost overbearing. When James visits him in the sponging house, for instance, we are given this poetic account:

> The unexpected Visit of a beloved Friend to a Man in Affliction, especially in Mr. *Booth's* Situation, is a Comfort which can scarce be equaled; not barely from the Hopes of Relief, or Redress, by his Assistance; but, as it is an Evidence of sincere Friendship, which scarce admits of any Doubt or Suspicion. Such an Instance doth, indeed, make a Man amends for all ordinary Troubles and Distresses; and we ought to think ourselves Gainers, by having had such an Opportunity of discovering, that we are possessed of one of the most valuable of all human Possessions. (330)

All the excessive language here, when the reader is already suspecting James' hypocrisy, points to how far short of any ideal actual friendship usually falls. Even as he articulates these values, moreover, the narrator does not seem able to resist exposing James, to the reader if not to Booth:

> In Truth, the Colonel, tho' a very generous Man, had not the least Grain of Tenderness in his Disposition. His Mind was formed of those firm Materials, of which Nature formerly hammered out the Stoic, and upon which the Sorrows of no Man living could make an Impression. A Man of this Temper, who doth not much value Danger, will fight for the Person he calls his Friend; and the man that hath but little Value for his Money will give it him; but such Friendship is never to be absolutely depended on: For whenever the favourite Passion interposes with it, it is sure to subside and vanish into Air. (331)

If what the narrator calls "the favourite Passion," in this case sexual intrigue, can cause all the value of friendship "to subside and vanish into Air," then a mind like James' is not really suitable to the nourishment of the kind of friendship that Fielding has articulated. The closest thing in the novel to a friend, as classically defined, James turns out to be a perverse and double-dealing enemy rather than anyone we would want to label "friend." In her wonderful book about Fielding, Jill Campbell notes the tension between two sets of values in the novel. For Campbell, Booth is often "paralyzed or isolated by a conflict between Christian ideals and the Cavalier or military code" and more modern and forward-looking versions of masculinity.[30]

---

[30] Jill Campbell, *Natural Masques: Gender and Identity in Fielding's Plays and Novels* (Stanford: Stanford University Press, 1995), 215.

This seems right to me, and by devoting himself to the friend who turns out to be false, Booth is trying to uphold values that are utterly outmoded.

We can see how outmoded they are by attending briefly to another friend: Colonel Bath. Bath is rendered ridiculous by the degree to which he is ready to rush into a duel for the sake of his "Honour." No friend is safe from the occasional ire of this fire-breather, who is at other times as sweet and charming as any friend could be. "The Man of Honour wears the Law by his Side" (354), Bath tells Dr. Harrison when the older man is trying to argue the speciousness of arguments in favor of dueling. Bath is not persuaded, and he leaves the novel bristling with irritation that shortly brings about his demise: "killed in a Duel" as the narrator announces (531). The older Cavalier values that Campbell mentions are mocked in the figure of Bath, and with James, equivalent libertine codes of sexual license are also questioned.

Male friendship is hampered by a conflict of codes and libidos in this way. Booth's friends are victims of these competing allegiances, but then so is Booth. He is as given to sexual jealousy as any other character in the novel, and he finds himself hounded by a sense of honor and what it demands of him in one situation after another. If friendship is only rivalry, as it often seems here, and male relations can only lead to conflict, however emotionally intense, then what hope is there for a culture that is structured around the flexibility of male relations?

Fielding considers a similar interplay between friendship and marriage in his play *The Modern Husband*, which was produced in 1730. As Martin Battestin notes in his biography of Fielding, "In *The Modern Husband*, Fielding risked a new kind of drama that ... dares even to be 'serious,' taking as its subject something intrinsically detestable, '*Modern Vice,*' and representing the Town 'vicious as it is.' " Battestin goes on to say, "Fielding was something of a rake in his youth: but he always regarded the institution of marriage as inviolable ... and adultery was so far from being with him the comical game of intrigue Restoration wits and modern gallants had made it, that in the period of his magistracy he openly deplored the lack of laws for punishing adulterers."[31] Adultery is the only lethal challenge to a married couple: other adversities can be overcome, but adultery gnaws at a marriage from within. This is what Fielding seems to argue in *The Modern Husband*, and he revisits the topic here with even more emotional delicacy.

---

[31] Martin C. Battestin, with Ruthe E. Battestin, *Henry Fielding: A Life* (New York: Routledge, 1989), 129.

Fielding offers two clear models of true friendship. Dr. Harrison stands out as a friend: the honorable older man supports Booth and Amelia and does his best to make their path easy. He challenges Booth when it seems he is going astray and he helps them discover the deceit that leads to the happy ending.

Sergeant Atkinson can also function as a friend, devoted as he is and as ready with his purse: when he can least afford to spare any cash he hands considerable amounts over to Booth. But Booth also treats him as little more than a servant, as Campbell reminds us. For her, "Assumptions about class and assumptions about the relative importance of homosocial and heterosexual bonds both influence Booth's understanding of Atkinson, whose actions and motivations he consistently either overlooks or mistakes" (221). Although Atkinson functions in this way, he remains a minor character whatever he does to distinguish himself as a stalwart friend and brother to the heroine.

For me, however, there is another friendship that stands out as the best and the most forward-looking relationship in the novel, and that friendship is the one between Booth himself and Amelia. Far from offering an idealized version of his first marriage, as is often suggested, Fielding uses this novel to examine the state of marriage itself; and far from sugarcoating it, he shows the stress it is under and the various ways in which it could easily fail. Unlike the relationship with James, however, that seems rooted in an idealized past, Booth's relationship with Amelia is not only rooted in the present, but it is constantly being redefined as the novel proceeds. Campbell reminds us that with "no more means than Booth to sustain her little family economically, but from quite early in their story, [Amelia] is given a sphere of honorable activity and self-definition in the labor of caring for their home and children" and that her "function as housekeeper and mother ... provides the present economic as well as moral anchor of the Booth household" (206–7).

If Linda Bree feels that Amelia "never converts [her] rhetoric [of devotion] into any practical action to improve the family's position," she nevertheless asserts, rightly, I think, "the scenes between Booth and Amelia offer a convincing representation of a husband and wife, who know each other well and are still in love with each other despite the pressures of a hostile world, whether they are exchanging informal intimacies, gossipy jokes, delicate half-truths, or uncomfortable lies."[32] Even more importantly, Amelia's "practical action" works to keep the family afloat when many things that Booth does could actually destroy it. Rather than merely passive, that is, Amelia works hard to see that her marriage and her family survive.

[32] Bree, "Introduction," 20, 17–18.

This "convincing representation" is in many ways the whole point of the novel.[33] The possibility of a mutual relationship based on respect that nourishes both members of the relationship and enables them to function together in a way that neither could function apart: this is the definition of marriage that Fielding offers, and it would be hard to find a better or more forward-looking definition of friendship. The degree that marriage is modeled on friendship in the later eighteenth century has only begun to be told.[34] Betty Rizzo reminds us that even so-called "companionate marriage" makes it clear that relations were askew to the point that wives felt subservient.[35] But what Fielding is offering is something else: something based on a model of friendship that celebrates mutual love and trust. Just to witness Booth and Amelia together is to see something that rarely appears in eighteenth-century fiction.

Some critics point out that deception creeps even into this relationship, but deception to protect is far different from the other kinds of deceptions that circulate in the novel.[36] When Amelia tricks Booth into thinking she has gone to the masquerade, she avoids having to admit her fears about James and involve Booth in them directly; moreover, she shows her faith in Booth in her knowledge that he will forgive and even celebrate her absence from the masquerade as he does. Booth transgresses with Miss Mathews while in prison, and Amelia both understands and forgives that behavior. She sustains the marriage, in turn, when Booth is unable to do so; and it is her inheritance that provides for them at the novel's conclusion. Booth's love might seem debilitating at times – as feckless as he often appears – but Amelia's faith in him is just that: faith that he can be the husband and friend who can sustain her in the world of multiplied dangers.

"Domestic Happiness is the End of almost all our Pursuits," Dr. Harrison says in his sermon on adultery (414), and that does seem to be the one lesson that this novel argues persuasively. Many critics have said that the novel was ahead of its time in dealing with social life as realistically as it does.[37] Even more important is this articulation of marriage as a kind of friendship. Fielding is an unlikely source for such an important advance in

---

[33] See George E. Haggerty, "Amelia's Nose; or, Sensibility and Its Symptoms," *The Eighteenth Century: Theory and Interpretation* 36 (1995): 139–56.

[34] Alan Bray, *The Friend* (Chicago: University of Chicago Press, 2003), 307–23

[35] Betty Rizzo, *Companions Without Vows: Relations Among Eighteenth-Century British Women* (Athens, GA: University of Georgia, 1994), 22–4.

[36] Bree, "Introduction," 15.

[37] See Martin C. Battestin, "Introduction," in *Amelia* (Middletown: Wesleyan University Press, 1983), xv–lxi (xxxix); and Battestin and Battestin, *Henry Fielding*, 535.

gender relations, but as one of the greatest novelists in the English literary tradition, it is suitable that he is.

The Abyss of Friendship in *Caleb Williams*

Works in the last decade of the eighteenth century sometimes seem to challenge the friendship ideal: William Godwin's *Caleb Williams*, like other Gothic novels, is teeming with violent emotions and vengeful plots, and would appear to tell a completely different story. However, if we look more closely at Godwin's 1794 novel, I think we will find that it fits crucially within the eighteenth-century tradition of erotic friendship.

Caleb Williams makes friendship so central to its harrowing conception of male relations that readers often miss its particular valence. Some critics, it is true, have suggested that a corrupted homosexual bond is what animates the conflict between Caleb and his patron/tormenter Mr. Falkland.[38] As provocative and at times persuasive as these readings are, and as seemingly true to the language of the text, they ignore the language of friendship that Godwin uses to give his account of human interaction a theoretical grounding in the romantic terminology with which he was so familiar. It may be true that homophobia was alive in the 1790s, but that does not mean that it is the first consideration in an analysis of complex emotional relationships between two men. Of course, in their own terms, by way of the friendship tradition, such bonds may be homoerotic, and excessively so. But even such intense friendships do not and cannot always give way to "homosexuality" in this era, nor are the most overtly emotional relationships necessarily more fruitfully described by using that twentieth-century terminology. Godwin makes clear in the manner in which he develops his plot, in its crisis, and in its resolution too, that friendship is what matters here.

What kind of friendship is it, though, when two characters are so long and destructively at odds that they come close to destroying each other? The enmity that Caleb and Mr. Falkland feel for each other does in fact haunt one version of "friendship" that can exist between two men. When two men are so deeply involved with each other that they uncover

---

[38] Among the most intriguing essays in this regard are: Robert Corber, "Representing the 'Unspeakable': William Godwin and the Politics of Homophobia," *Journal of the History of Sexuality* 1 (1990): 85–101; Alex Gold, Jr., "It's Only Love: The Politics of Passion in Godwin's *Caleb Williams*," *Texas Studies in Language and Literature* 19 (1977): 135–60; see also Ranita Chaterjee and Patrick M. Horan, "Teaching the Homosocial in Godwin, Hogg, and Wilde," in *Approaches to Teaching Gothic Fiction*, ed. Diane Long Hoeveler and Tamar Heller (New York: MLA, 2003), 127–32.

unpleasant truths that set them in opposition, they can become inseparable. These unpleasant truths are part of what determines the nature of friendship itself. As Jacques Derrida notes in *The Politics of Friendship*, "Friendship tells the truth – and this is always better left unknown. The protection of this custody guarantees the truth of friendship, its ambiguous truth, that by which friends protect themselves from the error or the illusion on which friendship is founded – more precisely, the bottomless bottom founding a friendship, which enables it to resist its own abyss."[39] Godwin wants to look more closely at the "error or illusion on which friendship is founded," and in doing so he is intent on pursuing friendship into this abyss. If Gothic fiction in general tries, in Victor Frankenstein's words, to pursue "nature in her hiding places," then Godwin, who might be called the godfather of *Frankenstein*, does the same with friendship.[40] He does not take it for granted, but he inverts it as a way of exposing its inner workings. Derrida calls this "politics," and Godwin is certainly writing about the politics of friendship in *Caleb Williams*. Godwin brings politics into the intimacy of friendship because that is where it has always already been from the time of Plato and Aristotle, through Montaigne and onto Derrida himself.[41]

Adam Smith says in *The Theory of Moral Sentiments*, "As we have no immediate experience of what other men feel, we can form no idea of the manner in which they are affected, but by conceiving what we ourselves should feel in the like situation."[42] Friendship offers the kind of identification that makes this sympathetic response possible. It would be a mistake to think, though, that this identification is always transformative in positive ways. *Caleb Williams* makes it clear how harrowing such identification can be.[43]

---

[39] Jacques Derrida, *The Politics of Friendship*, trans. George Collins (New York: Verso, 2005), 53.

[40] Mary Shelley, *Frankenstein, or The Modern Prometheus* (Oxford: Oxford University Press, 1980 [1819]). Victor Frankenstein is talking about the power of the modern philosophers who inspire him: "They penetrate into the recesses of nature, and show how she works in her hiding places" (47); Victor later says of his own research: "I pursued nature to her hiding places" (54).

[41] The classic works in the friendship tradition include Plato, *Symposium, Lysis,* and *Phaedrus* (*Plato: Complete Works,* ed. John M. Cooper [Indianapolis: Hackett, 1997]); Cicero, "De Amicitia" (Cicero, *De Senectute, De Amicitia, De Divinatione,* trans. William Armisted Falconer [Cambridge, MA: Harvard University Press, 1923], 103–211); and Montaigne, "On Affectionate Relationships" (Michel de Montaigne, *Complete Essays,* ed. and trans. M. A. Screech [London: Penguin, 2003], 205–19).

[42] Adam Smith, *The Theory of Moral Sentiments* (New York: Augustus M. Kelley, 1966 [1759]), 3. See also John Mullan, *Sentiment and Sociability: The Language of Feeling in the Eighteenth Century* (Oxford: Clarendon, 1988), 114–46.

[43] For Eric Daffron, the connection between the central characters is a form of "sympathy," and he connects this emotion to a specifically British context on account of the strong anti-Jacobin sentiment

From the first moment when Caleb is taken into the service of Mr. Falkland, he finds the older man fascinating in ways he does not completely understand: "His manner was kind, attentive, and humane. His eye was full of animation; but there was a grave and sad solemnity in his air, which, for want of experience, I imagined was the inheritance of the great, and the instrument by which the distance between them and their inferiors was maintained" (1.i; 61).[44]

Caleb observes "every muscle and petty line of his countenance seemed to be ... pregnant with meaning" (1.i; 61), and he hopes to bring this meaning forth, whatever the cost to himself or his patron. If he sees a "grave and sad solemnity," it is already implied that he will look deeply into Falkland's privacy in order to explain it. This is the nature of the attraction of friendship he feels for his patron, and of course it suggests an intense and clearly directed desire. This desire for knowledge is partly based in class distinction – Caleb might not be so interested if Falkland were not his social superior and his employer – but it is also grounded in an almost physical fascination that Falkland provides for his "inferior." This is not exactly the same thing as sexual desire, but it is equally powerful for an impressionable young man such as Caleb. He wants to know his master as intimately as possible. He sees discomfort, and he wishes to explain it. His aim is to know this man who has befriended him in every detail of his personal complexity.

Almost immediately after this, Caleb notes the ways in which his patron's personality seems affected by this deep "unquietness of mind": "The distemper which afflicted him with incessant gloom had its paroxysms. Sometimes he was hasty, peevish, and tyrannical ... Sometimes he entirely lost his self-possession, and his behaviour was changed into frenzy: he would strike his forehead, his brows became knit, his features distorted, and his teeth ground one against the other" (1.i; 63). It would almost be fair to say that Caleb is dealing with a madman, but these "paroxysms," as they are called, are not so frequent that they make intercourse impossible, nor so intense that they keep the men from each other. Caleb says that

to which Godwin and his friends were subjected. Sympathy of course connects more immediately and obviously to eighteenth-century notions of human intercourse through heightened sensibility, which writers like Adam Smith emphasize. For me the language of friendship has almost equal power and indeed is an older tradition; but that does not mean that the language of sympathy, as Daffron describes, is not at work here as well. See Eric Daffron, " 'Magnetical Sympathy': Strategies of Power and Resistance in Godwin's *Caleb Williams*," *Criticism* 37.2 (Spring 1995): 213–32.

44 William Godwin, *Caleb Williams* ed. Gary Handwerk and A. A. Markley (Peterborough, ONT: Broadview, 2000 [1794]). References to the novel include volume and chapter, as well as page in the Broadview edition.

Mr. Falkland rushed from the room when he was particularly overcome but otherwise could control his responses. Caleb is already on alert: he suspects that the man he admires and hopes to emulate is harboring a deep unhappiness that Caleb can only guess at. But as the intimacy between the two men grows, it takes on a darker cast: Caleb insists on uncovering Falkland's deepest secrets, however private or debilitating. For his part, Falkland almost insists that his secrets are there for Caleb to find, even as he resists the process and castigates Caleb for invading his privacy.

Very early in his tenure at Mr. Falkland's estate, Caleb wanders into Mr. Falkland's chamber and hears "a deep groan, expressive of intolerable anguish." There he finds Mr. Falkland in the process of slamming shut the cover of a trunk. Only Falkland would keep his most carefully kept secrets locked up in a trunk: it is almost too grossly available as a metaphor for his world of private guilt and torment. Be that as it may, Caleb happens upon him when this trunk is open, and he pays the price when he encounters Falkland's rage:

> at that moment a voice, that seemed supernaturally tremendous, exclaimed, "Who is there?" The voice was Mr. Falkland's. The sound of it thrilled my very vitals ... Mr. Falkland was just risen from the floor upon which he had been sitting or kneeling. His face betrayed strong symptoms of confusion. With a violent effort, however, these symptoms vanished, and instantaneously gave place to a countenance sparkling with rage. "Villain!" cried he, "what has brought you here?" I hesitated a confused and irresolute answer. "Wretch!" interrupted Mr. Falkland, with uncontrollable impatience, "you want to ruin me. You set yourself as a spy upon my actions; but bitterly shall you repent your insolence. Do you think you shall watch my privacies with impunity?" I attempted to defend myself. "Begone devil!" joined he. "Quit the room, or I will trample you into atoms." (1.i; 64)

Falkland wants to befriend Caleb, but he also sees their intimacy as a threat. This could be the result of Falkland's innate sense of superiority, inculcated by class difference, to be sure,[45] but it is also the product of the intensity of friendship: because of this very intensity, the language of friendship has been perverted into a kind of enmity. Intimacy breeds mutual suspicion, if not contempt.

Friendships between masters and servants are not unheard of – think only of Trim and Uncle Toby in *Tristram Shandy* – and there is no structural reason for Falkland and Caleb to be enemies. Derrida reminds us how deeply threatening friendship can be: he calls this the truth that is

---

[45] See Gary Handwerk, "Of Caleb's Guilt and Godwin's Truth: Ideology and Ethics in *Caleb Williams*," *ELH* 60 (1993): 939–60.

better left unknown. Mutual knowledge is as dangerous as it is wonderful for two men to share. Without trust, this knowledge can be lethal. Still, while Caleb has admitted curiosity about his patron's affairs, he has not (yet) been playing the spy or trying to catch Mr. Falkland in nefarious acts. He has no reason to imagine any. Instead, it is possible to say that Mr. Falkland has over-invested his relationship with Caleb with levels of suspicion that Caleb can only wonder about. He has projected intentions and motivations that are the products of his own guilt. The resulting threats are harrowing expressions of power – as it happens he uses the very words he repeats near the conclusion of the novel – and they leave Caleb speechless and afraid: speechless, afraid, and utterly engaged. Nothing could be more carefully calculated to draw the young man into Falkland's own power than this peremptory demand that Caleb absent himself. This very moment could be said to mark the beginning of Caleb's obsession with his master.

After this introductory chapter, Mr. Collins, Mr. Falkland's steward and a friend to Caleb, tells the elaborate account of Falkland's time in Italy; his return to the village and conflict with Barnabas Tyrrel; his friendship with Miss Melville and her death; the insults between Tyrrel and Falkland; and finally Tyrrel's death and Falkland's increasing depression: "From this time to the present Mr. Falkland has been nearly such as you at present see him … These symptoms are uninterrupted, except at certain times when his suffering becomes intolerable, and he displays the marks of a furious insanity … His domestics in general know nothing of him, but the uncommunicative and haughty, but mild, dejection that accompanies every thing he does" (1.xii; 174–5).[46]

Caleb is embarrassed by this information because he does not know how to respond. He is also embarrassed by the admiration he still feels: "I found thousand fresh reasons to admire and love Mr. Falkland" (11.i; 179). Either because of this love and admiration or in spite of it, Caleb soon begins to imagine that Mr. Falkland might have been the murderer. "It was but a passing thought, but … I determined to place myself as a watch on my patron": "The instant I had chosen this employment for myself, I found a strange sort of pleasure in it. To do what is forbidden always has its charms … To be a spy upon Mr. Falkland! … The more impenetrable Mr. Falkland was determined to be, the more uncontrollable was my curiosity" (11.i; 180–1).

---

[46] Other critics have talked at length about Falkland and Tyrrel. See for instance, Robert Kiely, *The Romantic Novel in England* (Cambridge, MA: Harvard University Press, 1972), 81–97; and Tilottama Rajan, "Wollstonecraft and Godwin: Reading the Secrets of the Political Novel," *Studies in Romanticism* 27 (1988): 221–51; see also her "Judging Justice: Godwin's Critique of Judgment in *Caleb Williams* and Other Novels," *The Eighteenth Century* 51 (2010): 341–62.

What is this "strange sort of pleasure" but an attempt to forge an intimacy even more intense than the one Mr. Falkland has offered? Caleb courts this forbidden knowledge because he understands that it is the secret Mr. Falkland holds most dear. This attempt to probe into Mr. Falkland's secrets backfires on Caleb, to say the least. But at the moment, he is motivated by the form of desire he calls "curiosity." This curiosity is a desire to know Falkland's secrets and to use them, Caleb hardly admits to himself, as a way of intensifying their bond. If, for Derrida, friends come together to keep silent about what they know they are destined to be – "dissociated, 'solitarized,' singularized, constituted into modadic alterities ... where, as the phenomenlogist says, what is proper to the *alter ego* will never be accessible *as such*"[47] – then what Caleb is in the process of discovering might be seen as the harrowing difference between self and other that the concept of alter ego may for a moment disguise.[48] He thinks that by forcing himself closer and closer to this man he so admires, he will finally "penetrate" the forbidding exterior. As thrilling as this potential bond might be, Caleb actually finds as he pushes closer to Mr. Falkland, in order to discover his deepest secrets, he is also pushing himself so far away from his admired friend that he will never find his way back to him.[49]

This dynamic is almost painful in the long series of scenes in which Caleb brings up murder as a topic of discussion, and Mr. Falkland engages him in conversation and tries to instruct him in the world which he is about to enter. After Caleb has been railing against Alexander as a murderer, Mr. Falkland responds with these kindly remarks. "Recollect his heroic confidence in Philip the physician, and his entire and unalterable friendship for Ephestion":

> The way of thinking you express, Williams, is natural enough, and I cannot blame you for it. But let me hope that you will become more liberal. The death of a hundred thousand men is at first sight very shocking; but what in

---

[47] Derrida, *The Politics of Friendship*, 54.
[48] Accounts of the function of Falkland and Caleb as the avatars of each other go back as far as Misao Miyoshi's wonderful study, *The Divided Self: A Perspective on the Literature of the Victorians* (New York: New York University Press, 1969), 1–45. For Miyoshi, Caleb Williams is "a voyeur with a touch of the morbid about him," and he adds that "The two locked together in their strange drama have little to do with the rest of society, and are isolated within it" (25).
[49] See Miriam L. Wallace, "Duplicitous Subjects and the Tyranny of Ideology: Godwin's *Things As They Are; or Caleb Williams* (1794) and Fenwick's *Secresy* (1795)," in *Revolutionary Subjects in the English "Jacobin Novel"* (Lewisburg: Bucknell University Press, 2009), 36–60. In this wonderful chapter, Wallace discusses the ways in which secrecy helps to determine subjectivity in the 1790s. "Both novels explore," she says, "the ways in which subjects and subjectivities are made ideologically coherent: through the legal-juridical discourse, through the language of gendered sensibility, and through the lure of detection," 38.

reality are a hundred thousand such men, more than a hundred thousand
sheep? It is mind, Williams, the generation of knowledge and virtue, that
we ought to love. This was the project of Alexander; he set out in a great
undertaking to civilise mankind; he delivered the vast continent of Asia
from the stupidity and degradation of the Persian monarchy; and, though
he was cut off in the midst of his career, we may easily perceive the vast
effects of his project. Grecian literature and cultivation, the Selucidae, the
Antiochuses, and the Ptolemies followed, in nations which before had been
sunk to the condition of brutes. Alexander was a builder, as notoriously as
the destroyer, of cities. (ii.i; 185)

This celebration of Alexander is thoughtful and suggestive. Basing his
appreciation, as he does, on the much-recounted friendship between
Alexander and Ephestion, Falkland offers Caleb an ideal of male relations
that Caleb cannot comprehend. Like Achilles and Patroclos or Antony
and Dolabella, these classical friendships are commemorated as bonds that
"surpass the love of women," and as such, they act as models of male–male
relations.⁵⁰ In other words, Falkland offers heroes of classical friendship
who are willing to die for each other; and instead Caleb perverts this ideal
by pushing even more aggressively at the issue of murder and responsibility. "Mr. Falkland ... gave me a penetrating look, as if he would see my
very soul. His eyes were then in an instant withdrawn. I could perceive
him seized with a convulsive shuddering which, though strongly counter-
acted, and therefore scarcely visible, had I know not what of terrible in it"
(ii.i; 187).

When Falkland turns this scorching look on Caleb – "as if he would see
my very soul" – he mimics Caleb's own pursuit. This is a terrible portrait
of what intimacy can evoke and the terror with which personal knowledge
is fraught. This is the dark underside of friendship, but it is exactly where
Caleb wants to be. "Is it possible," said I, "that Mr. Falkland, who is thus
overwhelmed with a sense of the unmerited dishonour that has been fas-
tened upon him in the face of the world, will long endure the presence of a
raw and unfriended youth, who is perpetually bringing back that dishonour to his recollection, and who seems himself the most forward to entertain the accusation?" (ii.ii; 188). Caleb insists on this confrontation, as if
exposure were the only route to gaining intimacy with Mr. Falkland; and
of course it may well be. This darkness, the dark privacy that is tantamount
here to a secret crime, is the crux of the friendship ideal after all: can the

---

⁵⁰ Such friends are discussed at length in David M. Halperin's study, *One Hundred Years of Homosexuality
and Other Essays on Greek Love* (New York: Routledge, 1989): 75–87. See also Haggerty, *Men in
Love*, 23–43.

friend be supported if he has done something immoral? Caleb assumes the answer to this question is yes, but Falkland knows why it has to be no.[51]

Whatever Caleb thinks he is doing, he certainly provokes Mr. Falkland to extreme expressions:

> "How came this conversation?" cried he. "Who gave you a right to be my confidant? Base, artful wretch that you are! learn to be more respectful! Are my passions to be wound and unwound by an insolent domestic? Do you think I will be an instrument to be played on at your pleasure, till you have extorted all the treasures of my soul? Begone, and fear lest you be made to pay for the temerity you have already committed!" (ii.ii; 193)

Mr. Falkland seems interested in confiding in Caleb: he seems almost to be ready to trust him with the secrets of his soul. But this intimacy quite understandably scares him, and his immediate and vitriolic put-down of Caleb is a measure of the threat that friendship always, and this friendship especially, poses. Derrida, citing Nietzsche, argues that "friendship had better preserve itself in silence, and keep silent about the truth," and that truth is what Falkland confronts here. Falkland's most violent expression is to put Caleb in his place as an "insolent domestic" and to insist on his social superiority.[52] But note that he does this only in such moments of crisis: for the most part, in these earlier sections of the novel, he almost seems ready to treat Caleb as an equal. Equality is of course key to the concept of friendship as it has evolved. Friends may not start out equal, as even Cicero attests, but equality results from their open dealing with each other.[53] This openness is starting to backfire here: Falkland's rhetorical questions – "Who gave you the right to be my confidant?" "Do you think I will be an instrument to be played on at your pleasure" – remind us how fully Falkland himself has been the author of this bond that now seems to torment him.

Caleb, sensing that he has struck a nerve, cannot give up his pursuit. Almost in spite of the admiration and love he feels for Mr. Falkland, he pushes his advantage; and before too many chapters, he has laid out the story as he heard it from Mr. Collins and implicitly asks Mr. Falkland to respond. Falkland's response is fascinating:

> The scene of that night, instead of perishing, has been a source of every new calamity to me, which must flow for ever! I am then, thus miserable

---

[51] This question is asked everywhere in the classic theories of friendship; see, for instance, Cicero, "De Amicitia," 185–9.
[52] Derrida, *The Politics of Friendship*, 53.
[53] See Cicero, "De Amicitia," 181.

and ruined, a proper subject upon which for you to exercise your ingenuity, and improve your power of tormenting? ... Misery itself has nothing worse in store for me, except what you have inflicted: the seeming to doubt of my innocence, which, after the fullest and most solemn examination has been completely established. You have forced me to this explanation. You have extorted from me a confidence which I had no inclination to make. But it is part of the misery of my situation, that I am at the mercy of every creature, however little, who feels himself inclined to sport with my distress. (II.iii; 196)

Friendship has become a scene of misery because Caleb pushes beneath the rugged surface of Falkland's "miserable and ruined" façade. Caleb's doubt is a product of the intimacy between the two men. He only "extorted a confidence" to the degree that Mr. Falkland found himself trusting him. This is the very extortion upon which friendship is based: what would friendship be if it did not extort secrets.[54] Here, however, it has shifted from mutual confidence into something more like forced confession. That shift is one that makes friendship a torment rather than a balm. Of course, Falkland knows the person with whom he is dealing, and he changes his tack to evoke his young protégé's guilt by emphasizing the agony of the procedure for himself: "Misery itself has nothing worse in store for me, except what you have inflicted." In this way, Falkland draws Caleb into the emotional stress of his position, and in a sense, he insists that Caleb share in his misery. This becomes clearer in the string of questions and responses with which Caleb follows this speech.

Caleb first offers to quit Falkland's service: "Let me go and hide myself where I will never see you more." Falkland takes this almost as an insult: "But you cannot bear to live with such a miserable wretch as I am!" The conversation then ventures into a zone that must be recognized as a moment of extreme passion:

"Oh, sir! do not talk to me thus! Do with me anything that you will. Kill me if you please."
"Kill you!" (Volumes could not describe the emotions with which this echo of my words was given and received.)
"Sir, I could die to serve you! I love you more than I can express. I worship you as a being of superior nature. I am foolish, raw, inexperienced, – worse than any of these – but never did a thought of disloyalty to your service enter into my heart." (II.iii; 196–7)

The intensity of the love that is expressed here – Caleb is not merely willing to die but ready to be killed by Falkland – is the love that resides

---

[54] Derrida, *The Politics of Friendship*, 62.

in the most celebrated male friendships. Caleb's praise of his master and the resulting self-abnegation bind him in a relationship that is more than he could ever have hoped for. Friendship calls for adoration, in this way, and silence about the doubts and fears of "dishonour." Derrida reminds us of the "Lie, mask, dissimulation, [which] the simulacrum [of friendship] bestows ... The sage, for friendship's sake ... takes on the disguise of a fool, and, for friendship's sake, disguises friendship in enmity." And he goes on to explain that if "the sage presents himself as an enemy in order to conceal his enmity. He shows his hostility so as not to hurt with his wickedness."[55] What we see here is a performance similarly positioned in and around enmity. When Caleb says, seemingly in self-contempt, "Oh, sir! do not talk to me thus! Do with me anything that you will, Kill me if you please," he is challenging Mr. Falkland with the suspicion of murder, and Mr. Falkland responds appropriately. But his demands that Caleb not leave his service are also a threat. These men are locked into a dance of respect and mutual admiration, which masks and holds in check their need and desire to destroy each other in the intensity of their love. "Sir, I could die to serve you!" Caleb does not realize how powerfully prophetic these words actually are.

Instead he finds himself recommitting himself to his master in a fit of rapture:

> Here our conversation ended; and the impression it made on my youthful mind it is impossible to describe. I thought with astonishment, *even with rapture*, of the attention and kindness towards me I discovered in Mr. Falkland, through all the roughness of his manner. *I could never enough wonder at finding myself, humble as I was by my birth, obscure as I had hitherto been, thus suddenly become of so much importance to the happiness of one of the most enlightened and accomplished men in England.* But this consciousness attached me to my patron more eagerly than ever, and made me swear a thousand times, as I meditated upon my situation, that I would never prove unworthy of so generous a protector. (ii.iii; 197; italics mine)

Caleb's raptures are a measure of his own transformation and how important he thinks he has become to the happiness of his patron. He hugs himself with the delusion that Falkland depends upon him. What he does not recognize is how deeply his own interior life is dependent on his master.

At the same time, these protests of devotion mask Caleb's unremitting attempts to expose Mr. Falkland at his most vulnerable, and hardly has the next chapter begun when he says: "It is not unaccountable that, in the

---

[55] Derrida, *The Politics of Friendship*, 60.

midst of all my increased veneration for my patron, the first tumult of my emotion was scarcely subsided, before the old question that had excited my conjectures recurred to my mind, Was he the murderer? It was a kind of fatal impulse, that seemed destined to hurry me to my destruction" (II. iv; 198). The "fatal impulse" seems to emerge directly from the raptures of devotion. Could they be connected? I would say, yes: Caleb's devotion – "the first tumult of ... emotion" – brings with it this desire to know Falkland to the depths of his soul. This is an instinctual impulse in friendship, the abyss that true friendship can always mask. Caleb and Falkland turn trust inside out, and as a result, friendship becomes a form of torment to them both.

Such torment becomes clear as Falkland starts slipping into a form of insanity. He disappears for long stretches, and as Caleb remarks, "It was by an obstinate fatality that, whenever I saw Mr. Falkland in these deplorable situations, and particularly when I lighted on him after having sought him among the rocks and precipices, pale, emaciated, solitary, and haggard, the suggestion would continually recur to me, in spite of inclination, in spite of persuasion, in spite of evidence, Surely this man is a murderer!" (II.iv; 202).

When shortly after this, there is a fire in Mr. Falkland's home, Caleb finds that by some "mysterious fatality" (II.vi; 210), his steps lead him to Mr. Falkland's room beyond the library, where he had seen Falkland closing a trunk in the first chapter. Now alone in this room, while everyone is running around to deal with the fire, Caleb finds himself confronting the trunk once more: "My mind was already raised to its utmost pitch. In a window-seat of the room lay a number of chisels and other carpenter's tools. I know not what infatuation instantaneously seized me. The idea was too powerful to be resisted. I forgot the business on which I came, the employment of the servants, and the urgency of the general danger" (II.vi; 210). Caleb calls his impulse an infatuation, and in a sense that is exactly what compels him to probe into the secrets of Mr. Falkland. It is not the truth itself but rather the discovery of the truth that motivates Caleb.

Caleb does not even manage to lift the lid and examine the contents before he is interrupted by Mr. Falkland, who has entered the chamber and confronts Caleb now:

> I was in the act of lifting up the lid, when Mr. Falkland entered, breathless, distracted in his looks! He had been brought home from a considerable distance by the sight of the flames. At the moment of his appearance the lid dropped down from my hand. He no sooner saw me than his eyes emitted sparks of rage. He ran with eagerness to a brace of loaded pistols

which hung in the room, and, seizing one, presented it to my head. I saw his design, and sprang to avoid it; but, with the same rapidity with which he had formed his resolution, he changed it, and instantly went to the window, and flung the pistol into the court below. He bade me begone with his usual irresistible energy; and overcame as I was already by the horror of the detection, I eagerly complied. (II.vi; 211)

The thrill of confrontation here – the culmination of all the indirection and insinuation of this section of the narrative – is almost a relief after all the subterfuge, and Caleb reacts so quickly that he almost seems to understand that. "My act was in some sort an act of insanity," he says. "The insatiable vengeance of a Falkland, of a man whose hands were, to my apprehension, red with blood, and his thoughts familiar with cruelty and murder" (II.vi; 211). Caleb understands the man whom he has challenged, and it adds to his thrill that he nearly excited this man to murder him. If the consummation of friendship is love, that of enmity is murder, or the fantasy of murder, as these scenes remind us.

What Caleb cannot perhaps imagine is what actually happens: Falkland confesses the murder of Tyrrel and his allowing the Hawkinses to take the blame for his act. Caleb "started in terror, and was silent" (II.vi; 213); but after the confession, Mr. Falkland makes his most important claim on Caleb so far:

> Do you know what it is you have done? To gratify a foolishly inquisitive humour, you have sold yourself. You shall continue in my service, but can never share my affection. I will benefit you in respect of fortune, but I shall always hate you. If ever an unguarded word escape from your lips, if ever you excite my jealousy or suspicion, expect to pay for it by your death or worse. It is a dear bargain you have made. But it is too late to look back. (II.vi; 215)

Falkland has made his confession concern Caleb rather than himself. Falkland has spoken, but Caleb has "sold himself." Even more to the point, friendship has given way to employment: "you shall continue in my service, but can never share in my affection." Falkland's language insists on friendship as loss. "I shall always hate you": this sustaining enmity is the other side of the love that friendship offers. The bond is every bit as intense, but the terms are more tormenting. Falkland talks as if he has possession of Caleb, and this is the abyss into which the young hero has fallen.

This abyss is the abyss of friendship. For no sooner has Falkland told him that "it is too late to look back," than Caleb is celebrating his patron and reminding himself of obligation and beneficence:

> This will not be wondered at, when it is considered that I had myself just been trampling on the established boundaries of obligation, and therefore

might well have a fellow-feeling for other offenders. Add to which, I had
known Mr. Falkland from the first as a beneficent divinity. I had observed
at leisure, and with a minuteness which could not deceive me, the excellent
qualities of his heart; and I found him possessed of a mind beyond comparison the most fertile and accomplished I had ever known. (II.vi; 217)

It is remarkable that Caleb can talk in these terms of the man who has just
threatened to deprive him of his freedom forever, but he does. It is almost
as if Falkland's threats fulfill Caleb's earlier desires. After all, they place him
in an unremitting relation to his master and they insure that he will never
be far from his master's thoughts. As he acknowledges here: "I had made
myself a prisoner"; but this prison is one that he has carefully constructed
of his own materials.

Of course as the novel proceeds into its darkest sections, it becomes clear
how much a prisoner Caleb really is. After a brief respite, when Falkland's
brother Forester is visiting and seems to befriend the young man, Caleb
becomes the consummate victim. As if to illustrate Caleb's psychological
disease, Caleb flees the Falkland household only to find himself wandering in a heath that is neither hospitable nor nurturing. It is a landscape as
disorienting as it is dispiriting:

> At length I roused myself, and surveyed the horizon around me; but I could
> observe nothing with which my organ was previously acquainted. On three
> sides, the heath stretched as far as the eye could reach; on the fourth I dis-
> covered at some distance a wood of no ordinary dimensions. Before me,
> scarcely a single track could be found, to mark that any human being had
> ever visited the spot. As the best expedient I could devise, I bent my course
> toward the wood I have mentioned, and then pursued, as well as I was
> able, the windings of the inclosure ... The sun was hid from me by a grey
> and cloudy atmosphere ... My thoughts were gloomy and disconsolate; the
> dreariness of the day, and the solitude which surrounded me, seemed to
> communicate a sadness to my soul. (II.viii; 227)

Caleb is as lost on the heath as he is in his dealings with Mr. Falkland, and
even if he does not recognize the meaning of this scene – grey and cloudy
atmosphere; gloomy and disconsolate thoughts – he is dreary, solitary, and
sad. Friendship has led him into this labyrinth of depression, but it will
also lead him into torments he can barely imagine. Here is the abyss of
friendship figured forth in the landscape of mental conflict. This is where
Caleb finds himself after his at first hopeful and later desolate dealings with
Mr. Falkland. No human being has walked on this heath, just as no one
has suffered through friendship as Caleb has. And of course, his unhappiness is barely beginning.

When Caleb emerges from the wood, he finds himself at the home of Mr. Forester, where Mr. Falkland shortly appears. Caleb tries to flee, but soon he is called back to face Falkland: "There was nothing I so ardently desired as the annihilation of all future intercourse between us, that he should not know there was such a person on the earth as myself" (ii.ix; 239). Caleb feels his innocence will defend him in the trial that ensues; but once Falkland condemns him as a "monster of depravity," who has stolen money and jewels from his master, Caleb is already guilty, even to himself.

After this so-called trial, Caleb is thrown into prison, and it would seem as if an entirely different story of incarceration and punishment has succeeded that of friendship and enmity. But Caleb no sooner finds himself in this new scene – "To me every thing was new, – the massy doors, the resounding locks, the gloomy passages, the grated windows, and the characteristic look of the keepers, accustomed to reject every petition, and to steel their hearts against feeling and pity" (ii.xi; 262) – than he recognizes that his former master is the mastermind of his incarceration here. Even as his case is postponed – and his execution delayed – Caleb feels the hand of his "persecutor": "My thoughts were full of irritation against my persecutor … In every view I felt my heart ulcerated with a sense of his injustice; and my very soul spurned these pitiful indulgences, at a time that he was grinding me into dust with the inexorableness of his vengeance" (ii.xii; 277). The amorphous fear of victimization, a staple of Gothic fiction, is here given so specific a cause that it becomes closer to a psychological thriller than a Gothic fantasy. The personal struggle between these two men, a struggle of life and death, has brought them into an intimacy as close as anything figured in even the most intensely personal Gothic fiction.

These prison scenes, then, as brutal as they are, function as a fulfillment of the expression of friendship between these two men. Caleb can only be a victim, which is what the intensity of Falkland's feeling for Caleb has rendered him. Falkland wanted Caleb as the young man he could control as he wished. But by defying that control, Caleb has begun to expose its ugliest features. The law becomes nothing more than an excuse for personal persecution, and Caleb is abject until he decides to manipulate the law for his own purposes.[56]

When Caleb does finally escape from the prison – after a failed attempt and solitary confinement – he finds he is never far from being discovered

---

[56] See John Bender, "Impersonal Violence: The Penetrating Gaze and the Field of Narration in *Caleb Williams*," in *Critical Reconstructions: The Relationship of Fiction and Life*, ed. Robert M. Polhemus and Roger B. Hinkle (Stanford: Stanford University Press, 1994), 111–26.

and rarely free from the pursuit of Falkland. James Thompson has written compellingly about "surveillance" in *Caleb Williams*, and these scenes are brilliantly devised to give the feeling that wherever Caleb turns he is being watched.[57] He disguises himself as a beggar – another telling metaphor – and even distorts himself as a way of escaping detection: "I adopted, along with my beggar's attire a peculiar, slouching and clownish gait, to be used whenever there should appear the least chance of my being observed, together with an Irish brogue which I had an opportunity of studying in my prison" (iii.v; 333). Caleb is a parody of himself precisely because he is trying to establish an independent existence, outside the one that Falkland was ready to provide for him.[58]

It is now no surprise that Caleb puts his extreme misery in terms of an absence of friendship – the consolations of friendship – but it is by giving in to his need for a friend that Caleb is finally undone.[59] Whatever he does here, he finds that Falkland is there, watching him and, as it were, pursuing him, turning him against himself: "I was shut up, a deserted, solitary wretch, in the midst of my species. I dared not look for the consolations of friendship; but, instead of seeking to identify myself with the joys and sorrows of others, and exchanging the delicious gifts of confidence and sympathy, was compelled to centre my thoughts and vigilance in myself" (iii.viii; 353). That bond between the two men is inescapable, however far Caleb strays from his master. Caleb may feel at times that he is escaping from Falkland, but it is clear that all his actions are still predicated on the bond between them. Reverence and esteem are trampled; he feels himself pursued by this fiend-like being. "One is the other," Derrida says, "One guards and guards himself in the other. One does violence to one-self, becoming violence."[60] In some ways, it almost seems as if Caleb is haunted by Falkland; but what could be more intimate than this kind of haunting. Caleb is courting his master even as he resists him. This trope of a kind of queer spectrality, familiar from Gothic fiction, works here

---

[57] James Thompson, "Surveillance in William Godwin's *Caleb Williams*," in *Gothic Fictions: Prohibition/Transgression*, ed. Kenneth Graham (New York: AMS Press, 1989), 173–98 (182–9).

[58] On the question of multiple selves in the novel, see Jacqueline T. Miller, "The Imperfect Tale: Articulation, Rhetoric, and Self in *Caleb Williams*," *Criticism* 20 (1978): 366–82.

[59] Shaftesbury, in his *Characteristics*, makes a similar observation: "Now if banishment from one's country, removal to a foreign place, or anything which looks like solitude or desertion, be so heavy to endure, what must it be to feel this inward banishment, this real estrangement from human commerce, and to be after this manner in a desert, and in the horridest of solitudes even in the midst of society?" (Anthony Ashley Cooper, third earl of Shaftesbury, *An Inquiry Concerning Virtue or Merit*, 1699. See *Characteristics of Men, Manners, Opinions, Times*, ed. Lawrence Klein (Cambridge: Cambridge University Press, 2001), 229.

[60] Derrida, *The Politics of Friendship*, 59.

to undermine Caleb's sense of his ability to make any determinations for himself.[61]

When shortly after this, he sees Falkland, he recognizes that Falkland has suffered as much, if not more, than he:

> when I last beheld this unhappy man, he had been a victim to the same passions, a prey to the same undying remorse, as now. Misery was at that time inscribed in the legible characters upon his countenance. But now he appeared like nothing that had ever been visible in human shape. His visage was haggard, emaciated, and fleshless. His complexion was a dun and tarnished red, the colour uniform through every region of the face, and suggested the idea of its being burnt and parched by the eternal fire that burned within him. (III.xii; 382)

This fiend-like character accosts Caleb and demands that he sign a retraction of the accusations he has tried to bring against Falkland. When Caleb refuses this final act of self-abnegation, Falkland becomes almost violent: "You defy me! At least I have a power respecting you, and that power I will exercise; a power that shall grind you into atoms" (III.xii; 386). In this repetition of his earlier threat, Falkland is starting to show the limits of his power, but Caleb does not recognize that and instead he finds himself confronting one ultimate attempt to clear his own name. When he realizes he will never escape Gines or feel less intensely the hand of Falkland, he decides to publish his tale. This feels like his last resort, but it is of course at the same time a final insult to his former patron.

"Tremble!" he says as he takes his story to a magistrate. When Falkland is brought before this magistrate at last, Caleb almost regrets what he has done:

> He was brought in in a chair, unable to stand, fatigued and almost destroyed by the journey he had just taken. His visage was colourless; his limbs destitute of motion, almost of life. His head reclined upon his bosom, except that now and then he lifted it up and opened his eyes with a languid glance; immediately after which he sunk back into his former apparent insensibility. He seemed not to have three hours to live. (III.xv; 426)

In this figure, the abyss of friendship takes on the quality that does little but threaten. The reality of friendship is this figure of death.

---

[61] On the topic of "queer spectrality," see Carla Freccero, "Queer Spectrality: Haunting the Past," in *A Companion to Lesbian, Gay, Bisexual, Transgender, and Queer Studies*, ed. George E. Haggerty and Molly McGarry (Oxford: Blackwell, 2007), 194–213, 195.

Caleb protests at first – "Mr. Falkland! I most solemnly conjure you to recollect yourself! Did I ever prove myself unworthy of your confidence?" (III.xv; 429) – but before long he is regretting his action and wondering how he could undo it:

> I have told a plain and unadulterated tale. I came hither to curse, but I remain to bless. I came to accuse, but am compelled to applaud. I proclaim to all the world, that Mr. Falkland is a man worthy of affection and kindness, and that I am myself the basest and most odious of mankind! Never will I forgive myself the iniquity of this day. (III.xv; 431)

This is Caleb's last word on Falkland. It is as if he recommits himself to the earlier friendship these men shared. And why shouldn't he? Both men are brought to the extreme here, and it seems that they have plumbed the abyss of friendship to the very bottom. Now Falkland can say only: "Williams, you have conquered! … You cannot hate me more than I hate myself" (III. xv; 433). Perhaps, but this pursuit has never been about hate, it has been about desire. As Caleb says here, after Falkland has already passed away, "Falkland, I will think only of thee, and from that thought will draw ever-fresh nourishment for my sorrows" (III.xv; 434).

As if this erotic love has always already been the valedictory love of the elegy, Caleb connects that love with sorrow and memory in the best elegiac tradition. As Derrida says, "a memory is engaged in advance, from the moment of what is called life, this strange temporality opened by the anticipated citation of the funeral oration"[62]: *Caleb Williams* has been all along anticipating this moment when Caleb could speak of Falkland with heartfelt funereal devotion. If this love is elegiac, that is because it could never find expression beyond this tale of mutually haunting desire. Erotics and desire are transformed into elegiac feeling when they cannot be adequately expressed before the grave. Friendship, as Derrida reminds us, commemorates loss, and what is *Caleb Williams* but a complex and harrowing saga of loss. Only friendship gives meaning to this loss and transforms the political tale of a master and his servant into a powerfully personal tale as well. The violence of this novel earns it a place in this section on erotic friendship because its elegiac demeanor becomes apparent only at the close. I cannot imagine a more complex dynamic of friendship than the one that Godwin presents us with here.

---

[62] Derrida, *The Politics of Friendship*, 5. See also George E. Haggerty, "Desire and Mourning: The Ideology of the Elegy," in *Ideology and Form*, ed. David Richter (Lubbock: Texas Tech University Press, 1999), 184–206.

The Horror of Friendlessness in *Frankenstein*

Early in Mary Shelley's 1831 edition of her masterpiece, we are told that Robert Walton, the lonely explorer in search of the unknown, has a deeply frustrated need that he must share with his sister:

> I have one want which I have never yet been able to satisfy; and the absence of the object of which I now feel a most severe evil. I have no friend, Margaret: when I am glowing with the enthusiasm of success, there will be none to participate my joy; if I am assailed by disappointment, no one will endeavour to sustain me in dejection. I shall commit my thoughts to paper, it is true; but that is a poor medium for the communication of feeling. I desire the company of a man who could sympathize with me; whose eyes would reply to mine. You may deem me romantic, my dear sister, but I bitterly feel the want of a friend. I have no one near me, gentle yet courageous, possessed of a cultivated as well as of a capacious mind, whose tastes are like my own, to approve or amend my plans. How would such a friend repair the faults of your poor brother! ... I greatly need a friend who would have sense enough not to despise me as romantic, and affection enough for me to endeavour to regulate my mind.[63]

This clear statement of need is never specifically answered in the novel – Victor Frankenstein himself, whom Walton meets soon after this, when he is taken into the explorer's vessel as a broken and desperate man, can hardly function in this capacity; nor can the creature, melancholy and suicidal, whom Walton meets at the end of the novel. It is almost as if these lines that characterize Walton so clearly are without any attention to the larger concerns of the novel. I would argue, though, that there is no greater concern in *Frankenstein* than this question of friendship. Walton seems schooled in the friendship tradition, and he places this ideal version of a friend before his sister as a claim on what he misses in human experience. Far more than a tease in Walton's letter to his sister, friendship looms in the novel as a need that can only be ignored at one's peril.

Walton's plea establishes a high mark for any friend to reach. This friend has to be strong in exactly those areas where Walton is weak, and he has to be sensitive to Walton's needs and understanding of his shortcomings. He cannot despise him as a romantic, even as he teaches him to regulate his mind. This friend emerges from the tradition of the perfect friend, as I have articulated it, and Walton's experience demonstrates how rarely that friend is to be found. It is of course the kind of friend familiar in the

---

[63] Shelley, *Frankenstein*, 28–9; further parenthetical references are to this edition.

writing of Montaigne, and Walton seems aware of that ideal, even if he does not refer to Montaigne specifically.[64]

What we discover as we move further into the novel, however, is that Victor Frankenstein has just such a friend. Clerval is described in these terms:

> Henry Clerval was the son of a merchant in Geneva, an intimate friend of my father. He was a boy of singular talent and fancy. He loved enterprise, hardship, and even danger, for its own sake. He was deeply read in books of chivalry and romance. He composed heroic songs, and began to write many a tale of enchantment and knightly adventure. He tried to make us act plays, and to enter into masquerades, in which the characters were drawn from Roncesvalles, of the Round Table of King Arthur, and the chivalrous train who shed their blood to redeem the holy sepulcher from the hands of the infidels. (43)

This description marks Clerval as the emotional and intellectual complement to Frankenstein, who is scientifically obsessed and who states clearly: "It was the secrets of heaven and earth that I desired to learn; and whether it was the outward substance of things, or the inner spirit and the mysterious soul of man that occupied me, still my enquiries were directed to the metaphysical, or, in its highest sense, the physical secrets of the world" (43). "Meanwhile," Frankenstein says immediately after this, "Clerval occupied himself, so to speak, with the moral relations of things. The busy stage of life, the virtues and heroes, and the actions of men, were his theme, and his hope and his dream was to become one among those whose names are recorded in history, as the gallant and adventurous benefactors of our species" (43). While Victor pushes at the limits of man's physical being, Clerval occupies himself with the "moral relations of things": his stories of gallantry and adventure pale beside Victor's scientific endeavors, but Clerval's moral compass is surely a safer guide than Victor's search for the "secrets of heaven and earth." When Victor begins his studies of the alchemical precursors of science, and when he witnesses the power of nature in the form of a wild lightning storm, he begins to question everything he knows about the world. Once he pursues his studies in Ingolstadt, Victor finds a professor, Waldman, who can nurture his desire to pursue the "mysteries of creation" (51). As his studies become more obsessive, his activities seem akin to those of a madman:

> To examine the causes of life, we must first have recourse to death. I became acquainted with the science of anatomy: but this was not sufficient; I must

---

[64] Montaigne, "On Affectionate Relationships," 205–19. See pp. 7–8, above.

also observe the natural decay and corruption of the human body … Darkness had no effect upon my fancy; and a churchyard was to me the mere receptacle of bodies deprived of life, which, from being the seat of beauty and strength, had become food for the worm. Now I was led to examine the cause and progress of this decay, and forced to spend days and nights in vaults and charnel houses … I saw how the fine form of man was degraded and wasted; I beheld the corruption of death succeed to the blooming cheek of life; I saw how the worm inherited the wonders of the eye and brain. (53–4)

Where is Clerval when Victor is obsessing over human decay? He had wanted to join Victor in his studies, but his own father, a trader, refused to allow it. Instead he sent Victor off with a handshake, and is now nowhere near his friend to offer advice or support. Victor has gone off on his own in solitary pursuit of his own fondest and most lurid dreams. Victor is not thinking of his friend right now, and that is a measure of his doom.

"I pursued nature to her hiding places," he says, "who shall conceive the horrors of my secret toil, as I dabbled among the unhallowed damps of the grave, or tortured the living animal to animate the lifeless clay?" (56). The solitary rape of the natural world would not have failed so spectacularly – that is, succeeded in the way it did – if Victor had allowed his friendship to guide him. But instead this solitary obsession sets him apart, and makes it clear that in order to succeed in his quest he is willing to sacrifice everything dear to him.

Chapter v of *Frankenstein* spells out the terms of his impending doom. In language that is famous in the annals of Gothic literature and science fiction, Victor says:

> It was on a dreary night in November, that I beheld the accomplishment of my toils. With an anxiety that amounted to agony, I collected the instruments of life around me, that I might infuse a spark of being into the lifeless thing that lay at my feet. It was already one in the morning, the rain pattered dismally against the panes, and my candle was nearly burnt out, when, by the glimmer of the half-extinguished light, I saw the dull yellow eye of the creature open; it breathed hard, and a convulsive motion agitated its limbs. (57–8)

Victor achieves this act of creation entirely on his own, and when he first looks at the being he has created, he finds it hideous: "His yellow skin scarcely covered the works of muscles and arteries beneath; his hair was of a lustrous black, and flowing; his teeth of a pearly whiteness; but these luxuriances only formed a more horrid contrast with his watery eyes … his shriveled complexion and his straight black lips" (58). Victor flees from this horrifying image and tries to compose himself in his room; there, he finally sleeps and dreams:

> I thought I saw Elizabeth, in the bloom of health, walking in the streets of Ingolstadt. Delighted and surprised, I embraced her; but as I imprinted the first kiss on her lips, they became livid with the hue of death; her features began to change, and I thought that I held the corpse of my dead mother in my arms; a shroud enveloped her form, and I saw the graveworms crawling in the folds of the flannel. (58)

Victor's act of creation involves him in these nightmare images of death and decay: death and decay of his fiancée and his mother, who are combined in this one grotesque transformation.

Often this dream is taken to mean that Victor has usurped his mother's right of giving birth and/or that he is sacrificing Elizabeth by devoting himself to this lurid creature.[65] Rather than usurping birth, however, I see this as a sacrifice of the female notions of love and domesticity and a turn instead to a more rugged world of masculine intimacy that the creature's appearance both mocks and invokes. Upon waking from this dream, Victor sees the creature at his bedside: "He held up the curtain of the bed, and his eyes, if eyes they may be called, were fixed on me. His jaws opened, and he muttered some inarticulate sounds, while a grin wrinkled his cheeks" (58). Victor flees, but not without this vivid image of the horror he has created. The creature's smile of invitation, though, might have forestalled the implicit horror in a bond of complicity. But that option does not seem open to the terrified and disgusted scientist.

Victor passes a miserable night: "mingled with this horror, I felt the bitterness of disappointment; dreams that had been my food and pleasant rest for so long a space were now become a hell to me; and the change was so rapid, the overthrow so complete!" (59). In this mood of bitterness, frustration, and defeat, Victor meets Clerval: "the Swiss diligence ... stopped just where I was standing; and on the door being opened, I perceived Henry Clerval, who, on seeing me, instantly sprung out. 'My dear Frankenstein,' exclaimed he, 'how glad am I to see you! How fortunate that you should be here at the very moment of my alighting!'" (60). Clerval's walking into

---

[65] See, for instance, Sandra M. Gilbert and Susan Gubar, *The Madwoman in the Attic: The Woman Writer and the Nineteenth-Century Literary Imagination* (New Haven: Yale University Press, 1979), 213–47; and Devon Hodges, "*Frankenstein* and the Feminine Subversion of the Novel," *Tulsa Studies in Women's Literature* 2.2 (Fall 1983): 155–64; Barbara Johnson, "My Monster/ My Self," in *The Barbara Johnson Reader: The Surprise of Otherness*, ed. Melissa Fruerstein, Bill Johnson González, Lili Porten, and Keja Valens (Durham, NC: Duke University Press, 2014), 179–90 (186–7); and see also Anne K. Mellor, "Possessing Nature: The Female in *Frankenstein*," in the Norton Critical Edition of *Frankenstein*, ed. Paul Hunter (New York: Norton, 2012), 355–68, esp. 355–8.

Victor's life at this crucial moment is more than coincidental. It reminds the reader, and it reminds Victor himself, of the values of friendship that Victor has sacrificed to his maniacal creativity: "I grasped his hand, and in a moment forgot my horror and misfortune; I felt suddenly, and for the first time during many months, calm and serene joy. I welcomed my friend, therefore, in the most cordial manner" (60).

This transformation in mood and sudden sense of calm seems inspired by the touch between these two men. This touch has been what Victor has been missing. They talk and chat, and Victor feels taken out of himself and brought into social relation for the first time in months. At first Victor is agitated and concerned, and his friend notes, "I did not before remark how very ill you appear; so thin and pale; you look as if you had been watching several nights" (60). When they return to Victor's room, they find no one there, and now Victor is manic: "It was not joy only that possessed me; I felt my flesh tingle with excess of sensitiveness, and my pulse beat rapidly. I was unable to remain for a single instant in the same place; I jumped over the chairs, clapped my hands, and alighted aloud" (61). Clerval reacts to this extreme behavior with concern, even as Victor collapses in a fit. As he recalls this scene, Victor laments:

> Poor Clerval! what must have been his feelings? A meeting, which he antici-pated with such joy, so strangely turned to bitterness. But I was not the witness of his grief; for I was lifeless, and did not recover my senses for a long, long time.
> This was the commencement of a nervous fever, which confined me for several months. During all that time, Henry was my only nurse. (61)

This role of nurse, so broadly ignored in most discussions of the novel, marks Clerval as a very special friend indeed. This kind of intimacy, as Holly Furneaux mentions in her discussion of Dickens, helps to fill out friendship with a mode of physical reality that it otherwise lacks. This is a wonderful example of what Furneaux describes. "If we recognize, how-ever, that homoerotics are not necessarily antithetical to or discontinuous with Victorian sexual mores," she says, "more tender, but no less prevalent, expressions of same-sex desire can be recognized."[66] I am not claiming that these relations are specifically homoerotic, but nevertheless they mark a friendship that is more intense than has otherwise been allowed. Clerval is a caring and nurturing friend, and as such, he stands in almost direct contrast to Victor's callous rejection of the creature.

---

[66] Holly Furneaux, *Queer Dickens Erotics, Families, Masculinities* (Oxford: Oxford University Press, 2009), 207–8; see below pp. 125–35.

As Victor recovers he plans to return home, and Henry helps him deal with family concerns. "The month of May had already commenced," he tells us, "and I expected the letter daily which was to fix the date of my departure, when Henry proposed a pedestrian tour in the environs of Ingolstadt … I was fond of exercise, and Clerval had always been my favourite companion in the rambles of this nature that I had taken among the scenes of my native country" (67). He then adds, "We passed a fortnight in these perambulations: my health and spirits had long been restored, and they gained additional strength from the salubrious air I breathed, the natural incidents of our progress, and the conversation of my friend" (67–8). This is another rarely remarked passage, but it is a measure of the intimacy of the relation between these two men. It represents an engaging and restorative moment of calm before increasingly desperate mental agony. The two friends spend their time walking and exploring in what could almost be called a celebration of mutual masculine endeavor.[67]

Immediately after this sojourn, Victor receives word that his young brother William has died. He and Clerval return home, and there Victor is confronted with the creature and the enormity of what he has done. Before that confrontation, however, Clerval expresses a brief eulogy for the murdered boy:

> "Poor William!" said he, "dear lovely child, he now sleeps with his angel mother! Who that had seen him bright and joyous in his young beauty, but must weep over his untimely loss! To die so miserably; to feel the murderer's grasp! How much more a murderer, that could destroy such radiant innocence! Poor little fellow! one only consolation have we; his friends mourn and weep, but he is at rest. The pang is over, his sufferings are at an end for ever. A sod covers his gentle form, and he knows no pain. He can no longer be a subject for pity; we must reserve that for his miserable survivors." (70)

This is an unremarkable eulogy, touching in its simplicity, but it verges on the appalling when we consider it a measure of Victor's own guilt. Even before he confronts the creature, Victor knows that this boy's death is his own responsibility.[68] Henry talks about death as final and an escape from pain, but Victor knows that there is no escape for him from the monstrous world he has created.

---

[67] For an engaging discussion of masculinity in the novel, see Bette London, "Mary Shelley, *Frankenstein*, and the Spectacle of Masculinity," *PMLA* 108.2 (March 1993): 253–65; reprinted in the Norton Critical Edition of *Frankenstein*, ed. Paul Hunter (New York: Norton, 2012), 391–403.

[68] See, for instance, William Veeder, *Mary Shelley & Frankenstein: The Fate of Androgyny* (Chicago: University of Chicago Press, 1986).

Victor's confrontation with the creature on the Sea of Glass near Mont Blanc undoes almost every consolation Henry has articulated. The creature confronts Victor with his own actions and pleads with him for understanding:

> I am thy creature, and I will be even mild and docile to my lord and king, if thou wilt also perform thy part, the which thou owest me. Oh, Frankenstein, be not equitable to every other, and trample on me alone, to whom thy justice, and even thy clemency and affection is most due. Remember, that I am thy creature; I ought to be thy Adam; but I am rather thy fallen angel, whom thou drivest from joy for no misdeed. Everywhere I see bliss, from which I alone am irrevocably excluded. I was benevolent and good; misery made me a fiend. (90)

This passage is the prologue to the creature's long account of his first experiences; his time in the hovel peering in on the De Laceys; and his more recent rampage, murdering William and implicating Justine. At the end of this long tale, he asks Frankenstein to create for him a mate. "I am alone and miserable; man will not associate with me; but one as deformed and horrible as myself would not deny herself to me. My companion must be of the same species, and have the same defects. This being you must create" (124).

What the creature is protesting in these two speeches is surely the failure of friendship. Victor may be the creator, but he has rejected the thing he created. What the creature really needs is a friend. His isolation and loneliness, recollecting as it does that dissatisfaction that Walton expresses in his letters to his sister, remind us of the abjection that friendlessness instills. The creature asks for a mate, and often there is talk of procreation and the threat of a race of monsters; Victor himself imagines that at the moment he destroys the second creature. But really all the creature needs or wants is a friend. That is what he has sought again and again, and that is what he has been denied. In this, as in so many things, he is a parody of his creator himself. For Victor chose solitary pursuits over his intimate relations, and the measure of his obsession is also the measure of his undoing.

This becomes clear at the moment I was just describing. After the creature has met Victor in the Alps and pleaded with him to make him a mate – a female creature like himself whom he can love and nurture as a companion – Victor almost relents. Before marrying Elizabeth, who now feels that marriage would be best for his health as well as their joint happiness, he says he has to travel so that he might "be restored to my family in peace and happiness" (131). He travels north with his friend Clerval – "the presence of my friend could in no way be an impediment, and truly

I rejoiced that thus I should be saved many hours of lonely, maddening reflection" (131) – and Clerval seems to embrace the journey, praising the landscape and celebrating the mountain landscapes. Frankenstein looks back on this moment with clear devotion:

> Clerval! beloved friend! even now it delights me to record your words, and to dwell on the praise which you are so eminently deserving. He was a being formed in the "very poetry of nature." His wild and enthusiastic imagination was chastened by the sensibility of his heart. His soul over-flowed with ardent affections, and his friendship was of that devoted and wondrous nature that the worldly-minded teach us to look for only in the imagination. (133)

Victor is lamenting Henry Clerval here, but he is also making a statement about friendship. This beautifully articulate version of friendship stands out in stark contrast to the relation between Victor and the creature. Rather than overflowing with ardent affections, Victor's soul has closed down as it has rejected the creature. This rejection is completed as he fails at his task of creating a mate. "But in Clerval," he says, "I saw the image of my former self; he was inquisitive, and anxious to gain experience and instruction … He was also pursuing an object he had long had in view … He was forever busy; and the only check to his enjoyments was my sorrowful and dejected mind" (135). Victor seems already to have built regret into his discussions of Clerval. It almost feels as if he could have saved himself if he had recognized what this friendship truly offered him. Instead, he cuts himself away and destroys them both.

Eventually he finds his way to the Orkney Islands of Scotland, where he will finally honor his pledge and create a second creature. As he sets to work here, he finds that he cannot complete this task:

> I grew restless and nervous. Every moment I feared to meet my persecutor. Sometimes I sat with my eyes fixed on the ground, fearing to raise them, lest they could encounter the object which I so much dreaded to behold. I feared to wander from the sight of my fellow-creatures, lest when alone he should come to claim his companion. (140)

Victor continues this act of creation while looking over his shoulder and fearing to see the creature he calls his "persecutor," and in a sense almost expecting him to appear "to claim his companion." When he does appear, Frankenstein cannot contemplate continuing work on this second being, and he destroys the new creature even before he manages to endow it with life:

> I sat one evening in my laboratory; the sun had set, and the moon was just rising from the sea; I had not sufficient light for my employment, and

> I remained idle, in pause of consideration of whether I should leave my labour for the night, or hasten to its conclusion by an unremitting attention to it. As I sat, a train of reflection occurred to me, which led me to consider the effects of what I was now doing ... I had before been moved by the sophisms of the being I had created; I had been struck senseless by his fiendish threats: but now, for the first time, the wickedness of my promise burst upon me; I shuddered to think that future ages might curse me as their pest, whose selfishness had not hesitated to buy its own peace at the price perhaps of the existence of the whole human race. (140–1)

In this change of heart, Victor rejects any claim of relation, friendship or otherwise, to talk himself out of the creation he had promised, and before he can even think beyond these first reactions, the creature torments him with his presence:

> I trembled, and my heart failed within me; when, on looking up, I saw, by the light of the moon, the dæmon at the casement. A ghastly grin wrinkled his lips as he gazed on me, where I sat fulfilling the task which he had allotted to me ... As I looked on him, his countenance expressed the utmost extent of malice and treachery. I thought with a sensation of madness on my promise of creating another like to him, and, trembling with passion tore to pieces the thing on which I was engaged. The wretch saw me destroy the creature on whose future existence he depended for happiness, and with a howl of devilish despair and revenge, he withdrew. (141)

Frankenstein deprives his creature of a future and in a single act also destroys his own. Victor was formerly a creator, but in this scene he does nothing but destroy. If he can destroy "the creature on whose future existence he [the creature] depended for happiness," then he rejects any future in favor of a present that is both unthreatening and resistant to the demands of procreation. If that earns the despair and revenge of the creature, Victor is willing to face that as long as he can avoid giving a future to the creature he detests. That creature threatens him with a resounding, "I go; but remember I will be with you on your wedding night" (142). Victor worries about his own future, never even imagining that the creature will destroy both Elizabeth and Clerval. But the creature understands how best to force his creator to confront him directly and answer for the failure of his promise.

When Victor realizes that the creature has murdered Henry Clerval, which happens almost immediately after the scene quoted above, he lapses into a heartfelt lament that spells out the terms of his transgression:

> I entered the room where the corpse lay, and was led up to the coffin. How can I describe my sensations on beholding it? I felt parched with horror, nor can I reflect on that terrible moment without shuddering and agony.

> The examination, the presence of the magistrate and witnesses, passed like a dream from my memory, when I saw the lifeless form of Henry Clerval stretched before me. I gasped for breath; and throwing myself on the body, I explained, "Have my murderous machinations deprived you also, my dearest Henry, of life? Two I have already destroyed; other victims await their destiny: but you, Clerval, my friend, my benefactor." (149)

Victor's sensations here – the sense of loss coupled with responsibility – unmans him (he is "carried out of the room in strong convulsions" [149]) and it also reminds him what his act of creation has really meant. This friendship with Clerval, this abiding and intimate relation, is now blasted. The very answer that Victor had to the creature's demands is now used against him. Victor laments this loss so bitterly because he knows that his refusal to create a second dæmon has broken the bond of friendship that has allowed him to flourish as he has. Friendlessness now looms as the deeply disturbing result of all his solitary longing.

Victor's masculine other understands him and knows that destroying this friendship will hit Victor at his core. It is significant that most film versions of the novel leave Clerval alive or neglect to tell the final story. His loss in the novel is almost more devastating to Victor than the loss of Elizabeth. Friendship is the key to what Victor loses, just as it is the key to what the creature lacked. That is why this loss and the devastating confrontation of the wedding night, when he finds Elizabeth strangled, can only lead him in a mad pursuit: the very pursuit, that is, that leads him into the frozen north and onto the very ship that Walton is piloting into the unknown.

As Victor laments to Walton:

> My imagination was vivid, yet my powers of analysis and application were intense; by the union of these qualities I conceived the idea, and executed the creation of a man. Even now I cannot recollect, without passion, my reveries while the work was incomplete. I trod heaven in my thoughts, now exulting in my powers, now burning with the idea of their effects. From my infancy I was imbued with high hopes and a lofty ambition: but how am I sunk! (176)

Victor knows his defeat and he also knows that he must depart without a resolution of any kind. Victor is not allowed to claim his creation or to position himself as the creative genius that the story has celebrated. Instead, he is broken and frustrated. "Now I am sunk!" Victor felt he could challenge the creator with his own creative power, but miserable and alone, finally friendless, he knows that he has really created nothing but the misery that surrounds him. He has challenged the very notion of God, and in doing so, he has deprived himself of all satisfaction, love, or friendship.

The surprising feature of the novel's closing pages is the creature's own sense of loss and the sudden and urgent meaninglessness of his own position.

> After the murder of Clerval, I returned to Switzerland, heartbroken and overcome. I pitied Frankenstein; my pity amounted to horror. I abhorred myself ... Evil thenceforth became my good. Urged thus far, I had no choice but to adapt my nature to an element which I had willingly chosen. The completion of demoniacal design became an insatiable passion. And now it is ended: there [pointing at Frankenstein's body] is my last victim. (182–3)

The creature is driven to destroy because he is not allowed the solace of any real companionship. He mimics Milton's Satan because he is shut out from the pleasures of sociability. The creature is "lost in the darkness and distance" at the end of the novel; we are forced to acknowledge that there is absolutely nothing else he could have done. This is the horror of the creature's friendlessness. He is truly lost.

CHAPTER 3

Platonic Friendship

Platonic friendship comes into clearest focus in the later nineteenth and early twentieth centuries. It is connected to the rediscovery of Plato in the halls of Oxford and Cambridge in the middle of the nineteenth century, especially by way of the rich and evocative translations of Benjamin Jowett.[1] For Dowling, "The great significance of Jowett's innovation ... would always have to do with the way Plato functioned within the machinery of the improved curriculum as a metaphysical basis for the liberalism of the Oxford reformers."[2] Richard Dellammora, the most recent of these friendship commentators, makes the important point, following Bray, that "in Greek and Roman philosophic and literary tradition, perfect friendship between two men is often taken as paradigmatic of the virtues that are necessary in a just polity." He says further that "within the Athenian institution of pederasty, a citizen and an adolescent joined in a mentor-protégé relationship, motivated by erotic attraction."[3] Platonic love has a real currency in English public schools and universities of the nineteenth and early twentieth centuries, as Forster's novels especially demonstrate. If classical scholars like Jowett, whose limpid translation of the Platonic dialogues was at least in part responsible for the great enthusiasm over these works that Linda Dowling describes, could popularize Plato, then sensitive readers at every level could take heart in his descriptions of male love.[4] Here is what Dowling says on this topic: "Oxford Hellenism provides the means of sweeping away the entire accumulation of negative associations with male love which had remained strong through the beginning of the nineteenth century."[5] Platonic love thus became a touchstone

---

[1] Linda Dowling, *Hellenism and Homosexuality in Victorian Oxford* (Ithaca: Cornell University Press, 1994), 32–66.
[2] Dowling, *Hellenism and Homosexuality*, 68–9.
[3] Richard Dellamora, *Friendship's Bonds: Democracy and the Novel in Victorian England* (Philadelphia: University of Pennsylvania Press, 2004), 21.
[4] See Dowling, *Hellenism and Homosexuality*, 67–103.
[5] Dowling, *Hellenism and Homosexuality*, 79.

for the first generation of same-sex activists, like John Aldington Symonds and Edward Carpenter. I would include in this group E. M. Forster, whose novels *The Longest Journey* and *Maurice* are deeply influenced by the dialogues of Plato. I hope to tease out some of the details of this influence and to show how platonic love, both in its larger cultural and philosophical context and in its more local and popular dissemination, had a profound effect on the history of sexuality as it emerged in the work of sexologists in the later nineteenth and early twentieth centuries.

If English writers did not read Plato in the original, his concepts were available, both in Cicero's Latin account of friendship, "De Amicitia," and in later years in the translations of Platonic dialogues that started to appear in Cambridge in the middle of the nineteenth century. Platonic love is a concept, moreover, that had currency in the Renaissance, when Neoplatonism was in fashion across Europe. Latin translations of Plato, by Ficino and others, were available from the fifteenth century. What Plato's concept of friendship offers is a richer mode of idealization that is usually recognized in the term "platonic love." Indeed, far from divesting these relations of any physicality, Plato's work makes it clear that no idealization is possible that does not begin in an erotically charged physical attraction. The novels I discuss in this chapter come closer than any others in the English literary tradition to articulating a modern version of platonic love.

Friendship and Marriage in *Great Expectations*

Great Expectations stands as a perfect nineteenth-century example of what I am trying to make clear: the meaning of male friendship in the English literary tradition. Friendship has rich literary and cultural tradition, but the ways Dickens has employed it have been under-theorized.[6] In pushing the rhetoric of friendship to include distinctly erotic energies, and to express those feelings as the love that is without much insistence recognizable as the very same love that animates the Western tradition and gives meaning to interpersonal relations, I think we are doing something that Dickens himself, and his contemporaries, would have understood. I do not think it is assimilationist to claim that the adjective "homoerotic" is not necessary to modify the description of the love between two men, like

---

[6] An important exception to the claim of anachronism is, of course, the rhetoric of masturbation, with which Dickens was familiar. One need only think of "Master Bates" from *Oliver Twist*. On this topic in *Great Expectations*, see William A. Cohen, *Sex Scandal: The Private Parts of Victorian Fiction* (Durham, NC: Duke University Press, 1996), 26–72.

the poet and the lost erotic object in Tennyson's *In Memoriam* or between Maurice and Scudder in Forster's *Maurice*. The loves that are expressed in *Great Expectations* are loves that emerge from the tradition of friendship and may point to some later configuration of desires that was not yet culturally available to Dickens or his readers. What was understood, though, was a rich tradition of male intimacy that gives male relationships in this novel meaning beyond their extraordinarily touching representation.[7] This is as close as Dickens comes to an articulation of platonic love, and he does so in a way that has eluded interpretation.

Much of the material I will talk about here has been noted elsewhere, and at times it has been cited to insist on a particular sexuality. For me, the full meaning of friendship in this novel has never been recognized. Friendship remains a vague and clumsy notion. But friendship does not stand as an alternative agenda or in oblique relation to the central plot of the novel; rather, it is tantamount to the central plot of the novel in so many ways that it is remarkable that readers have felt that the novel was about anything else. Plots are compellingly end-form driven, as Peter Brooks argued long ago, and it is hard to resist final resolutions wherever they appear. But as I argue in discussions of Gothic fiction, endings that dispel Gothic uneasiness are often unsatisfactory in the extreme. Think, for instance, of the happy marriage at the end of Ann Radcliffe's *The Mysteries of Udolpho*. The "happy ending" is muted and unsatisfactory precisely because the horrors raised in the novel cannot be completely dispelled. In *Great Expectations* almost the reverse is true. The novel resolves itself in so many ways before the ending that the ending itself is almost superfluous.[8] I do not want to go into detail about these alternative endings at this point, but even here it is possible to ask what Dickens puts in place of a definitive ending. What it seems to me that Dickens puts in its place is friendship.

First and foremost there is the friendship with Joe, at first the deepest cause of guilt in the novel and later the source of deepest affection; there is also the friendship with the bizarre and winning character Wemmick, who befriends the hero in his darkest moments and gives him a purpose;

---

[7] An essay that looks carefully at the narrative as well as autobiographical homoerotics of friendship in Dickens is Oliver S. Buckton, "'The Reader Whom I Love': Homoerotic Secrets in *David Copperfield*," *ELH* 64.1 (1997): 189–222.

[8] Holly Furneaux says, "The plausibility of marriage as a natural completing structure is ... challenged by the two endings of *Great Expectations* ... Paradoxically, though, this capitulation to readerly demands for closure through heterosexual union ... poignantly dramatizes not only the insufficiency of that union, but invalidates perceptions of marriage as the only closure, as an opposite alternative is both possible and plausible." See Holly Furneaux, *Queer Dickens: Erotics, Families, Masculinities* (Oxford: Oxford University Press, 2009), 174–5.

and finally there is the friendship with Herbert Pocket, to my mind one of the great friendships in nineteenth-century fiction. This friendship not only sustains Pip throughout the bulk of the novel, but it also changes him in such basic ways that Pip becomes a different person entirely. Friendship does many things in the novel: it challenges Pip and confronts him, it also caresses him and gives him purpose. Friendship takes the measure of him, and it allows him to grow. It ultimately makes him a better man than he otherwise would have been. And as it does these things for him, friendship transforms those around him as well. All these are the features of friendship in *Great Expectations*, and it seems to me that when the meaning of friendship in this novel is filled out with such detail, its function in the culture of the nineteenth century will be more fully revealed.[9]

The narrative clues that make Pip's relationship with Joe central to his identity are sprinkled throughout the first half of the novel. It is clear to the reader, and in a sense to Pip himself, that his rejection of Joe, in self-conscious embarrassment about his working-class ways, is a mistake. One example occurs at the beginning of Chapter xiv (Volume i):

> It is a most miserable thing to feel ashamed of home. There may be black ingratitude in the thing, and punishment may be retributive and well deserved; but, that it is a miserable thing, I can testify.
>
> Home had never been a very pleasant place to me, because of my sister's temper. But, Joe had sanctified it, and I had believed in it. I had believed in the best parlour as a most elegant saloon; I had believed in the front door; … I had believed in the kitchen; … I had believed in the forge … Within a single year, all this was changed. Now, it was all coarse and common, and I would not have had Miss Havisham and Estella see it on any account.[10]

The basics of the plot are well known. Not long after Pip has been accosted by a convict and persuaded to help him with some necessities, Pip is taken to the home of a rich, eccentric woman, Miss Havisham, and asked to "play" with her adopted daughter Estella, in her home, Satis House. Pip is so immediately impressed with Estella and with the trappings of wealth, however faded, he sees at Satis House, that he becomes dissatisfied with his own home. That dissatisfaction brings guilt because Joe, his foster

---

[9] One critic who looks askance at the simplistic depiction of childhood in Dickens and makes a claim for complex sexualities and victimizations is Susan Zieger, "Dickens's Queer Children," *Literature Interpretation Theory* 20.1–2 (2009): 141–57. Richard Dellamora looks at the politics of *Oliver Twist* in these terms: see chapter 1 ("Pure Oliver, or Representation without Agency") in *Friendship's Bonds*.

[10] Charles Dickens, *Great Expectations* (London: Penguin, 1996 [1860–1]), 106–7; further references are included parenthetically in the text.

father-brother and the one character who loves Pip unconditionally, must be left behind as Pip's ambitions grow.

Joe's affection for Pip is embarrassingly inarticulate at times, but no reader can doubt its sincerity or Pip's deep misery when he is untrue to this friendship. Perhaps the darkest moment in this relationship occurs after Pip has come into his great expectations and moved to London, where he is rooming with Herbert Pocket in an upper set of rooms in Barnard's Inn. Pip hears that Joe is coming to London and Pip says, "Let me confess exactly, with what feelings I looked forward to Joe's coming": "Not with pleasure, though I was bound to him by so many ties; no; with considerable disturbance, some mortification, and a keen sense of incongruity. If I could have kept him away by paying money, I certainly would have paid money" (218; II.viii). Critics often quote this passage in order to note how far Pip has distanced himself from his earlier love. "Merciless," one critic calls it, and it does seem an especially painful confession.[11] I would like to pause for a moment, though, over the issue of incongruity. Pip's ascension through both meeting Miss Havisham and receiving the financial support of his secret benefactor has caused him to feel disconnected from his earlier self. This sense of "incongruity" – this sense that he cannot put the parts of his life together – is what causes his own misery later in the novel. Until he can understand how the friendship with Joe is actually part of the person he is, a feature, that is, of his identity, in all its confusing messiness, he will never be whole enough to sustain anything like a narrative resolution. Only this knowledge can restore him to a meaningful relation with this first paternal figure in his life, his first friend.[12]

The person who helps him to this realization is, of course, Herbert Pocket. Pip meets Herbert first – although he knows him only as the "pale young gentleman" (90; I.xi) – in the courtyard at Miss Havisham's. And before he even knows what is happening, the two boys are fighting. It is an amusing scene, and Herbert's posturing and prancing are almost enough to intimidate Pip. It is certainly amusing to the reader:

> I was secretly afraid of him when I saw him so dexterous; but, I felt morally and physically convinced that his light head of hair could have had no business in the pit of my stomach, and that I had a right to consider it irrelevant when so obtruded on my attention … On his asking me if I was satisfied with the ground, and on my replying Yes, he begged my leave to

[11] David Trotter, "Introduction," in *Great Expectations* (London: Penguin, 1996), vii–xx (vii).

[12] Holly Furneaux remarks on "the yearning not to reproduce but to parent, a longing to restore and heal damaged bodies, and a range of non- (or not necessarily) genital physical intimacies and tenderness." See Furneaux, *Queer Dickens*, 12.

absent himself for a moment, and quickly returned with a bottle of water and a sponge dipped in vinegar. "Available for both," he said, placing these against the wall. And then fell to pulling off, not only his jacket and waist-coat, but his shirt too, in a manner at once light-hearted, businesslike, and bloodthirsty. (91–2; 1.xi)

This is a fascinating scene. As one critic says, "Herbert proves himself most efficient as a sponge boy."[13] Other critics have emphasized the violence of the scene and the gentlemanly terms of the "rules."[14] "Light-hearted, businesslike, and bloodthirsty": Pip's first impression of Herbert is depend-ent on a performance of gentlemanly behavior, or "masculinity," in Joseph Childers' terms, that is as instructive to Pip as it is distracting. That this fighting is a prelude to their later intimacy makes a certain sense, as well. For once he has stripped, and fought, and been bloodied by Pip, Herbert is ready to admit defeat and accept Pip on equal terms. There is no awkward-ness later on because the friendship is earned in this mockery of battle. As rivals, that is, they cut through various social obstacles between them, not least of which is class distinction and family background. When they meet on this field, they are equal, and equality is one of the tenets of the kinds of friendships I am describing.

The rivalry in question is clear, at least in retrospect. These two boys are rivals for Estella's hand. Herbert recounts later that he was brought there specifically to be offered to Estella, and Pip feels that he is being groomed for the same position.

"Miss Havisham had sent for me, to see if [Estella] could take a fancy to me. But she couldn't – at all events, she didn't."

I thought it polite to remark that I was surprised to hear that.

"Bad taste," said Herbert, laughing, "but a fact. Yes, she had sent for me on a trial visit, and if I had come out of it successfully, I suppose I should have been provided for; perhaps I should have been what-you-may-called it to Estella."

"What's that?" I asked, with sudden gravity.

He was arranging his fruit in plates while we talked, which divided his attention, and was the cause of his having made this lapse of a word. "Affianced," he explained, still busy with the fruit. "Betrothed. Engaged. What's-his-named. Any word of that sort."

"How did you bear your disappointment?" I asked.

"Pooh!" said he, "I didn't care much for it. *She's* a Tartar." (176–7; II.iii)

---

[13] Furneaux, *Queer Dickens*, 209.

[14] For a nuanced account of these fisticuffs, see Cohen, *Sex Scandal*, 49–52. See also, Joseph Childers, "'What do you play, boy?': Violence, Masculinity, and 'Beggaring your Neighbor' in *Great Expectations*," unpublished manuscript.

Both these scenes, which together comprise the first two meetings between Pip and Herbert, turn potential male rivalry into its comic alternative in friendliness and camaraderie. In the first instance, Pip's easy defeat of Herbert and the utter self-delusion with which Herbert hopes that he has not hurt Pip is amusing exactly to the degree that it is not serious. The second encounter, coming close to Pip's feelings as it does, again turns rivalry to comedy, and Herbert's refreshing "Pooh!" in reaction to his rejection by Estella is both welcome for the reader and delusion-popping, at least potentially, for Pip. The affection between the young men, moreover, immediate and powerful, makes it possible for them to talk about things that Pip has talked about to no one, and it creates a bond as unmistakable as it is irresistible:

> Herbert Pocket had a frank and easy way with him that was very taking. I had never seen anyone then, and I have never seen anyone since, who more strongly expressed to me, in every look and tone, a natural incapacity to do anything secret and mean. There was something wonderfully hopeful about his general air. (177; II.iii)

Herbert's open friendliness defuses rivalry almost instantaneously. And if Pip goes on to imagine that "something at the same time whispered to me he would never be very successful or rich" (177–8; II.iii), this almost endears him to Pip even more. And, indeed, it becomes the source of his first act of true generosity later on, when he secretly helps Herbert to his first break in business.

Herbert does not like "Pip" as a name, and he rechristens Pip Handel, in honor of the composer who wrote a piece called "The Harmonious Blacksmith" (179; II.iii). This is a deft act of recognizing origins while transforming them, and that is something that Pip has not yet learned how to do. Herbert, in other words, is teaching Pip how to be himself.

As Herbert charmingly corrects Pip's table manners and speech, he also cements a bond that will sustain Pip and give him the means of transforming himself. ("Take another glass of wine," Herbert says as they are discussing Miss Havisham, "and excuse my mentioning that society as a body does not expect one to be so strictly conscientious in emptying one's glass, as to turn it bottom upwards with the rim on one's nose" [180; II. iii].) Herbert is not just teaching Pip how to be a gentleman, of which these are the earliest and crudest examples, but he is also transforming him into someone he might eventually respect and who might actually come to respect himself. This transformation is not immediate – there are quite a few barriers to self-respect when two young men are trying to survive in a thriving metropolis – but Herbert's project is as long and as sustained as any domestic partnership based on deep personal attachment might be.

If gentleman-making is carried out by correcting table manners and demonstrating social ease, then character transformation happens through a communication of character that Pip comes only gradually to understand fully. With Estella everything is stilted and unsatisfying:

> There was no discrepancy of years between us, to remove her far from me; we were of nearly the same age, though of course the age told for more in her case than in mine; but the air of inaccessibility which her beauty and her manner gave her, tormented me in the midst of my delight, and at the height of the assurance I felt that our patroness had chosen us for one another. Wretched boy! (239; II.x)

This torment that Pip feels, this inevitable inaccessibility, is somehow built into the desire for Estella, from the first awkward meetings at Miss Havisham's until the last devastating encounters when she announces her engagement to Drummle.

Throughout this period, Herbert keeps Pip's spirits up and teaches him the meaning of hope. As they sit "with [their] feet upon the fender," just after Pip returns from Satis House, he confesses his love for Estella and Herbert responds mildly, "Of course I know *that*" (247; II.xi). Later Herbert goes on to explain:

> You have always adored her, ever since I have known you. You brought your adoration and your portmanteau here, together. Told me! Why, you have always told me all day long. When you told me your own story, you told me plainly that you began adoring her the first time you saw her, when you were very young indeed. (247; II.xi)

Herbert not only understands Pip, but he takes Pip's attraction to Estella as the very ground of their friendship. It is not an alternative to what they share, it almost seems to be a part of it. In this context, Herbert asks Pip who he is:

> "I am ashamed to say it," I returned, "and yet it's no worse to say it than to think it. You call me a lucky fellow. Of course, I am. I was a blacksmith's boy but yesterday; I am – what shall I say I am – to-day?"
>
> "Say, a good fellow, if you want a phrase," returned Herbert, smiling, and clapping his hand on the back of mine, "a good fellow, with impetuosity and hesitation, boldness and diffidence, action and dreaming, curiously mixed in him." (248; II.xi)

This intimate gesture and perceptive assessment of Pip's character, as he pronounces him a "good fellow," is the very version of friendship that will sustain Pip and offer him life (at first, at least) without Estella. "Good" has special resonance here, as I discuss below. But Herbert gives Pip hope, in describing his situation and explaining the obvious outcome of everything Pip has experienced so far. After challenging him with: "Not being bound to her, can you not detach yourself from her?" (250; II.xi). Pip's response is silent but powerful:

> I turned my head aside, for, with a rush and a sweep, like the old marsh winds coming up from the sea, a feeling like that which had subdued me on the morning when I left the forge, when the mists were solemnly rising, and when I laid my hand upon the village finger-post, smote my heart again. There was silence between us for a little while. (250; II.xi)

Friendship has led Pip to the very depth of feeling, and in so doing it creates a mood that even as it draws Pip into himself expands the intimacy between these two young men. This mood of the solemnly rising mists is Pip's deepest mood of loss and regret; but it is also a kind of hope; and that is what Herbert makes it here. This is the power of friendship. No sooner has Pip admitted his hopeful love than Herbert tells Pip of his own engagement to Clara, or at least his plan to marry her as soon as he "began to realise Capital" (252; II.xi).

Pip is a "good fellow," or he is becoming one, because male intimacy allows him to see himself clearly. With Estella everything is subterfuge and confusion, but with Herbert, mists rise and everything becomes clear. This is what friendship means in the novel: this is what male intimacy can offer. The "good" that Herbert speaks of has the potential of becoming a powerful abstraction in the novel. For now, it is merely descriptive; but later it becomes a significant measure of worth. Friendship signals an intimacy that elsewhere is beyond each. The bond between Pip and Herbert is unmistakable.

Holly Furneaux makes the reasonable case that we might label this relationship queer. In *Queer Dickens*, she argues that homoerotic friendship is a nearly fully articulated alternative to heterosexual fulfillment and that masculine relations are the ones with real significance and power in the novel. As Furneaux claims, she would not need to posit any rigid binaries since in her parlance a "queer" critique "moves us beyond the constricting binary of homo *or* hetero," and shows that "marriage and reproduction are not the only, or indeed the dominant or preferred, modes of being, and in doing so, [the term] undoes an unhelpfully narrow model of identity as determined by a fixed point of sexual orientation." For Furneaux, who sees the time during which Dickens was writing as just before the heyday of sexology and its categorizations, "there was greater flexibility in the thinking of the erotic, less focused on object choice, and better able to articulate desires that expand and expose the limits of what now registers as the sexual."[15] But even as she articulates a notion of queer indeterminacy in Dickens' novels, she does not hold herself to this queer indeterminacy as rigidly as even she might like. Throughout her book, she contrasts homo and hetero modes of expression while she amasses a great deal of material that she tries to fit under the not-always-fully-explanatory label "homoerotic." Furneaux shies away from labels as limiting and prescriptive. I too would like to avoid all the kinds of sexual definition that attach to sexual desire simply because whatever versions of homoerotic, homosexual, or heterosexual that we use, we drag the text into the twentieth or twenty-first century and insist on terms with meaning in those eras. Dickens has a lot to say about desire and intimacy without resorting to these recent models, of which he could not be aware. If he resorts to notions of friendship, even platonic friendship, then that may be because that is where, for him, such profound intimacy inheres.

After a long account of how deeply into financial debt the pair have fallen and how quickly Herbert has followed Pip into overspending, Pip approaches Wemmick and asks if he can help him to a way of aiding his friend. Before explaining Wemmick's solution for Pip, it is crucial to understand that Wemmick is a character who has divided public and private life absolutely. In the office of Mr. Jaggers, Pip's legal counsel and the agent of his benefactor, Wemmick is nothing but business. Once he has invited Pip to his fortress-like home and introduced him to the endearing "aged parent," Wemmick has shown Pip his private side. When Pip asks him in the office how he might help his friend, Wemmick answers bluntly that Pip should choose a bridge "and pitch your money into the Thames over the centre arch of your bridge, and you know the end of it. Serve a friend with it, and you may know the end of it too – but it's a less pleasant and profitable end" (291; II.vii). This is what happens to friendship in the marketplace or the world of business and law; but when Pip asks the same question when they are at Wemmick's home in Walworth, Pip finds Wemmick more amenable to his request. Pip tells Wemmick about the "advantages" that his association with Herbert have afforded him and about his own worries that he "had but ill repaid him." He praises Herbert for his generosity and for his position "far above any mean distrusts, retaliations, or designs":

> For all these reasons (I told Wemmick), and because he was my young companion and friend, and I had a great affection for him, I wished my own good fortune to reflect some rays upon him, and therefore I sought advice from Wemmick's experience and knowledge of men and affairs, how I could

[15] See Furneaux, *Queer Dickens*, 9–12.

best try with my resources to help Herbert to some present income – say of
a hundred a year, to keep him in good hope and heart – and gradually to
buy him on to some small partnership. (295; II.xviii)

The terms of Pip's request and the description of the relationship between
the two men is cast in a way to appeal to Wemmick's personal side. "I
had great affection for him" is the key to Pip's appeal, and it works well
on Wemmick who offers a plan that will assure Pip's anonymity. It is not
long after Wemmick answers Pip's plea that Herbert comes home with the
exciting news that he has been taken on by Clarriker's House, an import
concern. Pip is so happy that "I did really cry in good earnest when I went
to bed, to think that my expectations had done some good to somebody"
(299; II.xviii).

If Herbert is committed to Pip's development as a "good fellow," Pip is
deeply concerned about Herbert too. The spirit of generosity with which
he approaches the issue and the pleasure he takes from doing something
good for Herbert are both key to understanding the role that friendship
plays in this novel. To be good, truly good, Pip has had to grow and change.
Friendship is the context in which this growth can happen, and it seems to
be the only context in which this is true. That is the meaning of platonic
friendship, after all. In *Lysis*, Socrates says that the good is beautiful as he
tries to explain the friendship between Lysis and Menexenus. What he
means, of course, is that love seeks goodness, just as it seems to do here.[16]

Later on, Pip has the greater challenge of coming to terms with
Magwitch, but that would never have been possible if he had not learned
to value his friend in this way. Everything he says about Herbert is positive – and true to the character we have come to know – and touching in
its detail. Pip talks about Herbert "possessing a generous soul, and being
far above any mean distrusts, retaliations, or designs," but that is what he
is learning by and through Herbert himself. The depth of feeling between
these two men becomes the basis on which any kind of resolution is possible. If its goodness reaches into reservoirs of the platonic, that is where
such a configuration takes on most meaning.

When Magwitch appears and explains to Pip the sordid source of his
"expectations," that resolution seems more distant than ever. Pip is at first
appalled at discovering the source of his wealth. He believes Magwitch
when he has heard his tale, but he really doesn't want anything more to
do with him. Pip feels a horror even at being touched by Magwitch: "The

---

[16] See the discussion of *Lysis*, pp. 4–5 above.

abhorrence in which I held the man, the dread I had of him, the repugnance with which I shrank from him, could not have been exceeded if he had been some terrible beast" (319–20; II.xx). He does manage to make some decisions and even to plan where he can house Magwitch when Herbert returns. But his panic never leaves him and once, in the night, "I actually did start out of bed … and begin to dress myself in my worst clothes, hurriedly intending to leave him there with everything else I possessed, and enlist for India as a private soldier" (338; III.i). When Pip learns that Magwitch has defied the law and will face capital punishment if he is recognized and apprehended, Pip is even more frightened. He imagines absconding in this way as a means of hiding, perhaps, even from himself.

When Herbert comes home, however (he has been at business in Marseille), Pip's movements become clearer and his actions more purposeful. Once Herbert is apprised of this situation and sworn to secrecy, and once Magwitch has gone home for the night, "Herbert received me with open arms, and I had never felt before, so blessedly, what it is to have a friend" (341; III.ii); he and Pip sit down by the fire to discuss the matter. Pip insists he will take no more of Magwitch's money and worries how he will pay back all he has taken already. Then he wonders:

> "What am I fit for? I know only one thing that I am fit for, and that is, to go for a soldier. And I might have gone, my dear Herbert, but for the prospect of taking counsel with your friendship and affection."
>
> Of course I broke down there, and of course Herbert, beyond seizing a warm grip of my hand, pretended not to know it.
>
> "Anyhow, my dear Handel," said he presently, "soldiering won't do. If you were to renounce this patronage and these favours, I suppose you would do so with some faint hope of one day repaying what you have already had. Not very strong, that hope, if you went soldiering! Besides, it's absurd." (342–3; III.ii)

This moving scene, in which the two young men touch as a way of expressing their bond, suggests that Herbert will help Pip through this crisis, and he does. He persuades him that to drop Magwitch quickly might lead to some violent action on the part of the criminal, and he persuades Pip to try to get him out of the country:

> And you have, and are bound to have, that tenderness for the life he has risked on your account, that you must save him, if possible, from throwing it away. Then you must get him out of England before you stir a finger to extricate yourself. That done, extricate yourself, in Heaven's name, and we'll see it out together, dear old boy. (344; III.ii)

Herbert sees the situation clearly and he helps Pip to see what is right and at the same time what is in his own best interest. In a sense they are both seeing things more clearly now that they are involved in a real crisis and not their own financial confusion. It is only after this realization of what is right, and the more practical plans of how to get Magwitch out of the country, that Pip begins to see Magwitch as something other than a frightening burden.

As Pip and Herbert are preparing for the escape, Pip visits Miss Havisham, first as she is with Estella: this is when he finds that she is engaged to marry Bentley Drummle, Pip's nemesis from schooldays; and again, when she is alone and he asks Miss Havisham directly to provide the money to carry on his support of Herbert. After she agrees to do this, and hands Pip the tablets for that purpose, she is burned in a terrible conflagration at Satis House. In helping to save her, Pip's left arm and both hands are burned, and he returns to Herbert in no shape for pursuing their plan.

At this point Herbert nurses Pip. Furneaux makes the excellent point that this kind of caring runs in the face of those critics who would see only violence and rivalry in the novel. For her, there is a kind of homoerotics implicit in Dickens' nursing narratives. Furneaux quotes William Cohen, who emphasizes the violent fisticuffs in the novel and says:

> Violence has been a popular mode in historicist and psychoanalytic approaches to all sexualities because it both looks like, and does not look like, sex; it is both a recognizable component of sexual practice and a familiar coding of the erotic. If we recognize, however, that homoerotics are not necessarily antithetical to or discontinuous with Victorian sexual mores, more tender, but no less prevalent, expressions of same-sex desire can be recognized.[17]

I am very sympathetic with this reading, but I would also want to talk about the ways in which this amazing emphasis on love and care between men can also be seen as a fulfillment of the friendship dynamic at work here. That is not to distinguish friendship from the homoerotic but to claim that friendship always harbors erotic potential. Platonic friendship explains this erotic potential: friendship can be understood to extend male intimacy in the surprising physical dimensions that these scenes of care suggest.

For me, these male–male nursing scenes fill out the picture of friendship that Dickens expresses so well here. In the first instance, Herbert dresses

---

[17] Furneaux, *Queer Dickens*, 207–8.

Pip's wounds by the fire in scenes that are intensely both emotional and physical. As Furneaux says, "Dickens places increasing emphasis on the gentle physicality of Herbert's nursing: a bodily contact interspersed with, and ostensibly sanctioned by, a vocal exchange about the men's respective love interests. This alleged heterosexual interest is repeatedly interrupted by tender exchanges between the two men."[18] In this exchange, the "Provis" they talk about is really Magwitch:

> "And then you will be married, Herbert?"
>
> "How can I take care of the dear child otherwise? – Lay your arm out upon the back of the sofa, my dear boy, and I'll sit down here, and get the bandage off so gradually that you shall not know when it comes. I was speaking of Provis. Do you know Handel, he improves?"
>
> "I said to you I thought he was softened when I last saw him."
>
> "So you did. And so he is. He was very communicative last night, and told me more of his life. You remember his breaking off here about some woman that he had had great trouble with. – Did I hurt you?"
>
> I had started, but not under his touch. His words had given me a start.
>
> "I had forgotten that, Herbert, but I remember it now you speak of it."
>
> "Well! He went into that part of his life, and a dark wild part it is. Shall I tell you? Or would it worry you just now?"
>
> "Tell me by all means. Every word."
>
> Herbert bent forward to look at me more nearly, as if my reply had been rather more hurried or more eager than he could quite account for. "Your head is cool?" he said, touching it.
>
> "Quite," said I. "Tell me what Provis said, my dear Herbert."
>
> "It seems," said Herbert, " – there's a bandage off most charmingly, and now comes the cool one – makes you shrink at first, my poor dear fellow, don't it? but it will be comfortable presently – it seems that the woman was a young woman, and a jealous woman, and a revengeful woman; revengeful, Handel, to the last degree." (405; III.xi)

The delicacy of this conversation, its intimacy and intensity, point to a level of care and mutual concern that is rare in this novel. This scene is one of both physical and emotional intensity. Furneaux's point – about the interruption of heterosexual interest with tender exchanges – is welcome; and I hope it does not seem counterintuitive to make the complementary assertion that friendship is what makes it possible for these two characters to perform a loving scene at the same time that they discuss loves of a

---

[18] Furneaux, *Queer Dickens*, 209. Cohen makes this observation about the homoerotics of friendship: "Both Magwitch and Herbert partake of a homoerotic handling of Pip, and both must be retrofitted in order to discipline those desires" (*Sex Scandal*, 61). I am not certain that such retrofitting is required or even feasible.

different kind. The scene begins with the mention of Herbert's Clara, and it goes on to suggest the affair that is connected with Estella, still in rather nebulous ways. But as the men perform their friendship here, it can contain both the intimate touch and intense personal feeling that they share, as well as these other concerns about the women whom they love. There is not an either/or situation here: the young men would not be having this conversation if they were not the intimate friends they are. That they can touch in these ways is a measure of how close they are, and that closeness makes it also possible for them to talk about the absences – of Clara and Estella – that make these moments poignant. Homo/hetero erotic distinctions make no difference here. These loving friends express their love in ways that make these so-called different versions almost indistinguishable. This is the nature of the affection they share and it is what friendship comes to mean in this novel.

Later, after the escape fails, and Magwitch is captured, Herbert goes off to new responsibilities in Egypt.[19] He invites Pip to join him there, but Pip feels responsibility to Magwitch. Pip shows a new level of care himself, as he tends to Magwitch in prison. And when the convict is dying, Pip tells him that his daughter is alive and that she is the girl Pip has loved for many years. As in the scene I just quoted, here the friendship and love that Pip shows to Magwitch are reflected again in the love he bears for Estella.

Even more moving, though, are the scenes of Pip's own illness. He collapses after Magwitch's death just as debt collectors have come to take him to the sponging house. Joe appears to nurse him through this crisis, and as Furneaux argues, "Joe's nursing atones for Pip's suffering at the hands of the other members of the forge household. It comprises belated reparation for the child Pip's abuse by Mrs. Joe that Joe had felt powerless to prevent, as well as presenting a rewriting of Orlick's story of the brutal blacksmith." This project of reconciliation reverses the earlier "incongruity" in telling ways. "The moving reunion of Joe and Pip begins to heal the wounds of childhood trauma and class antagonism," Furneaux says, and she points to the "social and erotic reconciliation [that] are inextricable here, as they become literal bedfellows in Pip's sickbed."[20] As Pip recounts, "Joe had actually laid his head down on the pillow at my side and put his arm round my neck, in his joy that I knew him" (463; III.xviii).

[19] One interesting feature of the climax is that Magwitch's nemesis, Compeyson, is drowned. After the rivalry between these two men and the violence we witness between them, one suggestive essay to consider is Vybarr Cregan-Reid, "Bodies, Boundaries, and Queer Waters: Drowning and Prosopoeia in Later Dickens," *Critical Survey* 17.2 (2005): 20–33.
[20] Furneaux, *Queer Dickens*, 222–3.

The loving bond between Pip and Joe, represented here physically as well as emotionally, is the friendship that needs this full amplification in order to do what Dickens wants it to do in the novel. The depth and complexity that a scene like this gets us close to understanding is what Dickens must have in mind. After this moment, when Joe seems almost giddy at Pip's recovery, Pip looks across to him at the window and, "as my extreme weakness prevented me from getting up and going to him, I lay there, penitently whispering, 'O God bless him! O God bless this gentle Christian man!'" (463; III. xviii). This utter reversal of Pip's earlier embarrassment and shame over Joe is a testimony to his new consciousness, and it also marks this friendship as new again and as rich and wonderful as it had ever been. To say that this is a homoerotic moment or that the love between these men is an example of same-sex desire seems to me redundant. Friendship is by definition homoerotic in the ways that this novel has demonstrated. *Great Expectations* can help us to see all that friendship can mean to a character like Pip.

After his recovery, Pip goes off to live with Herbert and Clara in Egypt, and for nearly a dozen years they share a household and live the dream that was first articulated as an adventure worthy of the *Arabian Nights*. Furneaux puts it this way: "Pip, Herbert, and Clara finally settle in a triangular cohabitation in Cairo, forming a trio in which Pip's participation is unsanctioned by familial bonds … While a business relation between Herbert and Pip operates as ostensible rationale, the text firmly signals the queerness of this household." She goes on to remind us that "Peter Brooks has read Pip's final affection for Magwitch 'and his acceptance of a continuing existence without plot, as celibate clerk for Clarrikers' in Cairo as the 'real ending' of *Great Expectations*."[21]

In a sense, what Brooks says is true. For Pip's finding a life with Herbert and Clara, and his reclaiming himself through friendship in this way, is really what constitutes a resolution in this novel. Only friendship makes possible whatever other details one wants to include. If Pip meets Estella with young Pip, the son of Joe and Biddy, and regretfully parts from her at last, he still has the profound intimacy with Herbert to which to return. If he sees that "shadow of no parting from her" (484; III.xx) as he does in Dickens' revised ending, friendship is the foundation on which these clouds finally part. If he is simply being delusional about what she offers, that would also be in keeping with his earlier self-delusions regarding her.

---

[21] Furneaux, *Queer Dickens*, 173–4. See Peter Brooks, *Reading for the Plot: Design and Intention in Narrative* (New York: Alfred A. Knopf, 1994; reprinted Cambridge, MA: Harvard University Press, 2002), 137.

Whichever ending one prefers, that is to say, it is grounded in friendship and realized in terms that only friendship offers. *Great Expectations* truly is, in that sense, "a novel of friendship."[22]

Oscar Wilde's Platonic Dialogue in *The Picture of Dorian Gray*

> Sometimes you will find, even as I have found,
> that there is no such thing as a romantic experience;
> there are romantic memories,
> and there is a desire for romance, that is all. (Wilde, *Letters*, xx)

Oscar Wilde's *The Picture of Dorian Gray* first appeared in *Lippincott's Monthly Magazine* in July 1890. It was later revised and expanded in book form for Ward Lock, & Co., in 1891. The changes are so significant, especially in the scene I wish to discuss, that I will work from the earlier publication. The edition I am using also notes changes from the manuscript to the magazine publication, and I will have occasion to talk about those changes too.[23]

Chapter 1 of *The Picture of Dorian Gray* serves as a poetic set-piece that establishes all the terms that the novel will go on to pursue. Even more than that, it demonstrates a procedure and a manner of thought and expression that give this novel its very special quality, a quality I would place in relation to the other friendships I have discussed. This chapter invokes a philosophy of love and beauty that is unmistakably Platonic in structure and form. In using Plato in this way, Wilde articulates a theory of friendship that can serve to comment on all the other chapters in this study. Wilde redefines friendship in these pages.

The chapter opens with a lush description of an artist's studio. Tradition has it that it is the studio of Charles Ricketts (1866–1931), as Donald L. Lawler tells us, "an artist friend who designed several of Wilde's books, including *Dorian Gray*."[24] Whether or not the room really existed, the evocation of a particular mood is more precisely what Wilde is seeking here:

> The studio was filled with the rich odor of roses, and when the light summer wind stirred amidst the trees of the garden there came through the

---

[22] That phrase comes from the title of Bert G. Hornback, *Great Expectations: A Novel of Friendship* (Boston: Twayne, 1987).

[23] The edition I am using is Oscar Wilde, *The Picture of Dorian Gray*, the Norton Critical Edition, ed. Donald L. Lawler (New York: Norton, 1988). All textual references will be to this edition. I have also consulted Nicholas Frankel, *The Picture of Dorian Gray: An Annotated, Uncensored Edition* (New York: Belknap Press, 2011).

[24] Donald L. Lawler, "Keys to the Upstairs Room: A Centennial Essay on Allegorical Performance in *Dorian Gray*," in *The Picture of Dorian Gray*, the Norton Critical Edition, ed. Donald L. Lawler (New York: Norton, 1988), 431–57 (432).

open door the heavy scent of the lilac, or the more delicate perfume of the pink-flowering thorn.

From the corner of the divan of Persian saddle-bags on which he was lying, smoking, as usual, innumerable cigarettes, Lord Henry Wotton could just catch the gleam of the honey-sweet and honey-coloured blossoms of the laburnum, whose tremulous branches seemed hardly able to bear the burden of beauty so flame-like as theirs, and now and then the fantastic shadows of birds in flight flitted across the long tussore-silk curtains that were stretched in front of the huge window, producing a kind of momentary Japanese effect ... The sullen murmur of the bees shouldering their way through the unmown grass, or circling with monotonous insistence round the black-crocketed spires of the early June hollyhocks, seemed to make the stillness more oppressive, and the dim roar of London was like the bourdon of a distant organ. (173)[25]

The opening paragraph concentrates on the sense of smell, an almost overwhelming combination of aromas: rose, lilac, and thorn. This is not so much a particular studio as one vividly imagined as a place in which exquisite experience might transpire. The odors are moving with the breeze as well, as if the first action of the novel is this almost spiritual movement. Lilacs and pink-flowering thorn also throw a light suffusion of color onto the scene: the colors of the late afternoon, almost floating on the breeze as the aromas do.

The second paragraph intensifies these first impressions in very specific terms. Lord Henry, lying there and smoking, takes in the beauty even as he starts to judge it. At first the "gleam of the honey-sweet and honey-coloured blossoms of the laburnum" catch his eye; pendulous and richly colored, the "tremulous branches seemed hardly able to bear the burden of beauty so flame-like as theirs." This beauty is almost too rich and too overwhelming. As the chapter goes on to show, beauty can be so intense that it is debilitating, and Lord Henry uses the defense mechanism of irony, as we will see, to preserve himself from its full effect. As he lies motionless, smoking almost as if to combat the sweet aromas, he resists becoming part of the scene.

Natural beauty combines with the textures and colors of the manufactured silk curtains, as birds flit by and cast their shadows, "producing a kind of momentary Japanese effect." The sounds that follow add another dimension of sensuous pleasure: "the sullen murmur of the bees shouldering their way through the unmown grass, or circling with monotonous insistence round the black-crocketed spires of the early June hollyhocks." All this beauty is oppressive, or at least this stillness is, the narrator tells us, while "the dim roar of London was like the bourdon of a distant organ."

[25] In the Norton Critical Edition, the Lippincott version is published after the Lock and Co. book version. It begins on p. 173.

Wilde has evoked a mood of sensual luxury here, and a fitting prelude to his unveiling of the picture. If the sounds of London are like a distant organ, then that world of business and responsibility has been left far behind. Lord Henry may find this setting oppressive because he feels the pull of that world. For now the artist, as well as his model, are so caught up in their artistic endeavor that they think nothing of the world beyond.

Basil Hallward finds the whole world in the picture he has created:

> In the centre of the room, clamped to an upright easel, stood the full length portrait of a young man of extraordinary personal beauty, and in front of it, some little distance away, was sitting the artist himself, Basil Hallward, whose sudden disappearance some years ago caused, at the time, such public excitement, and gave rise to many strange conjectures.
>
> As the painter looked at the gracious and comely form he had so skillfully mirrored in his art, a smile of pleasure passed across his face, and seemed about to linger there. But he suddenly started up, and closing his eyes, placed his fingers on his lids, as though he sought to prison within his brain some curious dream from which he feared he might awake. (173)

The portrait is described simply as a "full length portrait of a young man of extraordinary beauty," but there it stands in the "centre of the room," as if it were the young man himself. In the same sentence we are introduced to the artist, Basil Hallward, who is sitting "some little distance away" in order to look "at the gracious and comely form he had so skillfully mirrored in his art"; and moreover, after being nearly betrayed by a "smile of pleasure," Basil "suddenly started up, and closing his eyes, placed his fingers on his lids, as though he sought to prison within his brain some curious dream from which he feared he might awake." Wilde's writing is deeply suggestive here. This first encounter with the artist includes suggestion of an intense relation with his subject: so deeply pleasurable, on the one hand, and so fraught with danger or at least secrecy, on the other. The "curious dream" with which this passage ends is really the subject of the later part of this chapter. For now, however, Lord Henry Wotton and Basil Hallward engage in a dramatic conversation that begins to take the shape of a Platonic dialogue.[26]

At first Lord Henry praises the picture and says that he must show it "next year" (173) at the Grosvenor Gallery. Basil demurs and says that he

---

[26] Nicholas Frankel makes the following important point about this scene: "No reader perhaps can fail to appreciate that *Dorian Gray* is a novel that abounds in commentary on painting and portraiture ... Wilde was greatly influenced in his writing of the novel by the cult of aesthetic portraiture that then dominated the transatlantic arts scene and that stands at the imaginative center of the novel" (*The Picture of Dorian Gray: An Annotated, Uncensored Edition*, 22).

has no plans to show it at all. Lord Henry insists and Basil continues to resist the suggestion until he is quite categorical:

> "I know you will laugh at me," he replied, "but I really can't exhibit it. I have put too much of myself into it."
> Lord Henry stretched his long legs out on the divan and laughed.
> "Yes, I knew you would laugh; but it is quite true, all the same."
> "Too much of yourself in it! Upon my word, Basil, I didn't know you were so vain; and I really can't see any resemblance between you, with your rugged strong face and your coal-black hair, and this young Adonis, who looks as if he was made of ivory and rose-leaves. Why, my dear Basil, he is a Narcissus, and you – well, of course you have an intellectual expression, and all that. But beauty, real beauty, ends where an intellectual expression begins … He is a brainless, beautiful thing, who should be always here in winter when we have no flowers to look at, and always here in summer when we want something to chill our intelligence. Don't flatter yourself, Basil: you are not in the least like him." (174)

Lord Henry's insistence in taking Basil's comment literally means that he can riff on beauty and intelligence as he does. The passage achieves several other things as well. In the first place, it gives a physical description of the artist – "rugged strong face and coal-black hair" – and his model – "this young Adonis, who looks as if he was made of ivory and rose leaves." Light and dark is contrasted, of course, but so is the pure delicacy of one image and the rough and rugged quality of the other. Lord Henry may not want to be picturing a parody of Greek love, but the very images he chooses almost do that for him. The brute masculine physicality of the artist makes his comments about the picture nearly as ludicrous as Lord Henry makes out. But the expression of a connection between that swarthy masculinity and the effete youth comes almost directly out of Plato.

The image of Dorian Gray calls to mind an early poem of Wilde's, in which he praised the exotic image of a handsome young man. The poem, which he published in *Kottabos*, the magazine of Trinity College, Dublin, was a response of Violet Troubridge's medieval-styled image of a slender young man:

> A fair slim boy not made for this world's pain,
> With hair of gold thick clustering round his ears,
> And longing eyes half veiled by foolish tears
> Like bluest water seen through mists of rain;
> Pale cheeks whereon no kiss hath left its stain,
> Red under-lip drawn in for fear of Love.[27]

---

[27] See Neil McKenna, *Oscar Wilde: An Intimate Biography* (New York: Basic Books, 2011), 14. This biography can be invoked to support much of what I argue here. Wilde's obsession with Pater is emphasized in McKenna: see the chapter "Tea and Beauties."

In this poem, Wilde emphasizes the almost diaphanous quality of the image: the boy's vulnerability is implicit in his beauty. If Basil sees Dorian in similar terms, as an untouchable beauty, Lord Henry seems more than ready not only to tamper with that vulnerability, but also to dismiss the almost sanctimonious celebration of beauty that Basil articulates.

When Lord Henry proceeds to discuss beauty, he does so in terms that underline the Platonic connection. Plato, after all, has Socrates discuss beauty in similar terms, in *Lysis* and *Phaedrus*, as well as in *The Symposium*, and his conclusions are not necessarily very different from Lord Henry's. In *Lysis*, for instance, when Socrates is demonstrating the ways to engage a beautiful young man in conversation, he tells Hippothales that you cannot engage a beautiful boy by writing poems and songs to his beauty, but instead you need to engage him in topics that are of interest to him, as he proceeds to do in the dialogue. When Lord Henry says, "Beauty, real beauty ends where an intellectual expression begins," he is challenging the artist in an analogous way: how can the artist approach such beauty without destroying it. Of course Lord Henry is only teasing Basil with these remarks, but he is also articulating an ideal of "real beauty" that the narrative will go on to explore more fully.

Basil responds as if to demonstrate that he is completely engaged in this dialogue, even as he rejects Lord Henry's analysis:

> You don't understand me, Harry. Of course I am not like him. I know that perfectly well. Indeed, I should be sorry to look like him. You shrug your shoulders? I am telling you the truth. There is a fatality about all physical and intellectual distinction, the sort of fatality that seems to dog through history the faltering steps of kings. It is better not to be different from one's fellows. The ugly and the stupid have the best of it in this world … Your rank and wealth, Harry; my brains, such as they are – my fame, whatever it may be worth; Dorian Gray's good looks, – we shall suffer for what the gods have given us, suffer terribly. (174–5)

Here Basil tries to articulate an attitude toward his model and a theory of beauty that can sustain him in his abject fascination. To talk about the "fatality" of beauty, though, is only his first attempt to give substance to what he feels. If at the beginning of his speech he seems to distinguish himself carefully from the boy – "Of course I am not like him" – by the end he talks about an "us" that includes the beautiful young man as well as Lord Henry. In their different forms of distinction, they will all suffer. "Even though Wilde's critique of an imperial England that would finally send him to jail is always charged by his memorable parodistic wit," Joseph Bristow tells us, "the narrative shape he frequently gives to his work repeatedly tends toward fatalism."[28] The fatality, or fatalism, that Basil talks about here, is implicit in the distinction of beauty or talent itself. Basil's own suffering is something he will say a lot more about before this chapter comes to a conclusion, but even here we begin to understand that this beauty is double-edged.

Lord Henry takes great pleasure that he has learned the young man's name, and Basil is angry with himself that he has let the name slip: "When I like people immensely I never tell their names to any one. It seems like surrendering a part of them. You know how I love secrecy. It is the only thing that can make modern life wonderful or mysterious to us. The commonest thing is delightful if one only hides it" (175). Basil explains the value of secrecy to private pleasure, and it would be fair to say that he is revealing more than he intends to; but very quickly, he is revealing even more.

> "Harry," said Basil Hallward, looking him straight in the face, "every portrait that is painted with feeling is the portrait of the artist, not of the sitter. The sitter is merely the accident, the occasion. It is not he who is revealed by the painter; it is rather the painter who, on the colored canvas, reveals himself. The reason I will not exhibit this picture is that I am afraid I have shown with it the secret of my own soul." (176)

Lord Henry laughs at this remark, as if he is afraid to take it seriously. But it is deadly serious. Basil knows that the feeling he put into the picture – the manuscript word here is "passion" – reveals more about himself than it does about Dorian.[29] The very beauty of the piece, then, is beauty that Basil has created. In a Platonic sense, this ideal of beauty is what the artist can create when he encounters a beautiful boy. In the *Symposium*, Diotima tells Socrates, "Love is wanting to possess the good forever," and lovers pursue this good by "giving birth in beauty, whether of body or soul."[30] Basil feels that his love for Dorian Gray, if we can call it that, has allowed him to create this beautiful image. But that beauty comes not really from Dorian but from the love the older man feels for him: this is what he means when he says that he puts into the picture something of himself.

Later he explains to Lord Henry about meeting Dorian and about being almost frightened to encounter the exotic youth.

> I had always been my own master; had at least always been so, till I met Dorian Gray. Then – But I don't know how to explain it to you. Something

---

[28] Joseph Bristow, *Effeminate England: Homoerotic Writing after 1885* (New York: Columbia University Press, 1995), 21.

[29] Lawler, *The Picture of Dorian Gray*, 176, n. 9.

[30] Plato, *Symposium*, trans. Alexander Nehamas and Paul Woodruff, in *Plato: Complete Works*, ed. John M. Cooper (Indianapolis: Hackett, 1997), 457–505 (489).

seemed to tell me that I was on the verge of a terrible crisis in my life. I had a
strange feeling that Fate had in store for me exquisite joys and exquisite sorrows. I knew that if I spoke to Dorian I would become absolutely devoted
to him, and that I ought not to speak to him. I grew afraid and turned to
quit the room. It was not conscience that made me do so: it was cowardice.
I take no credit to myself for trying to escape. (177)

Here Basil confronts his attraction to Dorian Gray in terms that any of
Socrates' interlocutors could understand. Desire for the beautiful is overwhelming in ways that outdistance even outright sexual desire, which it
might of course include. The lover recognizes beauty in the beloved when
he encounters it, and he is deeply affected and profoundly changed. In
Lysis, Hypothales' friends tell him what a fool he is making of himself,
"blushing and too embarrassed to tell Socrates the name [of the boy he
admires]," and then they add: "if he spends any time at all with you he'll
be driven to distraction hearing you say it [the boy's name] so often."[31] He
cannot stop thinking or talking about the boy, and this both thrills him
and torments him. Basil is talking about this kind of love and devotion –
in the manuscript he adds that "I would never leave him till either he or
I were dead" – and he describes an attraction that he cannot resist. His life
is changed in ways that he does not yet even understand.[32]

Neil McKenna discusses "the perfectly beautiful, wonderfully poetic,
and absurdly boyish looking John Gray" as the love object that inspired
this tale. "There can be no doubt in the minds of Oscar's friends and contemporaries," McKenna argues, "that John Gray was the model for Dorian
Gray; that Oscar had fashioned his exquisite amoral hero from the exquisite reality of John Gray."[33] Even more telling, McKenna notes that Wilde
added to John Gray's surname, the Christian name Dorian: "a name replete
with implicit *paiderastia*. The Dorians were a tribe of ancient Greece ...
famous for their custom of institutionalised *paiderastia*, by which an older
man became the lover and the teacher of a youth."[34] The Dorians, then,
are the quintessential Greek lovers, and Wilde clearly has this mode of
intimacy in mind. Dominic Janes also suggests sources for Lord Henry
and Basil Hallward, but he notes, "To identify the continuities between
The Picture of Dorian Gray and the relationships in Wilde's own life is not
to say that the novel is a *roman à clef* or an allegory of Wilde's own life."[35]

---

[31] Plato, *Lysis*, 689.
[32] Lawler, *The Picture of Dorian Gray*, 177, n. 5.
[33] McKenna, *Oscar Wilde*, 121.
[34] McKenna, *Oscar Wilde*, 122; see further pp. 122–5 for a reading of the novel in personal terms.
[35] Frankel, *The Picture of Dorian Gray: An Annotated, Uncensored Edition*, 14; see further pp. 12–15.

As their conversation continues, Lord Henry tries to defuse the situation by teasing Basil about friendship with his typical wit – "I choose friends for their good looks, my acquaintances for their characters, and my enemies for their brains" (178). Almost like Socrates who tells Hypothales that it is better to ignore the boy than to shower him with gifts and praise, Lord Henry refuses to take this adoration seriously. Basil continues in his serious and revelatory mode:

> "Tell me more about Dorian Gray. How often do you see him?"
>
> "Every day. I couldn't be happy if I didn't see him every day. Of course sometimes it is only for a few minutes. But a few minutes with somebody one worships mean a great deal."
>
> "But do you really worship him?"
>
> "I do."
>
> "How extraordinary! I thought you would never care for anything but your painting – your art, I should say. Art sounds better, doesn't it?"
>
> "He is all my art to me now." (179–80)

By equating Dorian with his art, Basil acknowledges that beauty I was talking about above. The artist finds his beloved himself an artistic object, and this is what Diotima tells Plato in the *Symposium*: "You see, the man who has been thus far guided in matters of Love, who has beheld beautiful things in the right order and correctly, is coming now to the goal of Loving; all of a sudden he will catch sight of something wonderfully beautiful in its nature; that, Socrates, is the reason for all his earlier labors."[36] When Basil continues this same speech, it is almost as if he is reading from a Platonic primer:

> But in some curious way – I wonder will you understand me? – his personality has suggested to me an entirely new manner in art, an entirely new mode of style. I see things differently, I think of them differently. I can now re-create life in a way that was hidden from me before. "A dream of form in days of thought," – who is it who says that? I forget; but it is what Dorian Gray has been to me. The merely visible presence of this lad – for he seems to me little more than a lad, though he's really over twenty, – his merely visible presence, – ah! I wonder can you realize all that that means? Unconsciously he defines for me the lines of a fresh school, a school that is to have in it all the passion of a romantic spirit, all the perfection of spirit that is Greek. The harmony of soul and body – how much that is! (180)

Donald L. Lawler tells us that "Basil's aestheticism is an ideal combination of the teaching of John Ruskin ('all the passion of the romantic spirit') and

---

[36] Plato, *Symposium*, 493.

Walter Pater ('all the perfection of the spirit that is Greek'). Both taught Wilde at Oxford in the 1870s."[37] Aside from imagining what it must have been like to have been at Oxford at that moment, it remains important to note that Jowett's concept of Greek love was also alive and well when Wilde was at Oxford. As Linda Dowling argues, "Jowett summarized Diotima's famous speech about the philosophy of love ... in *Symposium* 202–12 ... by offering a host of religious and literary analogues. So suggestive did Jowett's enhanced version of the philosophic eros become that Oscar Wilde would later copy the passage into his Oxford commonplace book."[38] Basil has found inspiration in Dorian's beauty: "the merely visible presence of this lad" – in the manuscript the "lad" is labeled a "boy" – emphasizes the very kind of inspiration that Plato talks about in *Symposium* and *Lysis*. Here Basil is at a loss for words: "ah! I wonder can you realize all that that means?" All that means is an idealization of the boy's image that charges Basil with a romantic vision that he has realized in this painting. "Unconsciously he defines for me the lines of a fresh school, a school that is to have in it all the passion of a romantic spirit, all the perfection of spirit that is Greek." It could hardly be clearer. The Greek passion, that perfection of spirit, is the idealization of male beauty that abstracts it from the individual boy and creates a new ideal. Basil seems to be achieving that ideal even as he clings to the very boy whose beauty he has created.

Soon after the speech, Harry responds enthusiastically, and as he does he points out this contradiction:

> "Basil, this is quite wonderful! I must see Dorian Gray."
>
> Hallward got up from the seat, and walked up and down the garden. After some time he came back. "You don't understand, Harry," he said. "Dorian Gray is merely to me a motive in art. He is never more present in my work than when no image of him is there. He is simply a suggestion, as I have said, of a new manner. I see him in the curves of certain lines. That is all."
>
> "Then why don't you exhibit his portrait?"
>
> "Because I have put into it all the extraordinary romance of which, of course, I have never dared to speak to him. He knows nothing about it. He will never know anything about it. But the world might guess it; and I will not bare my soul to their shallow, prying eyes." (180–1)

---

[37] Lawler, *The Picture of Dorian Gray*, 14, n. 4. See also, "Saint Oscar," in Dominic Janes, *Visions of Queer Martyrdom, from John Henry Newman to Derek Jarman* (Chicago: University of Chicago Press, 2015), 133–53. Janes makes the important point that "Wilde ... was ultimately interested in religion and religious style as the means to a form a self-actualization that had become dislocated from its achievement through spiritual salvation," 140. What the spiritual amounts to here, though, is purely aesthetic.

[38] See Dowling, *Hellenism and Homosexuality*, 71.

The "extraordinary romance" is what Basil has been describing, and he is as deeply enthralled as any besotted lover, even though he protests that Dorian represents suggestion and nothing more. He may offer Basil the suggestions of color and form, of beauty, but he can only be those things because of the love Basil feels for him. In the manuscript version of this scene, when Basil says, "the world might guess it," there he adds: "where there is merely love, they would see something evil. Where there is spiritual passion, they would suggest something vile."[39] This is a helpful gloss, to be sure, but perhaps Wilde removed it because it is not necessary. It is already clear what Basil is feeling and why he is afraid to show the picture publicly.

As this conversation draws to a close, Basil says:

> "As long as I live, the personality of Dorian Gray will dominate me. You can't feel what I feel. You change too often."
>
> "Ah, my dear Basil, that is exactly why I can feel it. Those who are faithful know only the pleasures of love: it is the faithless who know love's tragedies." (182)

Lord Henry admires Basil's devotion to Dorian, but that will not stop him from asserting himself in the boy's favor and stealing him, as it were, from his friend. It is almost as if Basil understands that, but for now all he says is:

> "Don't spoil him for me. Don't try to influence him. Your influence would be bad. The world is wide, and has many marvelous people in it. Don't take away from me the one person that makes my life absolutely lovely to me, and that gives to my art whatever wonder or charm it possesses. Mind, Harry, I trust you." He spoke very slowly, and the words seemed wrung out of him almost against his will. (183)

If the chapter concludes with this almost desperate plea of Basil's, it has also already made clear the faithlessness of Lord Henry and the absolute pointlessness of this trust. But that has been a given all along. Basil talks as the smitten, distressed, and almost maddened lover; while Lord Henry has all the sangfroid of the ironic friend who cannot understand the high flights of this aesthetic theory except insofar as it promises some sensual satisfaction. Lord Henry's ironic perspective takes over the novel after this, as Dorian falls from this glorious ideal, but that does not mean that this opening Platonic articulation of ideal beauty is not something to make us pause and think what this novel really says. Basil's platonic love is sacrificed to the exigency of sordid dealings in the modern world of which

[39] Lawler, *The Picture of Dorian Gray*, 181, n. 9.

Lord Henry is the Mephistophelian master of ceremonies. Basil becomes a literal sacrifice to this transformation, as does Dorian himself. The full tragedy of Dorian's fall does not emerge until the novel's close, but it commences when he walks in to this room on that sunny afternoon and is introduced to Lord Henry Wotton.

Platonic Love in *The Longest Journey* and *Maurice*

Early in *The Longest Journey*, E. M. Forster's second novel, Rickie Elliot is discussing, with his Cambridge friend Stewart Ansell, the nature of male friendship:

> [Rickie] was thinking of the irony of friendship – so strong it is, and so fragile. We fly together, like straws in an eddy, to part in the open stream. Nature has no use for us: she has cut her stuff differently. Dutiful sons, loving husbands, responsible fathers – these are what she wants, and if we are friends it must be in our spare time. Abram and Sarai were sorrowful, yet their seed became as sand of the sea, and distracts the politics of Europe at this moment. But a few verses of poetry is all that survives of David and Jonathan.

And after thinking these thoughts, Rickie says, "I wish we were labelled":

> He wished that all the confidence and mutual knowledge that is born in such a place as Cambridge could be organized. People went down into the world saying, "We know, and like each other; we shan't forget." But they did forget, for man is so made that he cannot remember long without a symbol; he wished there was a society, a kind of friendship office, where the marriage of true minds could be registered.[40]

---

[40] E. M. Forster, *The Longest Journey*, ed. Elizabeth Heine (London: Penguin, 2006 [1907]), 64. Further parenthetical references are to this edition. This passage became a starting point for David M. Halperin's discussion of friendship in *One Hundred Years of Homosexuality*. Halperin registers his appreciation for Forster's account of "the irony of friendship" and "its paradoxical combination of social importance and social marginality, its indeterminate status among the various forms of social relations. Friendship is the *anomalous* relation: it exists outside the more thoroughly codified social networks formed by kinship and sexual ties; it is – 'interstitial in the social structure' of most Western cultures. It is therefore more free-floating, more in need of 'labeling' (as Forster puts it) – more in need, that is, of social and ideological definition" (David M. Halperin, *One Hundred Years of Homosexuality and Other Essays on Greek Love* [New York: Routledge, 1989], 75. Internal quotation is to Dorothy Hammond and Alta Jablow, "Gilgamesh and the Sundance Kid: The Myth of Male Friendship," in *The Making of Masculinities: The New Men's Studies*, ed. Harry Brod [Boston: Allen & Unwin, 1987], 241–58 [243]). See also: Susan Ackerman, *When Heroes Love: The Ambiguity of Eros in the Stories of Gilgamesh and David* (New York: Columbia University Press, 2005). Halperin's comment reminds us of some of the crucial issues besetting friendship studies. See, for instance, Alan Bray, who has tried to correct a tendency to sexualize friendships; and his posthumous study, *The Friend*, argues for a public and social function for friendship throughout the early modern period. He challenges all private expressions of intimacy as mere public formulae for recognition and advancement. (Alan Bray, *The Friend* [Chicago: University of Chicago Press, 2003], 6–10.)

In the passage quoted above, Rickie begins by talking about the inability of friends to produce progeny or claim inheritance from one generation to the next. In doing so, Rickie echoes a traditional account of the limitations of friendship.[41] As Forster puts it: "Abram and Sarai were sorrowful, yet their seed became as sand of the sea, and distracts the politics of Europe at this moment. But a few verses of poetry is all that survives of David and Jonathan." The mention of David and Jonathan would seem to invoke loving friends as biblically and historically important as their prolific forebears, but Susan Ackerman reminds us that there is no guarantee that "the biblical book of 1 Samuel, in which the stories of David and Jonathan occur, contains a basically accurate account of ancient Israelite history."[42] Even more importantly for Ackerman, the "apparently homoeroticized language and images" of the David and Jonathan stories "need to be analyzed according to the paradigms of the sexual relations operative in the biblical world and not according to the terms in which we have categorized sexual interactions and identity in ours."[43] While I applaud Ackerman's scholarly acumen and celebrate the rigor of her study, I disagree with the pressure of this need when we are talking about the appearance of the reference at a moment like this. Equally important to the truth of Israelite history is also the tradition of the role of David and Jonathan in the popular imagination and through the eighteenth and nineteenth centuries where they are repeatedly represented as an ideal of loving male friendship. Ruth Smith reminds us, in her discussion of Handel's *Saul*, how the Biblical story of

[41] Descriptions of friendships often founder on the eroticism of the language that is used to express intimacy. Either, the erotic potential is explained away and/or it is argued that men addressed each other in these terms as a matter of course; or, intimate expressions are seen as expressive of nothing less than homosexual desire. Even this last explanation, as welcome as it might sometimes be, can obfuscate the details of intimacy and deprive friendship of some of its distinctive richness: what might be described as intensely erotic but not at all, or in any obvious way, sexual. See David M. Halperin, *How to do the History of Homosexuality* (Chicago: University of Chicago Press, 2002), 104–37. Halperin is certainly right to say that Forster is grappling with questions concerning the nature of friendship in *The Longest Journey*. Rather than jumping to a sexual interpretation of what is going on in the novel, as Wendy Moffat's recent biography might encourage, it is better to look at this novel on its own terms and to consider what Rickie means by his provocative outburst and try to show that this novel offers us ways to understand that the intimacy friendship implies can be measured in ways other than the simply sexual. See also Wendy Moffat, *A Great Unrecorded Life: A New Life of E. M. Forster* (London: Picador, 2011). Many earlier critics who interpreted Rickie's lameness as a metaphor for his homosexuality read the novel as a veiled account of homosexual desire. See, for example, James J. Miracky, *Regenerating the Novel: Gender and Genre in Woolf, Lawrence, Forster, Sinclair, and Lawrence* (New York: Routledge, 2003); Tariq Rahman, "Alienation and Homosexuality in E. M. Forster's *The Longest Journey*," *The Literary Half-Yearly* 27.1 (1986): 44–65. See also: Carola M. Kaplan, "Absent Father, Passive Son: The Dilemma of Rickie Elliot in *The Longest Journey*," in *E. M. Forster*, ed. Jeremy Tambling (New York: St. Martin's Press, 1995), 51–66.

[42] Ackerman, *When Heroes Love*, 153.

[43] Ackerman, *When Heroes Love*, 198.

David and Jonathan functioned as the perfect model of friendship. "As an exemplary relationship of great heroes," Smith asserts,

> the friendship of David and Jonathan was for the eighteenth century a touchstone, on a par with that of Achilles and Patroclus, but even more exemplary, sanctioned by being in the Bible. Yet while it was heroic and canonical it was also intensely human, the material of sentimental drama, as the response of contemporary biblical commentators indicates. The apotheosis and commemoration of the friendship, David's lament for Saul and Jonathan, was celebrated as one of the greatest Old Testament lyrics, was frequently paraphrased, and was obvious material for musical setting.[44]

To a certain extent, this Biblical model stands behind various representations of "heroic" friends in drama and fiction. And it is surely this version of the story that Forster is invoking at this moment in *The Longest Journey*.[45]

For Rickie, the friends cannot reproduce nor can they claim any central function in the history of Europe. But is this really true? If Forster were thinking of Plato, the Plato, especially, of the *Symposium*, then certainly it is not. Forster's interest in Plato is deeply central to the novel, as Elizabeth Heine, his Abinger editor has suggested.[46] In his own "Author's Introduction," Forster says the following:

> Cambridge is the home of Rickie, the elder brother, the legitimate, his only true home: the Cambridge of G. E. Moore which I knew at the beginning of the century: the fearless uninfluential Cambridge that sought for reality and cared for truth. Ansell is the undergraduate high-priest of the local shrine, Agnes Pembroke is its deadly debunker. Captured by her and by Sawston, Rickie goes to pieces, and cannot even be rescued when Ansell joins up with Stephen and strikes. The Cambridge chapters are still romantic and crucial for me, and I still endorse Ansell's denunciation of the Great World.[47]

Before addressing this denunciation, it is important to discuss the almost religious presence here of the philosopher G. E. Moore.[48] Moore was

---

[44] Ruth Smith, "Love Between Men in Jennens' and Handel's *Saul*," in *Queer People: Negotations and Expressions of Homosexuality, 1700–1800*, ed. Chris Mounsey and Caroline Gonda (Lewisburg: Bucknell University Press, 2007), 226–45 (226–7). The final reference is to *David's Lamentation over Saul and Jonathan* (1736), a cantata; also set by J. C. Smith junior, 1738 (not performed until 1740).

[45] Dominic Janes makes a similar point: "The trope of 'the love of David and Jonathan' appears to have circulated in Anglo-Catholic circles as a model for eroticized same-sex relationships. As the status of Platonic love between men became increasingly problematic in the nineteenth century, the Biblical example of the love of David for his best friend was increasingly stressed to emphasize the supposed purity of such alliances" (*Visions of Queer Martyrdom*, 157).

[46] Elizabeth Heine, "Editor's Introduction," in E. M. Forster, *The Longest Journey*, Vol. 2, Abinger edition (London: Edward Arnold, 1984), vii–lxv.

[47] Forster, *The Longest Journey*, lxviii.

[48] In her introduction, Heine says that "Through the pairing of Rickie Elliot and Stewart Ansell, Moore's influence on *The Longest Journey* is ineradicably associated with the mystical, poetic,

deeply influenced by Plato, and Forster himself was interested in the Platonic account of male relations, as conversations between Maurice and Clive make clear in Forster's later novel *Maurice*.[49] Without belaboring the details of this understanding, we can look directly at the *Symposium*, which Maurice and Clive discuss and which, if it is not mentioned specifically in this passage, is almost surely in Forster's mind when he is discussing the value of friendship.

Platonic love is a topic that baffles many readers of Plato. This love between friends: how can it be defined in ways that are instinctive for modern readers? Any discussion of this topic can benefit from a reminder about a couple of the peculiarities of the Greek language. Notably, the verb *philein*, to love – to love parents, siblings, relations of various kinds, and FRIENDS – is also the verb "to make love" as one does with a spouse or someone else in an intimate relation. This is not the same verb as *balein* – to have sex, to screw – and it is not linked to eros or the erotic directly; but it does have a cognate in the noun *philia*, or friendship. In what ways, we might then ask, do friends make love in a way that is distinct from eros?

What Plato offers in the *Symposium* is precisely the registry of friendship that Rickie is seeking. As the dialogue develops, Diotima talks about a special form of love. "Love is wanting to possess the good forever," Diotima says, and lovers pursue this good by "giving birth in beauty, whether of body or soul."[50] Diotima extends this remark to a notion of pregnancy: "All of us are pregnant, Socrates, both in body and soul, and, as soon as we come to a certain age, we naturally want to give birth." And further: "what Love wants is not beauty," but "reproduction and birth in beauty." Later talking more about reproduction, Diotima says, "For among animals the principle is the same as with us, and mortal nature seeks so far as possible to live forever and be immortal. And this is possible in one way only: by reproduction, because it always leaves behind a new young one in place of the old."[51] After talking about birth and love for one's offspring, Diotima distinguishes different ways of being pregnant: some prefer pregnancy in the body and turn to women

Hegelian idealism that gave way to his disciples' painstaking analyses of the worldly realities of individual 'states of mind' and personal 'relationships'" (Heine, "Editor's Introduction," xxxi). In her "Afterword" to the Penguin edition of the novel, Heine offers a different emphasis: "In *The Longest Journey*, Rickie Elliot embodies [Goldsworthy Lowes] Dickinson's, a mystic and poetic variant of McTaggart's Hegelianism and much influenced by Plato, Plotinus, and Shelley, and very different in style from Moore's closely reasoned linguistic analyses." See "Afterword," in *The Longest Journey*, 313.
49 E. M. Forster, *Maurice*, ed. David Leavitt (London: Penguin, 2005 [1971]), 42, 51–5.
50 Plato, *Symposium*, trans. Alexander Nehamas and Paul Woodruff, in *Plato: Complete Works*, ed. John M. Cooper (Indianapolis: Hackett, 1997), 457–505 (489).
51 Plato, *Symposium*, 490.

and childbirth, but others are pregnant in their souls, "because there surely *are* those who are even more pregnant in their souls than in their bodies." In the next sentence she refers to "Wisdom and the rest of virtue, which all poets beget, as well as craftsmen who are said to be creative."

> When someone has been pregnant with these in his soul from early youth, while he is still a virgin, and, having arrived at the proper age, desires to beget and give birth, he too will go about seeking the beauty in which he would beget; for he will never beget in anything ugly. Since he is pregnant, then, he is much more drawn to bodies that are beautiful than to those that are ugly; and if he also has the luck to find a soul that is beautiful and noble and well-formed, he is even more drawn to this combination; such a man makes him immediately teem with ideas and arguments about virtue ... In my view, you see, when he makes contact with someone beautiful and keeps company with him, he conceives and gives birth to what he has been carrying inside him for ages.[52]

To reconsider Rickie's comment about David and Jonathan, then, is to answer his complaint that "a few verses of poetry is all that survives" with something like Diotima's notion that souls are reproduced in the beauty of the poetry they create and, in turn, inspire. Physical reproduction is not the only kind of immortality available to men who are friends. The literature of friendship suggests that there is something more, as, to a certain extent, do the friends themselves. This may be what Forster means by a "marriage of true minds," alluding as he does to Shakespeare's Sonnet 116.[53] David and Jonathan may not have physical offspring, but they have inspired generations of friends who have turned to them as models, both of friendship and of the poetic expression of that friendship.

---

[52] Plato, *Symposium*, 491–2.
[53] Let me not to the marriage of true minds
Admit impediments. Love is not love
Which alters when it alteration finds,
Or bends with the remover to remove:
O no! it is an ever-fixed mark
That looks on tempests and is never shaken;
It is the star to every wandering bark,
Whose worth's unknown, although his height be taken.
Love's not Time's fool, though rosy lips and cheeks
Within his bending sickle's compass come:
Love alters not with his brief hours and weeks,
But bears it out even to the edge of doom.
         If this be error and upon me proved,
         I never writ, nor no man ever loved.
William Shakespeare, Sonnet 116, in *William Shakespeare: Complete Sonnets and Poems* (Oxford: Oxford University Press, 2002), 613.

In Plato's *Symposium*, this friendship begins in physical attraction – Diotima makes it clear that "A lover who goes about this matter correctly must begin in his youth to devote himself to beautiful bodies" – but it becomes deeply meaningful in ways that we have come to understand as "platonic": something more than the merely physical. Diotima says: "You see, the man who has been thus far guided in matters of Love, who has beheld beautiful things in the right order and correctly, is coming now to the goal of Loving; all of a sudden he will catch sight of something wonderfully beautiful in its nature; that, Socrates, is the reason for all his earlier labors."[54]

This kind of platonic love is at the heart of *The Longest Journey*. As Rickie and Stewart Ansell explore the deep and abiding friendship that gives meaning to both their lives during their time at Cambridge, they hardly recognize how much is at stake. Sitting in the dell, which is to Rickie "a kind of church ... where everything you did would be transfigured," Rickie weaves wreaths of flowers for his own and Ansell's brow – "he had plaited two garlands of buttercups and cow-parsley, and Ansell's lean Jewish face was framed in one of them" – in one of the most touching love scenes in the novel (18). Later, he complains that Cambridge is too small: "where is the great world?" he asks his friend. Stewart answers:

> There is no great world at all, only a little earth, for ever isolated from the rest of the solar system. The little earth is full of tiny societies, and Cambridge is one of them. All the societies are narrow, but some are good and some are bad – just as one house is beautiful inside and another ugly ... To compare the world to Cambridge is like comparing the outsides of houses with the inside of a house. (62–3)

Rickie does not understand Ansell fully, but he understands enough to say, "There'll never again be a home for me like Cambridge. I shall only look at the outsides of homes. According to your metaphor I shall live in the street, and it matters very much to me what I find there" (63). Rickie feels loss, in other words, as if leaving Cambridge the place means leaving the relationships that he formed there. And almost as if on cue, after their conversation about friendship, Rickie says that he has to go and meet Agnes, the woman with whom he is about to become engaged. They argue about this briefly and desultorily and then: "Rickie laughed, and suddenly overbalanced into the grass. Ansell, with his usual playfulness, held him prisoner. They lay there for a few minutes, talking and ragging aimlessly. Then Rickie seized his opportunity and jerked away" (65).

---

[54] Plato, *Symposium*, 493.

What Stewart Ansell is offering Rickie is an alternative to marriage with Agnes, a platonic friendship – playfully physical, probingly intellectual, emotionally intense – that could partake of the beauty of Cambridge and elicit from these men some of their greatest work. Rickie's stories and Stewart's scholarship could emerge from this playful moment as something powerful and significant. But Rickie hides his stories, and Stewart does not know how to stop Rickie from falling into middle-class normalcy. The novel marks this missed opportunity as a moment of loss – Rickie jerks away from Stewart's grasp – and it takes almost the entire novel for this break to be repaired.

As the relationship between Rickie and Agnes gets more serious and it becomes clear that Rickie will marry her, Stewart writes Rickie a letter in which he urges the inadvisability of this marriage. Stewart does not think Rickie suited to marriage and he refuses to countenance a relationship that seems to him fundamentally false. When Stewart says that Rickie is "not a person who ought to marry at all," he is talking ostensibly about Rickie's congenital lameness and his avowed unwillingness, discussed in Cambridge circles earlier, to pass that lameness on.[55]

More to the point, however, is Stewart's Shelleyan dictum that "you are also unfitted in soul 'You never were attached to that great sect' who can like one person only, and if you try to enter it you will find destruction" (81). Stewart's quotation is from Shelley's poem *Epipsychidion*, and it is this very passage that Rickie comes upon later when opening the book at random:

> I was never attached to that great sect
> Whose doctrine is that each one should select
> Out of the world a mistress or a friend,
> And all the rest, though fair and wise, commend
> To cold oblivion – though it is the code
> Of modern morals, and the beaten road
> Which those poor slaves with weary footsteps tread
> Who travel to their home among the dead
> By the broad highway of the world – and so
> With one sad friend, perhaps a jealous foe,
> The dreariest and the longest journey go.[56]

---

[55] For a discussion of "homosexuality" as a congenital illness, see Heine, "Afterword," 305–7.
[56] Percy Bysshe Shelley, *Epipsychidion* (1821). For a discussion of which edition of the poem Forster used, see *The Longest Journey*, 834n. For a modern edition of the poem, see *Shelley's Poetry and Prose*, Donald A. Reiman and Neil Fraisat (New York: Norton, 2002 [1821]), 390–407. For Heine "the interconnections between light and love in the novel, like its title, are drawn most directly from Shelley's *Epipsychidion*" (Heine, "Afterword," 317).

Forster's insistence on this passage, both here and in a key scene later on, as well as his use of it for the novel's title, all suggest that it offers a key to the meaning of the novel or, more specifically, the meaning of friendship in the novel. In her Afterword, Elizabeth Heine argues that "in Shelley's metaphor our life is our longest journey, and the problem is our choice of companions, symbolized further as a matter of main route or detour."[57] But Stewart's emphasis is slightly different. He rejects marriage for Rickie because not marrying Agnes will make him freer: freer for friendship but also freer in body and spirit, freer to think, freer to write, freer to be. Forster does not seem to embrace Shelley's notion of love beyond marriage. Instead he posits life without marriage for someone like Rickie. Forster's version of free love resists marriage altogether in its celebration of a masculine and intellectual ideal.

Stephen Wonham, a ward of Rickie's Aunt Emily, and it turns out, Rickie's half-brother, bears the brunt of the soul-searching that overtakes Rickie after marriage; and his role in the novel, if a bit overdetermined, at least reveals some of Forster's narrative priorities. Stephen is a man of the earth, a kind of Pan figure in the parlance of the novel, and he puts Rickie to shame at their first encounter – when they are pushed out horseback riding together, with disastrous results – and only embarrasses him or threatens to embarrass him throughout. There are several scenes that show the two men simply at odds. In his stories, Rickie is always creating characters who are "in touch with nature"; but Stephen is himself so intimately in touch with nature that he is hardly aware of any distinction between himself and the natural world. When he looks at Rickie's story, he sees that it is about a girl who turns into a tree (like Daphne), and he exclaims:

> In touch with Nature! The girl was a tree! He lit his pipe and gazed at the radiant earth. The foreground was hidden, but there was the village with its elms, and the Roman Road, and Cadbury Rings. There, too, were those woods, and little beech copses, crowning a waste of down. Not to mention the air, or the sun, or water. Good, oh, good!
>
> In touch with Nature! What cant would the books think of next? His eyes closed. He was sleepy. Good, oh good! Sighing into his pipe, he fell asleep. (119–20)

Rickie's obsession is nature as represented in the classics, and his tales tell of Ovidian transformation reimagined in the modern world. Stephen cannot make much of them, and his only commentary is to fall asleep while Rickie's pages settle in the gutter. Stephen, the natural man, has no time

---

57 Heine, "Afterword," 317.

for the gleanings of Rickie's imagination, at least not yet. Rickie is not the only one who resists this friendship. Stephen's anti-bookish elementalism has its limits too.

Stephen haunts the second half of the novel. Once Rickie hears that Stephen is his brother – and he assumes that the man is the illegitimate son of his father – he rejects him, with Agnes' help, and moves on to Sawston, where Agnes' brother runs a school, in the hope of suppressing the relation between himself and this sign of illegitimacy and keeping the information about his brother's existence a secret.

All this is exploded when Stephen, having been turned out at Agnes' urging and sent off to Canada, instead finds his way to Sawston and decides to tell Rickie about his parentage, of which he assumes Rickie is unaware. At first approach, though, he is turned from the door. Later, as he sits in the garden, he meets Stewart Ansell, who has come to Sawston to see whether there is anything he can do to reverse the dreadful process of deterioration he fears has taken place in Rickie because of marriage and the school.

The encounter between the would-be Cambridge philosopher and the man of nature is almost comical. Stephen tries to catch Stewart's attention, but Stewart is reading and cannot be bothered. Stephen ends up throwing clods of earth at him and then hurling him into the bushes, and he leaves the confused and very excited Stewart feeling amazed at this unusual encounter, if a bit ruffled and dirty. When Stewart discovers that Stephen is Rickie's brother, he is excited to break the news to his friend. He finds not only that the way is barred, but also that Rickie had already known about Stephen and that Agnes and her brother, who is in some authority at the school, are conspiring to keep Stephen from Rickie. In a burst of anger, Stewart charges into the dining hall, where teachers and students are assembled, and, the text says, as if "transfigured into a Hebrew prophet passionate for satire and the truth" (225) accosts Rickie publicly in these terms:

> Don't be afraid. I bring good news. You'll never see him [Stephen] nor anyone like him again. I must speak very plainly, for you are all three fools … Stephen is a bully; he drinks; he knocks one down; but he would sooner die than take money from people he did not love. Perhaps he will die, for he has nothing but a few pence that the poor gave him and some tobacco, which, to my eternal glory, he accepted from me. Please listen again. Why did he come here? Because he thought you would love him, and was ready to love you. But I tell you, don't be afraid. He would sooner die now than say that you were his brother. (225)

The "love" that Stewart throws at Rickie in this climactic scene is precisely what Rickie has been unable to discover in his marriage or in his relations with students and colleagues. This love is held up as the ideal to which Rickie has aspired, not just in his friendship with Stewart, but in his art and in his imagination. Stewart is arguing for a different life from the one he is living: a life that Stephen represents and Stewart is ready to support. This is the love that Rickie needs, not the stultifying and deceptive love of Agnes and her brother. For them, love is public and has meaning only for what they can achieve with it. They try to buy Stephen off ("They had not anticipated his claim would exceed two pounds" [221]) but he wants nothing of their subterfuge. For Stewart, and for Stephen, and increasingly for Rickie too, love is something that pulls people together and makes them one. Stephen tries to persuade Rickie to join him:

> "Come with me as a man," said Stephen, already out in the mist. "Not as a brother; who cares what people did years back? We're alive together, and the rest is cant. Here am I, Rickie, and there are you, a fair wreck. They've no use for you here – never had any, if the truth was known – and they've only made you beastly. This house, so to speak, the rot. It's common sense that you should come." (257)

It is out of this love that Rickie's stories finally emerge: this trio of friends brings them forth, even if Rickie dies, as it were, in childbirth. Rickie has nurtured the notion of publishing his stories long before his marriage to Agnes, and especially in the first year of their marriage, before teaching at Sawston. This passage, which takes place just after that first break with Stephen, suggests how deeply the stories are in part tied up with that first encounter: "The rest of the year was spent by Rickie partly in bed – he had a curious breakdown – partly in the attempt to get his little stories published. He had written eight or nine, and hoped they would make up a book, and that the book might be called *Pan Pipes*" (140).

Pan Pipes is Rickie's way to give poetic voice to his deepest desires. He sees the transformations in nature as an answer to the brutality of the modern world. But Stephen himself is a kind of Pan, as the novel makes clear, and Rickie's refusal to recognize him in those terms, at least until the very end of the novel, is the measure of his undoing.[58] The love that Stephen offers is a deep and elemental love, the love connected to the mother who, as it turns out, he and Rickie share – once Stewart informs him from which

---

[58] See, for instance, Peter Jeffreys, *Eastern Questions: Hellenism and Orientalism in the Writings of E. M. Forster and C. P. Cavafy* (Greensboro: ELT Press, 2005), 16; for Jeffreys, *The Longest Journey* is the "most ambitious literary expression of Western Hellenism ... Forster took his title from a line out of Shelley's Hellenizing *Epipsychidion,* a poem suffused in Hellenic thought and steeped in Romantic Hellenism," 37.

parent this brother comes – and the love that will free Rickie from the infertile gloom of his marriage to Agnes. As Forster quotes in those lines from Shelley: Rickie is one of "those poor slaves with weary footsteps… / Who travel to their home among the dead / By the broad highway of the world." Stewart and Stephen are giving Rickie a chance to choose life – "We're alive together, and the rest is cant" – and at first he is unable to see how close this is to what he has been desiring all along.[59]

After that dining hall encounter, Rickie recognizes that he must leave Agnes and go off – somewhere, anywhere – in order to ask Stephen to forgive him and to make a kind of life with him. If that cannot succeed for Rickie, and the novel makes it clear that in some ways it does not, then that is because he looks backward and tries to fit Stephen into an image of his mother. When Stephen drinks and breaks his promises, Rickie feels that he has failed. What has failed, momentarily, is his understanding of what love entails. He loves Stephen, but he is afraid to accept him for who he is and instead keeps trying to change him: to stop his drinking and carousing and make him take life more seriously.

One scene during their painful last encounters reaches beyond the misunderstanding and frustration in a tender and deeply touching moment of intimacy. Rickie and Stephen have been wandering in Wiltshire, having left the train on impulse and hoping to have some kind of experience. Rickie is pondering the meaning of romantic love, when Stephen calls from the edge of the stream they have approached:

> Stephen called from the water for matches: there was some trick with paper that Mr. Failing had showed him, and he would show Rickie now, instead of talking nonsense. Bending down, he illuminated the dimpled surface of the ford, "Quite a current," he said, and his face flickered out in the darkness. "Yes, give me the loose paper, quick! Crumple it into a ball."
>
> Rickie obeyed, though intent on the transfigured face. He believed that a new spirit dwelt there, expelling the crudities of youth. He saw steadier eyes, and the sign of manhood set like a bar of gold upon steadier lips. Some faces are knit by beauty, or by intellect, or by a great passion: had Stephen's waited for the touch of the years?
>
> But they played as boys who continued the nonsense of the railway carriage. The paper caught fire from the match, and spread into a rose of flame.

---

[59] Claude J. Summers, *E. M. Forster* (New York: Macmillan, 1983), 65. This passage is also quoted in Jeffreys, *Eastern Questions*, 37. As Claude Summers claims, "it is as the natural embodiment of the Greek spirit of life – as localized in Wiltshire – that Stephen inherits England. Stephen's intuitive absorption of the Greek spirit contrasts with Rickie's studied literary Hellenism. Rickie's artificial idealization of the ancient Greeks falsifies and distances, whereas Stephen's unconscious Hellenism translates ancient ideals into living values."

"Now gently with me," said Stephen, and they laid it flower-like on the stream. Gravel and tremulous weeds leap into sight, and then the flower sailed into deep water, and up leapt the two arches of a bridge. "It'll strike!" they cried; "no, it won't; it's chosen the left" and one arch became a fairy tunnel, dropping diamonds. Then it vanished for Rickie; but Stephen, who knelt in the water, declared that it was still afloat, far through the arch, burning as if it would burn for ever. (272–3)

This magical moment brings these men together playing as boys, and as they gaze into the fairy arch, they are united as they have never been. The richness of the image, coupled with Stephen's suddenly transfigured beauty, makes this a transformative moment for Rickie and Stephen both. This is the friendship they have been searching for: rooted in beauty, it is playful and intimate, and at the same time, it charms the present and even reaches toward a charming future. The passage begins to suggest a hope that has eluded them up to now and that would again elude them as Stephen – "a law to himself" (281) – slips off into drunkenness again.

In the end Rickie sacrifices himself for Stephen, in a resigned act of "duty" (282), which could also be understood as an act of love: when the intoxicated Stephen is in danger of being hit by a train, Rickie throws himself on the tracks in an effort to push Stephen out of its way. It is almost as if this act alone earns him the right to survive. He does not survive the accident, but he nonetheless achieves a kind of immortality, not through his death but through the art that connected him to nature.

In the last chapter, set sometime after Rickie's death, Agnes' brother Herbert and Stephen meet to do some last arrangements for the volume of Rickie's stories they are publishing under the name of *Pan Pipes*. Herbert is persuaded that these stories are in fashion now and that they will be a great success. Stephen argues for better financial terms, and it is clear that he is as committed to the publication as anyone. It is also clear that he is married and that he has a young daughter; that Stewart Ansell is with them, whether visiting or living with them is unclear; and, finally, that Stephen has named this child after his and Rickie's mother. After Herbert leaves, he looks down on his daughter, and:

He gave her one hand, and she was asleep before her fingers had nestled in its palm. Their touch made him pensive, and again he marvelled why he, the accident, was here. He was alive and had created life. By whose authority? Though he could not phrase it, he believed that he guided the future of our race, and that, century after century, his thoughts and his passions would triumph in England. (289)

Stephen assumes he is the future, and in one way, of course, he is. Through his daughter, he continues the line of love that began in his and Rickie's mother, and in so doing he begets life for the twentieth century. Stephen's triumph offers Rickie a version of inheritance too, through the mother whom he loved.

But Rickie has himself given posthumous birth to this volume of stories, through which his name will live on in a different way. What is so important about this publication is the sense that Stephen has been its inspiration, even if unwittingly. Rickie acknowledged Stephen through his stories about nature. Stephen is nature in the parlance of the novel, and in that sense he is in the pages that Rickie has written. Stewart Ansell, too, has joined with Stephen in editing and preparing the volume for publication, and now together they produce a volume that gives Rickie life anew.

Rickie has triumphed here in the very terms that Diotima outlines in Plato's *Symposium*. He has given birth to something whole and sound and beautiful. The publication of *Pan Pipes* is as great an accomplishment, in its way, as Stephen's having a beautiful child. "Now, some people are pregnant in body," Diotima says in Plato's *Symposium*, "while others are pregnant in soul – because there surely *are* those who are even more pregnant in their souls than in their bodies, and these are pregnant with what is fitting for a soul to bear and give birth." Rickie was not able to live anywhere but in his imagination, but there he has given birth to something beautiful.

The Longest Journey is a novel about friendships that almost fail because Rickie cannot recognize the love that is all around him. He is celebrating it in his stories, but he risked missing it entirely in his life. *Pan Pipes* might have been a mere act of sublimation and a sign of his inability to accept the loving friendships that were offered him. Instead, though, he acts in a way that suggests that he is trying to reclaim the love that he had almost lost. In that attempt, in the momentary wresting of success from failure, Rickie achieves the kind of connection that had eluded him throughout the novel. And *Pan Pipes* instead becomes the sign of what he has sacrificed for his friends. *Pan Pipes* defies the tragedy of Rickie's death with the hope of the kind of immortality that Forster himself imagined. Born in beauty, these stories have a life of their own.

Forster has articulated an ideal of friendship here, platonic friendship. Richly intimate and deeply connected in intellectual and physical ways, these friendships defy the simple definition of "friends," and yet they are not the same as homosexual relationships either. They are erotic, but not merely that. Instead they suggest a bond that is constituted in love and determined by physical intimacy, in that they are like a marriage, "a marriage of true minds," that emerges from Plato with an ideal that is rarely realized; but when it is, as it almost is here, it is rich and fruitful and the closest thing to male pregnancy that the friendship tradition offers. Rickie and Stewart and Stephen may never fully realize these ideals of friendship, but they certainly make clear how very much they matter.

Forster's later novel, *Maurice*, works very similar concerns to a different conclusion: he goes even further in contrasting platonic love to something even more intense: the expression of erotic love between men. It has long been recognized that the real enemy in *Maurice* is not the straight world in any familiar configuration, but rather the figure of Clive Durham and the seductive but ultimately both dissatisfying and betraying version of Greek love that he offers Maurice. Clive has learned about Greek love by reading Plato – the *Symposium* and the *Phaedrus* – and he has asked Maurice to read Plato too. Maurice cannot quite understand what he reads, but he sees how much it means to Clive, and he attempts to abide by the teaching of the Greek philosopher. The relationship between the two men is intense, but the novel also makes us understand that its physical dimension is severely limited by Clive's understanding of Plato. Clive's version of Greek love is one that idealizes male relations at the same time that it makes male–male physicality almost unthinkable. To examine how Forster is using this concept of platonic love – how it is represented in the novel – is to say something about the Hellenism of Cambridge and what it takes for Maurice to move beyond it.

In *One Hundred Years of Homosexuality*, David M. Halperin makes a crucial observation, not just about *Maurice*, or Forster, but for an entire generation or more of English gentlemen, who were educated in the Classics and who knew what kinds of male relations were typical of the Greeks. Talking about "temperate and exquisite expression of homoerotic feelings" to be found in Plato, Halperin says: "Study of the Greeks, especially Plato, has enabled this young man [Clive] gradually to accept himself and his desires as he has never been able to do in the course of his religious upbringing; the Greeks provided an ideological weapon against the condemnatory reflexes of his own Christian conscience, offering him, in its place, 'a new guide to life.' "[60] This is not the experience of one literary character alone. Others in the late nineteenth century, from writers and thinkers like Walter Pater and John Addington Symonds to other novelists, politicians and philosophers, mostly educated in a similar tradition at Oxford or Cambridge, had experiences similar to those that Forster described. Linda Dowling has given us a sense of the depth of this education and the meaning of Hellenism for a generation of the English before the First World War.[61] This knowledge

---

[60] Halperin, *One Hundred Years of Homosexuality*.
[61] Dowling, *Hellenism and Homosexuality*.

was remarkably general among the university-educated, and many of the assumptions Forster's character expresses were shared by a variety of writers from Shelley to Wilde. In talking about this novel in particular, Deborah Raschke says that "The specific weaving of Plato's *Phaedrus* and *Symposium* with Maurice's sexual encounters (both physical and rhetorical) suggests that metaphysics and sexuality are inextricably linked."[62] Raschke makes a persuasive argument that Forster is rethinking Western metaphysics in *Maurice*, as he pits Clive's Hellenism against Maurice's increasingly sexualized understanding of male relations – as Raschke puts it, "Maurice's recognition of Platonism as an impediment to physical love and human relationships presages Luce Irigaray's critique of Western metaphysics in *Speculum*" – and that Hellenism fails in the novel to offer Maurice a viable alternative to his oppressive Christian upbringing.[63] I would like to look again at these questions in the novel and to consider what is it specifically that causes Greek love to fail Maurice in this novel. I am interested in how an understanding of the Greeks is articulated, and what Greek love comes to mean when it is introduced into the drawing rooms of early twentieth-century England.[64]

[62] Deborah Raschke, "Breaking the Engagement with Philosophy: Re-envisioning Hetero/Homo Relations in *Maurice*," in *Queer Forster*, ed. Robert K. Martin and George Piggford (Chicago: University of Chicago Press, 1997), 151–65 (152); also see her "Re-Envisioning the Platonic Ideal: Forster's *Passage to India and Maurice*," in *Modernism, Metaphysics, and Sexuality* (Selinsgrove: Susquehanna University Press, 2006), 102–27.

[63] Raschke, "Breaking the Engagement," 152.

[64] *Maurice* was written just before the First World War. Foster says he completed it in 1913–14, which in his career falls between the great novels *Howards End* (1910) and *A Passage to India* (1924); and although it was not published until after Forster's death in 1970 – he did tinker with the novel over the intervening years – it can still usefully be read in the context of the early twentieth century. (See: E. M. Forster, *Maurice* (New York: Norton, 1993); further references are to this edition. It should be noted that in his "Terminal Note" to *Maurice*, written in 1960, Forster said that he would not publish the novel "unless the Wolfenden Report becomes law" [250].) By the time *Maurice* appeared in 1971, Gore Vidal's *City and the Pillar* (1948), James Baldwin's *Giovanni's Room* (1956), and Christopher Isherwood's *A Single Man* (1962) had all been published, while in 1914, Wilde's trials were fresh in the public memory and even Radcliffe Hall's *The Well of Loneliness* (1928) had not been conceived. As David Leavitt's introduction to the Penguin edition of *Maurice* makes clear, reviews when the novel did appear were condescending and superior about what Forster was trying to do and say. (See: David Leavitt, "Introduction," in E. M. Forster, *Maurice* (London: Penguin 2005), xi–xxxvi.) If the novel had appeared in 1914 – if Forster had been willing to publish it then – it would have had a far different reception, not only because such a plot would have been unfamiliar to contemporary readers, but also because some of the metaphysics of the novel might in fact have been more familiar. Contemporary readers might have understood more instinctively what Forster was doing with Greek love and why Clive, its major proponent in the novel, has to be shunted off into married country life misery at the end of the novel, while Maurice is able to strike out into the greenwood with his lower-class lover Alec. (When I say "lower class," I mean lower than Maurice's upper-middle class. Alec can be described as lower-middle class, I suppose. Conversations in the novel make it clear that he is considered of a different class from Clive and Maurice. As Maurice says at a moment of crisis with Alec, "The feeling that can impel a gentleman towards a person of lower class stands self-condemned" [150].)

The first specific mention of Greek love in *Maurice* occurs in a translation class at Cambridge:

> Towards the end of term they touched upon a yet more delicate subject. They attended the Dean's translation class, and when one of the men was forging quietly ahead Mr. Cornwallis observed in a flat toneless voice, "Omit: a reference to the unspeakable vice of the Greeks." Durham observed afterwards that he ought to lose his fellowship for such hypocrisy.
>
> Maurice laughed.
>
> "I regard it as a point of pure scholarship. The Greeks, or most of them, were that way inclined, and to omit it is to omit the mainstay of Athenian society."
>
> "Is that so?"
>
> "You've read the *Symposium*?"
>
> Maurice had not, and did not add that he had explored Martial.
>
> "It's all in there – not meat for babes, of course, but you ought to read it. Read it this vac." (51)

Whether or not the Dean is being hypocritical, this sense that even for Mr. Cornwallis the Greek classics revealed at times an "unspeakable vice" merely reminds us of the level of resistance to what Clive calls "the mainstay of Athenian society." To say, "the Greeks, or most of them, were that way inclined" gives a substance to the unspeakable, and because of that openness, Maurice feels "a breath of liberty." Of course, Clive's exhortation that Maurice *read* Plato's *Symposium*, which would be a reasonable suggestion among his intellectual peers, is probably a mistake. It may not be "meat for babes," but it is nevertheless difficult even for an adult, or advanced adolescent, like Maurice, to read without the supervision or engagement of a mentor. Maurice's preference for Martial suggests a simpler mode – Martial is famous for his scurrilous epigrams – and his lack of intellectual seriousness suggests that Clive would do better to read the text with Maurice, since he means it as a kind of communal experience and as a text that Bible-like will guide their actions. Because of this carelessness, or his shyness about the topic at hand, their next meeting after the vacation is something of a fiasco.

Forster's description of Maurice's time at home – as he makes decisions for the family and seems to become the man of the house (his father has been dead since his youth) – hardly prepares him for the encounter with Clive that happens shortly after their return:

> With half a dozen others he was starting for the theatre after hall when Durham called him.
>
> "I knew you read the *Symposium* in the vac," he said in a low voice.

> Maurice felt uneasy.
>
> "Then you understand – without my saying more – "
>
> "How do you mean?"
>
> Durham could not wait. People were all around them, but with eyes that had gone intensely blue he whispered, "I love you."
>
> Maurice was scandalized, horrified. He was shocked to the bottom of his suburban soul, and exclaimed, "Oh, rot!" The words, the manner, were out of him before he could recall them. "Durham, you're an Englishman. I'm another. Don't talk nonsense. I'm not offended, because I know you don't mean it, but it's the only subject absolutely beyond the limit as you know, it's the worst crime in the calendar, and you must never mention it again. Durham! a rotten notion, really – ". (58–9)

One has to feel a little sorry for Clive here. It seems in retrospect silly of him to have asked Maurice to read Plato if this was to be the result. He almost sheepishly utters this simple expression of love, somehow hoping that Maurice's reading will make him understand. As pathetic as this is, it is also important to note that Clive has, in spite of himself perhaps, fallen in love with his friend. And he is surely the first character in English fiction to give such unmistakable expression to the love between men, stated in such a way that even dull Maurice cannot be confused about what Clive means. For this, as awkward and ineffective as his gesture is, I think Clive should be celebrated.

Of course, Maurice's response is nothing like a celebration. "Shocked to the bottom of his suburban soul," he calls what Clive has said "nonsense" for two Englishmen. In other words, Maurice's deeply middle-class conscience makes it impossible for him to accept Clive's words for what they say. He may have read the *Symposium*, but he is not ready to accept the expression of love that one man addresses to another. He thinks this is a "rotten notion" because as an Englishman brought up in a Christian tradition, he has been taught to think this way, and Clive is challenging him to think differently.

It does not happen all at once – Maurice does not change his way of thinking overnight – but Clive's words do affect him, and it is not long before he is reconsidering what Clive has said.

> A slow nature such as Maurice's appears insensitive, for it needs time even to feel. Its instinct is to assume that nothing either for good or evil has happened, and to resist the invader. Once gripped, it feels acutely, and its sensations in love are particularly profound. Given time, it can know and impart ecstasy; given time, it can sink to the heart of Hell. Thus it was that his agony began as a slight regret; sleepless nights and lonely days must intensify it into a frenzy that consumed him. It worked inwards, till

it touched the root whence body and soul both spring, the "I" that he had been trained to obscure, and, realized at last, doubled its power and grew superhuman. For it might have been joy. New worlds broke loose in him at this, and he saw from the vastness of the ruin what ecstasy he had lost, what a communion. (60)

This wonderful description of the creaky movements of Maurice's feelings that gradually lead him to something like a "frenzy," realizing finally the "I" that had always been obscured, in fact expresses the full reaction to Clive's simple words, "I love you." What this is not, Forster makes clear, is an intellectual love. Clive may have been swept away intellectually by reading about the Greeks, but Maurice has not; instead he starts to imagine a response, from a careful search to the depth of his soul, to his friend's expression of love. This is the friend Maurice has imagined, and Clive has offered a bond that Maurice never dreamed would be possible in this world.

Since Maurice's first response to Clive was brutal, it does take some time for the other young man to respond to Maurice's new-found appreciation or to imagine that he is doing anything but mocking him. These kinds of misunderstanding are in part a result of feeling a love that "dare not speak its name"; speaking it, it seems, can only lead to confusion and misdirection. But it is also speech that Maurice imagines will lead them out of this wilderness.

> As the term went on he decided to speak to Durham. He valued words highly, having so lately discovered them. Why should he suffer and cause his friend suffering, when words might put all right? He heard himself saying, "I really love you as you love me," and Durham replying, "Is that so? Then I forgive you," and to the ardour of youth such a conversation seemed possible, though somehow he did not conceive it as leading to joy. He made several attempts, but partly through his own shyness, partly through Durham's, they failed. (63–4)

Failure is of course understandable given both the pressure on them to conform to a different set of values and a mutual shyness about the only issue that really matters to them at this juncture. Clive is mortified that his friend might have taken his expression the wrong way and judged him by it. The simple forgiveness and mutual love that Maurice imagines is inconceivable because an entire culture militates against it. Not just their shyness prohibits such a conversation, but everything that they have learned has taught them one way to approach one another, and that way does not include the simple expressions of love that Maurice imagines. But what about Plato's *Symposium*? In what sense does Plato's work encourage that

expression in a different way? What does it mean, that is, when Clive is
described, as he is later on, as an Hellenist, which for his country pastor, is
more dangerous than an atheist?[65]

As Dowling points out in her study of Victorian Oxford, Plato had
become central to the academic curriculum, or Greats, as the Classics are
called, under the direction of Benjamin Jowett. Dowling centers on John
Addington Symonds to make her point. Symonds had read the *Symposium*
and the *Phaedrus* when he was in public school, and as he himself records,
"Here ... I discovered the true *liber amoris* at last, the revelation I had been
waiting for."[66] Dowling comments:

> Symonds, who had earlier been both a witness to appalling scenes of the
> rankest schoolboy sex as well as a queasy recipient of caresses from his head-
> master, now realized that the erotic dream of idealized male love which he
> had cherished since early boyhood remained untainted by the brutalities
> of contemporary Harrow: "It was just as though the voice of my own soul
> spoke to me through Plato, as if in some antenatal experience I had lived the
> life of [a] philosophical Greek lover."[67]

What is there in Plato to give a young man like Symonds this new-found
purpose?

Raschke makes the point that "For Plato, the body and all materiality
become a position of illusion and nontruth. In the *Phaedo*, Socrates notes
that the 'true philosopher' must 'dissever the soul from the communion
of the body,' that the body provides knowledge of nothing." Raschke then
goes on to argue, reasonably: "That the body and materiality (that which
is to be escaped) become associated with femininity/passivity further cor-
roborates the difficulty Platonic philosophy poses as a paradigmatic homo-
eroticism."[68] Raschke cites several feminist theorists with whom she shares
the skepticism, and to their number could be added Halperin, who makes
a similar argument from a different perspective.[69]

---

[65] See p. 186 in chapter 17 for Borenius' pronouncement.
[66] John Addington Symonds, *The Memoirs of John Addington Symonds: The Secret Homosexual Life
of a Leading Nineteenth-Century Man of Letters*, ed. Phyllis Grosskurth (Chicago: University of
Chicago Press, 1986), 99; see also, Dowling, *Hellenism and Homosexuality*, 67.
[67] Symonds, *Memoirs*, 99; Dowling, *Hellenism and Homosexuality*, 67.
[68] Raschke, "Breaking the Engagement," 153; also, *Phraedus* in Plato, *The Dialogues of Plato in Four
Volumes*, trans. Benjamin Jowett (Oxford: Oxford University Press, 1892), 2.203–6.
[69] Raschke cites primarily Luce Irigaray, Hélèn Cixous, Catherine Clément, and Judith Butler in this
regard: see "Breaking the Engagement," 164–6, n. 5, 6, 10, 11. Forster's own knowledge of Greek was
such – he did Classics as his undergraduate degree at Cambridge – that he might have read Plato
in the original. If he did not, or even if he wanted to look at an English translation, he would have
looked at the same Jowett translation that I cite in footnote 14. Because Jowett's translation was the
standard from the late nineteenth until the mid-twentieth centuries, I may use his translation in

One must wonder, though, what late nineteenth- and early twentieth-century writers and thinkers found in Plato when they turned to him, much in the way Clive does, in order to find lessons of life and the meaning of love. John Addington Symonds, for instance, cites this passage from the *Phaedrus* when attempting to describe that higher form of love that he calls Greek love. In this passage Plato is describing the lover's soul:

> Wherever she thinks that she will behold the beautiful one, thither in her desire she runs. And when she has seen him and bathed herself in the waters of desire, her constraint is loosened and she is refreshed, and has no more pangs and pains, and this is the sweetest of all pleasures at the time, and is the reason why the soul of the lover will never forsake his beautiful one, who he esteems above all.

Symonds comments on this paragraph as follows: "These passages show how real and vital was the passion of Greek love. It would be difficult to find more intense expressions of affection in Western literature. The effect produced upon the lover by the presence of his beloved was similar to that inspiration which the knight of romance received from his lady."[70] In other words, what Symonds sees in passages like this is the representation of love. This love, he seems to say, is just like the most profound accounts of love that have been recorded. It is interesting that Symonds does not talk about the love being divorced from the body or removed into a spiritual plane. It is clearly of the body, even if it is not immediately expressed in physical intercourse. Love, for Symonds, involves an overwhelming feeling of longing and desire that can barely be satisfied. It is soothed in the presence of the beloved, as if "bathed in the waters of desire." This description is hardly un-physical, nor does it, for the moment reach into any other realm but the physical. Whether or not Symonds is correct in discussing Greek love in this way, it is where his own study of the classics has led him.

Symonds' is surely the notion of love that Clive clings to as well. He has read Plato in the very spirit that Symonds offers, and what he finds there must be equally soothing and promising to him. When Clive sends Maurice to Plato's *Symposium*, he clearly means him to find there an ideal

various places as I proceed. The implicit misogyny, of these materials and the use Forster makes of them can be inferred by Raschke's reference to French feminist theorists.

[70] John Addington Symonds, *A Problem in Greek Ethics, Being an Inquiry into the Phenomenon of Sexual Inversion: Addressed Especially to Medical Psychologists and Jurists* (London, 1901) 8–9; quotation from the *Phaedrus*, Benjamin Jowett, p. 252. This passage is translated as follows in *Plato: Complete Works*, 528–9: "But when it [the soul] looks upon the beauty of the boy and takes in the stream of particles flowing into it from his beauty (that is why it is called 'desire' [see note]), when it is watered and warmed by this, then all its pain subsides and is replaced by joy." [note about "desire": "'Desire' is *himeros*: the derivation is from meré ('particles'), *ienai* ('go') and *rhein* ('flow')."]

of love. His "I love you" outburst (58) is based on the love that Plato articulates, and if Maurice's response is directed at Clive rather than at Plato, it is still Plato's ideal of love that has shaped the terms these two men use as they declare their feelings for one another. But what is the ideal of love that is articulated in Plato's *Symposium*? Countless classical scholars and literary and cultural critics have weighed in on this topic, but that should not prohibit a fresh look at a recent translation of Plato's masterpiece to discover what Clive may have been hoping Maurice would find there.[71] Platonic love is the mainspring of much of the action in this novel, and it is also, in some sense, the reason that the relationship between Clive and Maurice breaks down.

Diotima's description of love and beauty is surely the basis of Clive's expression of love for Maurice.[72] Diotima defines love as desire for the beautiful; and as she builds her argument, we begin to see what special form this love will take. "Love is wanting to possess the good forever," Diotima says, and lovers pursue this good by "giving birth in beauty, whether in body or soul" (489).

Diotima continues,

> A lover who goes about this matter correctly must begin in his youth to devote himself to beautiful bodies. First, if the leader [i.e., Love] leads aright, he should love one body and beget beautiful ideas there; then he should realize that the beauty of one body is brother to the beauty of any other and that if he is to pursue beauty of form he'd be very foolish not to think that the beauty of all bodies is one and the same. (492)

When she comes to summing up her argument, she says,

> So when someone rises by these stages, through loving boys correctly, and begins to see this beauty, he has almost grasped his goal. This is what it is to go aright, or be led by another, into the mystery of Love: one goes always upwards for the sake of this Beauty, starting out from beautiful things and using them like rising stairs: from one body to two and from two to all beautiful bodies, then from beautiful bodies to beautiful customs, and from customs to learning beautiful things, and from these lessons he arrives in the end at this lesson, which is learning of this very Beauty, so that in the end he comes to know just what it is to be beautiful. (493)

---

[71] One of the best discussions of this topic is that to be found in Halperin, *One Hundred Years of Homosexuality*, 113–52: "Why is Diotima a Woman?" For an opposing and equally provocative account of the *Symposium*, see James Davidson, *The Greeks and Greek Love: A Bold New Exploration of the Ancient World* (New York: Random House, 2007), 321–3.

[72] Plato, *Symposium*, 484. Further parenthetical references are to this edition.

This profound understanding of beauty and this ability to learn from beautiful things is not as divorced from the body as some commentators have led us to believe. Diotima, at least, bases her entire scheme of love on the love of the beautiful body; and not only that, she insists that it is the lover who is capable of attaining the vision of Beauty that will make all experience pale before its visionary power. But this cannot happen without the love of the beautiful. Given the terms of this evening conversation, then, this love is the love of a beautiful boy or young man, whom one transforms in love into something more than a simple object of desire. The beloved in this configuration takes part in the birth of something new.

Cambridge Neoplatonists of the last years of the nineteenth and first years of the twentieth centuries would have found a helpful gloss on these ideas, if not outright inspiration, in the writing of G. E. Moore (1873–1958), the Cambridge philosopher whose *Principia Ethica* (1903) became the vade mecum of the Bloomsbury Group and the rallying cry for more than a generation of that elite secret society of Cambridge intellectuals, known as the Apostles, of whom Moore was one and for whom he wrote many papers that preceded and were later worked into *Principia*. One such paper, perhaps not directly imported into his philosophical masterpiece, but hovering somewhere behind it, was a paper he wrote in 1894 called "Achilles or Patroclus," which was an exploration of love and friendship. Paul Levy, writing about the obviously "homosexual" implications of this discussion, says that, "This tone [of homosexuality] was purely a verbal matter, a tradition that in the discussion of sexual questions it was obligatory to make the humorous assumption that all sexual relations were homosexual ones, so that even heterosexual love had to be treated as only a special case of the Higher Sodomy."[73] Steeped as they were in classical learning, and inspired as some of them, like Moore himself and Goldsworthy Lowes Dickinson (1862–1932), were by Plato, the Higher Sodomy was a catch word of writers like Lytton Strachey (1880–1932) that clearly referred to the nearly inaccessible ideal of platonic love.

In his Apostle presentation on "Achilles or Patroclus," Moore talks about friendship and gives it, according to his ethical scheme, the designation as a "Good," in that it contributes to pleasure, and Moore was still (in 1894) prepared to see pleasure as a high, if not the highest, good. At

---

[73] Paul Levy, *Moore: G. E. Moore and the Cambridge Apostles* (London: Weidenfeld & Nicolson, 1979), 140; see 139–46.

the time, the conversation about the paper was lively, and one of the group reported the following details of that conversation:

> Last night Moore read on friendship and Trevy, Mayor, and Theodore came up so that we had a very good meeting. Wedgwood and Mayor differed from the rest of us in thinking that the fact of copulation made an essential difference whereas we thought that love and friendship graduated into one another and that copulation was of secondary importance. But we differed further and a great deal as to how far it was important, symbolically or otherwise.[74]

That a discussion of love and friendship among this group might turn to the question of copulation is perhaps not surprising. What strikes me is that friendship and the notion of physical intimacy would have been on the tongues of these Cambridge intellectuals, who had not only the literary tradition of friendship but their own personal relationships to consider. This suggests to me, moreover, that these great friendships from literature, like that between Achilles and Patroclus, were always open to the interpretation that these seemingly erotic bonds were erotic in fact. I am not disagreeing with those scholars who argue that friendship was not physical; but I am noting that whatever classical sources said or did not say, a degree of eroticism was assumed, if only for the purposes of argument.[75]

In *Principia Ethica*, Moore does not return directly to this topic, but in defining the good, as he does in the last chapter of his study, he features love among those emotions that he is willing to give the highest designation. He no longer ranks goods, as he might have done in his earlier writing, but he is still ready to designate some activities as good in themselves. He places friendship in this category. But he also, in the much-discussed fifth chapter of his work, suspends the force of traditional morality and opens the door to self-determination in matters of "duty." This is what his Bloomsbury fans latched onto and that is how he became the guiding light of sexual liberation.[76] Moore's own Platonic obsession is behind these philosophical ideas, and Forster would have understood them implicitly, as he read Moore (or read about him) and thought about his notion of the good. Needless to say, Forster was skeptical, and what happens to Clive

---

[74] C. P. Sanger to Bertrand Russell, November 11, 1894. Quoted in Levy, *Moore*, 142. "Trevy," is R. C. Trevelyan (1872–1951), "Mayor" is Robin John Grote Mayor (1869–1947), and "Theodore" is Theodore Llewelyn Davies (1871–1905).

[75] See, for instance, Halperin, *How to Do the History of Homosexuality*, 117–21.

[76] This story is vividly told in Tim Regan, *Bloomsbury's Prophet: G. E. Moore and the Development of His Moral Philosophy* (Philadelphia: Temple University Press, 1986), 217–50.

would seem to be something that might happen to intellectuals who get too caught up in notions of the Higher Sodomy.[77]

At first it seems as if Clive understands something like Moore's version of platonic love and has marshaled it in his desire for Maurice. Early scenes between the two men suggest as much. And they also suggest that Maurice understands Clive and loves him in return. One powerful love scene that these men share and that we are witness to is the escapade of taking a motorbike out into the country, for which violation of college rules Maurice is "sent down"; but that is not before these two men have had a wonderful afternoon.

> They swirled across the bridge and into the Ely road. Maurice said, "Now we'll go to Hell." The machine was powerful, he reckless naturally. It leapt forward into the fens and the receding dome of the sky. They became a cloud of dust, a stench, and a roar to the world, but the air they breathed was pure, and all the noise they heard was the long drawn cheer of the wind. They cared for no one, they were outside humanity, and death, had it come, would only have continued their pursuit of a retreating horizon. A tower, a town – it had been Ely – were behind them, in the front of the same sky, paling at last as though heralding the sea. "Right turn" again, then "left," "right," until all sense of direction was gone. There was a rip, a grate. Maurice took no notice. A noise rose as of a thousand pebbles being shaken together between his legs. No accident occurred, but the machine came to a standstill among the dark black fields. The song of the lark was heard, the trail of dust began to settle behind them. They were alone.
> "Let's eat," said Clive.
> They ate on a grassy embankment. Above them the waters of the dyke moved imperceptibly, and reflected interminable willow trees. Man, who had created the whole landscape, was nowhere to be seen. (76)

This image of two men together on a motorbike, outside time and revving toward the horizon is so familiar that it is hard to imagine that it was E. M. Forster who first offered it as an image of aberrant masculine love. These two men have found something beyond the limits and confines of their families, beyond the limits and confines of Cambridge; and they find themselves together: "a cloud of dust, a stench, and a roar to the world, but the air they breathed was pure, and all the noise they heard was the long drawn cheer of the wind. They cared for no one, they were outside humanity, and death, had it come, would only have continued their pursuit of a retreating horizon." Later, when they sit by the water, there is no

---

[77] See G. E. Moore, *Principia Ethica* (Cambridge: Cambridge University Press, 2000 [1903]), chapters 5 and 6, 192–273.

one around them, and when a farmer passes, he does not even notice them. It is as if they have become one with nature. That oneness is a new position for them, and if they could take it in the right spirit it would liberate them. Liberate them into the beautiful, Plato might say, and indeed, this freedom could be the freedom to pursue the beauty that they see in one another. But almost immediately they are brought into the world of family and Cambridge once again. Maurice is sent down, and this results in a crisis with his family, which Maurice's attitude about not apologizing only exacerbates. But when Clive and Maurice work out that his apology and a return to Cambridge will give them both another year together, Maurice agrees to swallow his pride and apologize.

This conversation occurs during Maurice's important visit to Clive's house at Penge, where in a study, set between their bedrooms, fitted out to remind them of Cambridge, they talk long into the night. They talk about love and art – Clive talks about why he has two roads to the appreciation of Michelangelo – and they seem as much in love as ever:

> And their love scene drew out, having the inestimable gain of a new language. No tradition overawed the boys. No convention settled what was poetic, what absurd. They were concerned with a passion few English minds have admitted, and so created untrammelled. Something of exquisite beauty arose in the mind of each at last, something unforgettable and eternal, but built of the humblest scraps of speech and from the simplest emotions.
> "I say, will you kiss me?" asked Maurice, when the sparrows woke in the eaves above them, and far out in the woods the ringdoves began to coo.
> Clive shook his head, and smiling they parted, having established perfection in their lives, at all events for a time. (93)

The love, as it is first described, seems true. Foster articulates the kinds of challenges facing these young men who are trying to love in so unconventional a way that there are neither rules nor conventions for them to follow. But in doing so, they are able to discover "something of exquisite beauty … something unforgettable and eternal, but built of the humblest scraps of speech and from the simplest emotions." Then there is the question of the kiss and Clive's smiling denial of the one thing Maurice really needs to sustain him in this new-found happiness. Nothing is said now, but Clive's refusal of the kiss and his later refusal to express love physically, is the measure of his own tragedy.

After this experience, we hear of their ensuing years of "happiness":

> During the next two years Maurice and Clive had as much happiness as men under that star can expect. They were affectionate and consistent by nature, and, thanks to Clive, extremely sensible. Clive knew that ecstasy

cannot last, but can carve a channel for something lasting, and he contrived a relation that proved permanent. If Maurice made love it was Clive who preserved it, and caused its rivers to water the garden … Their happiness was to be together; they radiated something of their calm among others, and could take their place in society. (98)

Many critics forget these two seemingly happy and domestically satisfying years. Clive is given credit for being "sensible" and for managing a life in a context that militates against the happiness of two men together. We learn later that these two men have nights together in the city and that Maurice also visits Penge. The two families have become close, and there is an ease of movement where there might have been awkwardness – for reasons of class and background – before. Right in the center of this novel, then, Forster posits two grown men sharing a life together and loving each other to the exclusion of all else. They see themselves as a couple, even if they maintain separate residences and masquerade their true affection. They are happy, or at least as happy as "men under that star can expect"; but even with that qualification, the word happy is clear and the duration is significant. Still, the tension of such a life, the constant pressure of hiding your true self from the world, must have been intense: this might have been enough to cause Clive's later breakdown. But Forster has also already planted a deep seed of discontent. Clive's love, it seems, is not physical, and if this relationship fails, I think it is reasonable to believe that we can trace that failure back to Clive's refusal to kiss. We are only rarely privileged to encounter Clive's inner thoughts, but from things that Forster says now and others that appear when he is later confronting the loss of Maurice, we understand that Clive is afraid of physicality. In the night of their long and deep conversation, as other critics have noted, Clive seems to express disgust with the physical.[78] But that is not what is said here, when Clive and Maurice have managed to put together a life that they share:

> Their happiness was to be together; they radiated something of their calm amongst others, and could take their place in society.
>   Clive had expanded in this direction ever since he had understood Greek. The love that Socrates bore Phaedo now lay within his reach, love passionate but temperate, such as only finer natures can understand, and he found in Maurice a nature that was not indeed fine, but charmingly willing. He led the beloved up a narrow and beautiful path, high above either abyss. It went on until the final darkness – he could see no other terror – and when that descended they would at all events have lived more fully than either saint or sensualist, and would have extracted to their utmost the nobility and sweetness of the world. (98)

---

[78] Raschke, "Breaking the Engagement," 160.

Clive seems in this passage to have held himself and his beloved to a
Platonic standard of love, which he understands in the terms he outlines
here: "passionate but temperate," leading the beloved "up a narrow and
beautiful path," meant to avoid the extremes of saint or sensualist, thereby
extracting "to their utmost the nobility and sweetness of the world." This
is all well and good as an ideal, but it is impossible not to wonder how
Clive has understood Plato and what this noble love actually amounts to.
Diotima talks about an upward movement from the love of beautiful bodies to the love of beauty in general; but she does not make this sound as
an automatic climb or one that is always successful. For this ascent to be
successful, it has to be based in Love: but Clive cannot help but be afraid
of the love that he is trying to celebrate. This may be why Clive collapses,
as he does, when dining with Maurice and his family, too soon after a
bout of influenza. When Maurice bends over and kisses him, he is clearly
appalled; and this hint of nervous instability grows even more threatening
when Clive visits Greece and starts even to question his love for Maurice.
In almost an instant he changes from loving men to loving women. This
happens, ironically, when he is sitting amid the ruins of ancient Greece.

In a sense, the scenes in Greece could almost be said to predict this
shift. He does not find the land romantic or inspiring in any way. Instead,
he finds the place dissatisfying and antipathetic, and he almost surprises
himself with his change of erotic direction:

> Clive sat in the theatre of Dionysus. The stage was empty, as it had been
> for many centuries, the auditorium empty; the sun had set though the
> Acropolis behind still radiated heat. He saw barren plains running down
> to the sea ... But he saw only dying light and a dead land. He uttered no
> prayer, believed in no deity, and knew that the past was devoid of meaning
> like the present, and a refuge for cowards.
>
> Well, he had written to Maurice at last. His letter was journeying down
> to the sea ... "Against my will I have become normal. I cannot help it." The
> words had been written.
>
> He descended the theater wearily. Who could help anything? Not only
> in sex, but in all things men have moved blindly, have evolved out of slime
> to dissolve into it when this accident of consequences is over. μη φυναι
> τον απαντα νικα λογον sighed the actors in this very place two thousand
> years before. Even that remark, though further from vanity than most, was
> vain. (116)[79]

---

[79] The Greek quote is explained in David Leavitt's Penguin edition: "Not to be born, is past all prizing
best" (Willard R. Trask, trans. from Sophocles, *Oedipus at Colonnus* (l. 1225)).

Clive is in a kind of despair, and this letter to Maurice is cowardly, thoughtless, and aggressive. Confronted with the scene of Greek love, Clive finds that it is virtually meaningless to him. For the meaning of Greek love, the love itself, is necessary before any other of its transformative powers can be experienced. Clive lacks that love. It is not platonic love or Hellenism that fails Clive. What fails Clive is friendship, which for him is finally neither true nor transformative. He understands what Maurice needs, and it is a kind of love he cannot offer. If he could simply approach Maurice on his own terms and offer him a true friendship, of the kind Stewart offers Rickie in *The Longest Journey*, then they might have reached a richer understanding. Instead, Clive has tried to find some "Higher Sodomy," intellectually realized, divorced from the physical, and poised on idealistic transformation. But he tries to do that without even being able to kiss his friend. Rather than see the kiss as a collapse into the erotic, it is possible to see the kiss as a sign of true love, of the love that friends can share. In rejecting that physical touch and turning instead to the spiritual, Clive corrupts the spiritual and renders it meaningless. That is what happens in Greece. Because the friendship fails, the love fails as well. Clive's later collapse in Maurice's arms is a measure of how much that failure has cost him.

Maurice on the other hand has learned to love from Clive, but his love, neither intellectual nor couched in anything but his actual feelings for his friend, cannot be given up as easily or even sacrificed as willingly as Clive's can be. Maurice suffers, to be sure, but when he calls out in his pain – as he does on two different nights from his upper chamber at Penge – he is answered by the young groundskeeper who bounds through the window and takes him in his arms. Maurice at first is afraid of his feelings for Alec Scudder, whom he discovers at Penge when his attempts at mesmerism, his last attempt to change who he is, fail before the reality of this physical love. What Maurice feels about Alec, who comes to him in the night and with whom he is allowed to express love in physical terms at last, are the things he has been taught: Alec is uneducated and from a lower class. For Maurice there is transgression even in considering a bond with such a person. When he tries to ignore his feelings for Alec, and then hears from the boy, this is what he is forced to imagine:

> A nice situation! It contained every promise of blackmail, at the best it was incredible insolence. Of course he shouldn't answer, nor could there be any question now of giving Scudder a present. He had gone outside his class, and it served him right. (207)

On the one hand he feels that he has been a "traitor" to his family (206) and here, in a way, to his class. He also imagines that it is impossible to cross the class boundary and find happiness. Even at his most worried, however, about Scudder's class difference, Maurice knows that he offers something distinct from what Clive offered him. For one thing: "By pleasuring the body Maurice had confirmed – that very word was used in the final verdict – he had confirmed his spirit in its perversion, and cut himself off from the congregation of normal man" (214). As the novel reaches its denouement, this fear of class difference at first seems to put these two men at cross purposes, and when they meet at the British Museum, and Scudder unfolds his plan to blackmail him, Maurice knows that it is all a "muddle" (226), and he seems to come to an understanding of what it means for two men of different classes to love one another. Maurice recognizes Alec as someone who deserves his full attention:

> "Oh, let's give over talking. Here – " and he held out his hand. Maurice took it, and they knew at that moment the greatest triumph ordinary man can win. Physical love means reaction, being panic in essence, and Maurice saw now how natural it was that their primitive abandonment at Penge should have led to peril. They knew too little about each other – and too much. Hence fear. Hence cruelty. And he rejoiced because he had understood Alec's infamy through his own – glimpsing, not for the first time, the genius who hides in man's tormented soul. (226)

Physical love is "panic in essence," perhaps, because all the protective language of platonic love is abandoned and the men touch each other without any barriers of language. Once Maurice can take Alec seriously and speaks to him directly, these two men discover how much they can share. It is not an easy connection, but it is one that can triumph over this fear and find a bond that breaks the barriers to love that had haunted Maurice's relation with Clive.

After this encounter, Maurice and Alec still nearly misunderstand one another – Maurice goes to the ship that is to take Alec to the Argentine, and Alec sends Maurice a telegram he never receives, but still they find one another in the end. That is, they find themselves together in the boat house once again. Maurice approaches the structure in need of rest:

> The boathouse offered itself conveniently for that purpose. He went in and found his lover asleep. Alec lay upon piled up cushions, just visible in the last dying of the day. When he woke he did not seem excited or disturbed

and fondled Maurice's arm between his hands before he spoke. "So you got the wire," he said.

"What wire?"

"The wire I sent off this morning to your house, telling you...." He yawned. "Excuse me, I'm a bit tired, one thing and another ... telling you to come here without fail." And since Maurice did not speak, indeed could not, he added, "And now we shan't be parted no more, and that's finished." (240)

But once they go off together, it is Clive who finds he is alone and desperate. When Maurice at last confronts Clive and tells him what he plans, Clive can hardly believe him. He treats Maurice, in fact, as if this announcement doesn't really matter:

> He invited Maurice to dine with him the following week in his club up in town.
>
> A laugh answered. He had always liked his friend's laugh, and at such a moment the soft rumble reassured him ...
>
> His last words were "Next Wednesday, say at 7:45. Dinner-jacket's enough, as you know."
>
> They were his last words, because Maurice had disappeared thereabouts, leaving no trace of his presence except a little pile of the petals of the evening primrose, which mourned from the ground like an expiring fire ...
>
> He did not realize that this was the end, without twilight or compromise, that he should never cross Maurice's track again, nor speak to those who had seen him. He waited for a little in the alley, then returned to the house, to correct his proofs and to devise some method of concealing the truth from Anne. (246)

The novel ends with Clive plotting a deception for Anne, a self-deception, as it were. Even his assumptions that Maurice will be available for the regular round of clubs and dinners are utterly unfounded. Maurice has moved beyond him. As Clive stands there with his thin plans for the future – a loveless marriage, dinner at the club, a friendship that mocks the meaning of the word – he can almost demand our sympathy. How many thousands of men have made a similar choice – out of fear or panic or disgust – that drives them from their true selves into a masquerade that can persuade everyone that they are not what they fear: everyone but themselves, that is. Clive is that man who does not know how to love, and as a result he sacrifices the very people who might have saved him.

These two novels speak to each other, to be sure. But they also speak to us over the century since they were written. They remind us why platonic love was so important in the late nineteenth and early twentieth centuries.

They also shine light into the tunnel of gay history, offering us a glimpse of what at least one early gay pioneer was bold enough to imagine. That Forster was ready to have *Maurice* published at all is a sign that he understood its place in twentieth-century sexual liberation. And by insisting on this tension between platonic and erotic love, Forster reminds us of how crucial friendship remains to the history of sexuality.

Epilogue
Queer Friendship in A Single Man

Christopher Isherwood's *A Single Man* (1962) begins and ends in death. Early in the novel, George, its hero, remembers his lover who was killed in a car crash some time before:

> Breakfast with Jim used to be one of the best times of their day. It was then, while they were drinking their second and third cups of coffee, that they had their best talks. They talked about everything that came into their heads – including death, of course, and is there survival, and, if so, what exactly survives.[1]

This mention of death does not in itself constitute an obsession, but as the novel proceeds, the hero, George, thinks about little else. He has lost his partner Jim and now he thinks about how long he can survive without him. Death becomes a constant presence in the novel. Claude Summers says, "the awareness of death heightens the need to live fully and to love."[2] Here, for instance, is what George thinks when he visits his friend Doris (really Jim's friend Doris), who is dying of cancer: "Jim used to moan and complain and raise hell over a head cold, a cut finger, a pile. But Jim was lucky in the end – the only time when luck really counts. The truck hit his car just right. He never felt it" (95). He thinks about his own mortality too, in the bathroom, in the gym, and when he is thinking about how much he misses his lover.[3]

---

[1] Christopher Isherwood, *A Single Man* (Minneapolis: Minnesota University Press, 2001 [1964]), 15. Further references are included parenthetically in the text.

[2] Claude Summers, " 'The Waters of the Pool': Christopher Isherwood's *A Single Man*," in *Gay Fictions Wilde to Stonewall* (New York: Continuum, 1990), 195–214 (213).

[3] In the recent film of *A Single Man*, directed by Tom Ford and starring Colin Firth, this obsession with death is expressed by George's almost comic attempt to plan his own suicide throughout the film. Some viewers objected that this was not "in the novel," but it is there in this obsession, and I think Ford found a very useful way to dramatize those feelings that George mostly articulated only internally.

Elegiac in its way, this opening may suggest a debilitating melancholic encounter with the figure of loss and George's frustrated realization that his life is behind him; but that is not what transpires at all. Isherwood transforms the elegiac here: melancholy gives way to a more present life, while death becomes a kind of challenge that will lead George to new discoveries of what life can mean. Elegiac friendship, erotic friendship, and platonic love are all at work in this novel, and it almost seems as if Isherwood was interested to see how these various traditions might play out in a single novel covering a single day. George pushed friendship as far as it can be pushed, and then it almost seems to push back at him.

His confrontation with death does not stop George from finding himself sexually aroused; in fact, it seems to heighten his excitement. For he does get turned on both when he sees some sexy tennis players engaged in a game on the courts of Cal State San Tomas, where he teaches, and when he gazes out at the undergraduates as he walks to class. He is also clearly aroused by Kenny, the student who pursues him home at the end of the novel. And just before the heart attack that separates him from his body, he has a satisfying fling of masturbatory sex, thinking about both Kenny and the tennis players. His obsession with death does not stop him, that is, from such immediate and continual, if momentary, pleasures.

Instead a version of death (or what might even be called a rejection of life and futurity) is expressed throughout the novel by means of George's hatred of children and the "breeders" that surround him in the Santa Monica hideaway that he had shared with Jim. He is not just opposed to the presence of the children as an annoyance in aggregate, but he also has deep hatred for individual monsters who torment him:

> Ah, here's Benny, hammer in hand. He hunts among the trash cans set out ready for collection on the sidewalk and drags out a broken bathroom scale. As George watches, Benny begins smashing it with his hammer, uttering cries as he does so; he is making believe that the machine is screaming with pain. And to think that Mrs. Strunk, the proud mother of this creature, used to ask Jim, with shudders of disgust how he could bear to touch those harmless baby king snakes! (23)

George's not-so-subtle demonization of the child, which happens here and elsewhere in *A Single Man*, is almost shocking to a twenty-first-century gay culture in which the child and reproduction are being claimed as basic gay rights. For George, and for Isherwood himself, I would argue, this push for gay marriage and gay adoption would be an anathema. His sexuality makes him an outsider, and he may share outsider status with other minorities, but that does not mean that he wants to have all the rights that the majority has. I would argue that he prefers to be different.[4] Like other mid-twentieth-century gay crusaders, Isherwood did not seek assimilation or acceptance: he preferred the privacy and exoticism of outsider status.[5]

Of course George makes claims for his lover Jim, and he insists that their relationship be seen as a relationship in and of itself. At one point in the novel he tells his neighbor, an author of a book that offers simplistic psychological explanations for George's "condition" "your book is wrong, Mrs. Strunk … when it tells you that Jim is the substitute I found for a real son, a real kid brother, a real husband, a real wife. Jim wasn't a substitute for anything. And there is no substitute for Jim, if you'll forgive my saying so, anywhere" (29). George rejects easy psychoanalytic explanations in favor of the reality of the experience that the two men shared. But this also says that he did not want Jim as a husband or a wife any more than he wanted him as a father or a son. He loved Jim as Jim.

This is as different from recent neo-liberal gay politics as it could be. The figure that Isherwood creates is closer to being a "desiring machine" of the Deleuze and Guattari model than he is to being a Freudian case study.[6] Jim or no Jim, for instance, his immediate attraction to the tennis players, especially to the darker player – "he is Mexican, maybe, black-haired, handsome, catlike, cruel, compact, lithe, muscular, quick and graceful on his feet" – suggests that he is not talking about sexual desire that could be packaged according to any specific category or agenda.

That refusal to categorize is of course central to his refusal – Isherwood's refusal, I think – to give a name to George's sexuality. George articulates the queer epithet that one of the neighbors might throw at him – "Mr. Strunk, George supposes, tries to nail him down with a word. *Queer*, he growls" (27) – but he never uses that or any other name for himself. Much

---

[4] George's fantasy of destruction does not account for the possible return of these children as ghosts, but as Kathryn Stockton reminds us, gay child ghosts abound in twentieth-century literature. See, *The Queer Child: Or Growing Sideways in the Twentieth Century* (Durham, NC: Duke University Press, 2009), 17–22. She sees "proto-gay" children as "hovering, barely surfacing … threatening to depress or scare their parents" (18).

[5] See Summers, "The Waters of the Pool." In a *Gay Sunshine* Interview with Charles Henri Ford in 1974, we can find this interchange: "Ira Cohen [Interviewer]: So you think in spite of all the so-called changes in America, and talk about sexual revolution and bisexuality, gay liberation, you feel it's still pretty contorted and not very successful? Ford: I don't know, maybe for others it's been a great liberation but sex is still kind of sick in New York, as far as I can see. Lots of drinking and lots of cruising and lots of hustling. It doesn't have the naturalness that Greece has" (*Gay Sunshine Interviews*, ed. Winston Leyland (San Francisco: Gay Sunshine Press, 1978), 51). Ford, born in 1910, was a near-contemporary of Isherwood, and it helps to see this attitude, even if it is different from Isherwood, it suggests how many different attitudes might exist at that one historical moment.

[6] Gilles Deleuze and Félix Guattari, *Anti Oedipus: Capitalism and Schizophrenia*, trans. Robert Hurley (New York: Penguin, 2009).

later in the novel, when he is talking to Kenny, he protests against categories in these terms:

> Look – things are quite bad enough anyhow, nowadays – we're in quite
> enough of a mess, semantically and every other way – without getting our-
> selves entangled in these dreary categories. I mean what is this life of ours
> supposed to be *for*? Are we to spend it identifying each other with cata-
> logues, like tourists in an art gallery? Or are we to try to exchange *some* kind
> of signal, however garbled, before it's too late. *You* answer *me* that! (174)

George is talking specifically about the category "dirty old man," which
he imagines Kenny might suspect him of being, but of course his speech
applies to categories in a more general way, and especially about the topic
just under the surface in this conversation with Kenny: what category do
we use for our mutual sexual desire?

George's obsession with death, his hatred of children and of the breeder
culture around him, his refusal to see his relationship with Jim in the categories that straight culture offers him, and his rejection of any form of
sexual label makes this as queer a text, if not queerer, than any others in
this study. George in fact calls to mind that queer figure that haunts Lee
Edelman's *No Future*. Edelman's concern with outsider status is evident
in his diagnosis of political failure: "The structuring optimism of politics
to which the order of meaning commits us, installing as it does the per-
petual hope of reaching meaning through signification, is always, I would
argue, a negation of this primal, constitutive, and negative act."[7] Edelman's
argument involves a rejection of what he calls "reproductive futurity." For
Edelman, "The Child … marks the fetishistic fixation of heteronormativity: an erotically charged investment in the rigid sameness of identity that
is central to the compulsory narrative of reproductive futurism."[8]

Interestingly enough, the tensions of heteronormativity lead Isherwood's
George to imagine a fantasy terrorist role for himself. As he imagines some
of the hateful characters in his own world – a newspaper editor who is
attacking "sex deviates" and a hawkish senator who would like nothing
more than to attack Cuba with a nuclear missile – George decides:

> we must launch a campaign of systematic terror. In order to be effective, this
> will require an organization of at least five hundred dedicated individuals.
> The head of the organization will draw up a list of clearly defined, simple
> objectives, such as the removal of that apartment building, the retirement

---

[7] Lee Edelman, *No Future: Queer Theory and the Death Drive* (Durham, NC: Duke University Press, 2004), 4–5.
[8] Edelman, *No Future*, 21.

of that senator, regardless of the time taken or the number of casualties. In each case, the principal criminal will first receive a polite note, signed "Uncle George," explaining exactly what he must do before a certain deadline if he wants to stay alive. (38–9)

George has this fantasy as he is driving to work along the California freeways. This fantasy of power – the kind of power that is expressed by its very impossibility – offers something to thrill this isolated queer man. George opts out in a similar way, but he elects to celebrate his choice with the violence implicit in widespread assassination.

If the queer embraces the death drive in order to resist the overwhelming cultural force of reproductive futurism; if being true to one's queer self means accepting the symptom of this future obsessed cultural moment, confronting death as a statement about life; then this death is really a different kind of life.[9] This is what happens to Isherwood's George in *A Single Man*, and it seems to be the lesson that George learns after his long and exhausting day of personal interactions.

In *A Single Man*, Isherwood confronts this cultural impasse in a number of different ways. In the first place, we notice a narrative obsession with bodily waste. George empties his bladder and moves his bowels with great narrative fanfare. He sweats at the gym, and he urinates after masturbating at bedtime. These bodily processes serve to remind us, not of abjection, as this constant attention to physical waste might, but of the very physicality of George, his mortal being, as it were, that has its finite place in the world, and nowhere else.[10] This comes through most vividly, I think, in a scene that takes place just after his hours at the university. He is pleased with how his class has gone, and he has been talking with colleagues and remembering some intense conversations he has had with some of them. He steps off the public stage, as it were, into a kind of anonymity. Then the narrator tells us how George is feeling:

> Together with this anonymity, George feels a fatigue coming over him which is not disagreeable. The tide of his vitality is ebbing fast, and he ebbs

---

[9] "Only by renouncing ourselves can queer escape the charge of embracing and promoting a 'culture of death,' earning the right to be viewed as 'something far greater than what we do with our genitals' … This, I suggest, is the ethical burden to which queerness must accede in a social order intent on misrecognizing its own investment in morbidity, fetishization, and repetition: to inhabit the place of meaninglessness associated with the sinthome; to figure an unregenerate, and unregenerating sexuality whose singular insistence on jouissance, rejecting every constraint imposed by sentimental futurism, exposes aesthetic culture – the culture of forms and their reproduction, the culture of Imaginary lures – as always already a 'culture of death' intent on abjecting the force of a death drive that shatters the tomb we call life" (Edelman, *No Future*, 47–8).

[10] The richest connection between bodily waste and abjection is that found in Julia Kristeva, *Powers of Horror: An Essay on Abjection* (New York: Columbia University Press, 1982).

with it, content. This is a way of resting. All of a sudden, he is much, much older. On his way out to the parking lot, he walks differently, with less elasticity, moving his arms and his shoulders stiffly. He slows down. Now and then his steps actually shuffle. His head is bowed. His mouth loosens and the muscles of his cheeks sag. His face takes on a dull dreamy placid look. He hums queerly to himself, with a sound like bees around a hive. From time to time as he walks, he emits quite loud, prolonged farts. (93)

In this passage, which in some ways is meant to convey the notion of physical decay, something more than abjection is at work here. George settles into his older version of himself with a kind of easy relaxation. This bowed, shuffling creature is actually humming pleasantly, *queerly*, to himself. He might almost be called happy, or at least self-satisfied, in spite of his obvious physical decay. The "loud, prolonged farts," with which the passage ends, are an emanation of that satisfaction, even as they are indicative of age and lack of self-control. George is more deeply, almost aggressively, physical than other characters I have considered. As such, he reminds us of the physicality of experience and of the physical in all the friendships we may have wanted to spiritualize. George is a physical being first, and a physical being last, if it really comes to that.

This kind of deep confrontation with physicality in all its manifestations, suggests to me that George is himself the symptom of everything the Southern Californian culture of sun, and health, and family, would repress.[11] What more obvious example of this reversal of perspective could there be than George. George denies the appeal of a fantasy of futurity even as he mocks those public figures who are installing bomb shelters and urging war with the Soviet Union. George's bodily functions, as much, if not more, than his emotional turmoil, are a measure of George: who and what he is. This makes him a fascinating figure in many ways, but it also makes him an implicitly threatening one. George is bodily present in this novel – more bodily present than any other character I have considered – and that places him more definitely and defiantly in the world he occupies.

Much later in the novel, George talks with his middle-aged ex-pat English friend Charlotte, or Charley, about the past and the future, and he talks about both those things, and the present, too, in his drunken conversation with Kenny. In the first instance, while he momentarily seems nostalgic about his life with Jim, after she has been talking about going back to

---

[11] For Edelman, "denying the appeal of fantasy, refusing the promise of futurity that mends each tear, however mean, in reality's dress with threads of meaning … offers us fantasy turned inside out, the seams of the costume exposing reality's seamlessness as mere seeming, the fraying knots that hold each sequin in place now usurping that place" (*No Future*, 35).

England, "Sort of going back to the place where I turned off the road, do you see?" He says to Charley:

> "No. I don't see."
>
> "But, Geo-the *past!* Surely you can't pretend you don't know what I mean by that?"
>
> "The past is something that's over."
>
> "Oh really – how *can* you be so tiresome?"
>
> "No, Charley, I mean it. The past is over. People make believe that it isn't, and they show you things in museums. But that's not the past. You won't find the past in England. Or anywhere else, for that matter."
>
> "Oh, you're tiresome!" (141)

This is a desultory conversation at the end of a drunken evening, but still George gets at something that Charley cannot understand. There is no past for George because he is learning to live in the present. Now is what George is ready to experience – not more, not less. His memories of Jim are not the past so much as they are part of his present moment, and without them he would not be the person he is. This insistence on now, the rejection of melancholic nostalgia, seems almost to embrace the green-wood that Forster holds out as a possibility at the end of *Maurice*. He is creating a magical space of his own.

While he is with Charley, a little before this discussion of the past, he in fact remembers his conversation with an uncle of Jim's who phoned to tell him the news of Jim's accident.

> And then, at least five minutes after George has put down the phone, when the first shock wave had hit, when the meaningless news suddenly meant exactly what it said, his blundering gasping run up the hill in the dark, his blind stumbling on the steps, banging at Charley's door, crying blubbering howling on her shoulder, in her lap, all over her; and Charley squeezing him, stroking his hair, telling him the usual stuff one tells. (126)

This event from the past is with them during this evening that they share, even if George never articulates his sense of loss openly to Charlotte. He remembers that on that miserable night he at first felt he had betrayed Jim by running to Charley, but now he says: "that night, in purest ignorance, she taught him a lesson he will never forget – namely that you can't betray (that idiotic expression!) a Jim, or a life with Jim, even if you try" (127). It is not that there is no "life with Jim" to be betrayed, but rather that the life with Jim had its existence in the past, and it has no actual relation to what has happened since Jim's death. George does not especially want to go on living, the novel makes clear, but that is not the same thing as living in the past. It is the present that he feels willing to accept, even at his peril.

Even later, in his long encounter with Kenny that nearly closes the
novel, George returns to the theme of past and present. In his Platonic
dialogue with Kenny – "you have to be symbolic figures – like, in this case,
Youth and Age" (154) – George challenges Kenny about his distance from
events that transpired in the past. Of course, it is more than suggestive that
George thinks of a Platonic dialogue, since it is in Plato's *Symposium* that
the very ideal of the erotic mentor/mentee relationship is articulated and
explored, and in more or less the very terms that George employs in this
increasingly challenging conversation with Kenny. At this moment, Kenny
is saying that he is not terribly interested in the things out of the past that
George teaches:

> "I guess," [Kenny says,] "that's because we don't have any pasts of our own –
> except stuff we want to forget, like things in high school, and times we acted
> like idiots – "
> "Well, fine! I can understand that. You don't need the past, yet. You've
> got the present."
> "Oh, but the present's a real drag! I just despise the present – I mean, the
> way it is right now – I mean, tonight's an exception, of course – What are
> you laughing at, sir?"
> "Tonight – *sí!* The present – *no!*" George is getting noisy. Some people
> at the bar turn their heads. "Drink to tonight!" He drinks, with a flourish.
> "Okay," says George. "The past – no help. The present – no good.
> Granted. But there's the future. You can't just sneeze that off."
> "I guess we are. What's left of it. There may not be much, with all these
> rockets – "
> "Death."
> "Death?"
> "That's what I said."
> "Come again, sir. I don't get you."
> "I said death. I said do you think about death a lot?" (156–7)

Their conversation leads inevitably to death, as any conversation about
time must. George reminds Kenny that they will both die, George rather
sooner than Kenny, perhaps, but they will both die, as death is the lot of
all. The answer to death is, of course, the emphasis on the power of the
present. George wants to explain this to Kenny, but Kenny is too young
to understand what George is getting at. That is probably why he turns
to death.

That George could use this dilation on death as a mode of seduction is
a measure of his sudden queer strength. George wants Kenny to see him
as another physical being, as a body with desires, and Kenny seems almost
afraid to make that leap. For now, however, as George begins to talk about

the relative value of experience – "I, personally, have gotten steadily sillier and sillier" (160) – Kenny suggests that they go swimming in the Pacific. George takes Kenny up on that, and he has an amazing experience that has all the features of a consummation of everything that has been happening.

> George staggers out once more, wide-open-armed, to receive the stunning baptism of the surf. Giving himself to it utterly, he washes away thought, speech, mood, desire, whole selves, entire lifetimes; again and again he returns, becoming always cleaner, freer, less. He is perfectly happy by himself; it's enough to know that Kenny and he are the sole sharers of the element. The waves and the night and the noise exist only for their play. (162–3)

"Cleaner, freer, less": George celebrates this stripping away of layers and this reduction to a basic element. The freedom is in fact not undermined by George's near drowning, which happens next. In a sense, that is the fulfillment that George is seeking. It is not that he wants to die, but rather that he accepts the notion of his own demise. That is not a "death wish," but it is so close as to be almost indistinguishable.

After this experience in the sea, George and Kenny go back to George's place. Earlier, he chided himself at the idea of inviting Kenny back "(A voice inside George says, *You could invite him to stay the night at your place. Tell him you'll drive him back in the morning.* What in hell do you think I am? George asks it. *It was merely a suggestion*, says the voice)" (153); but now the suggestion is unrehearsed: " 'Can we go back to your place, sir,' he [Kenny] asks. 'Sure. Where else?' " (164).

Once at George's house – after the ritual of swimming has stripped George "clearer, freer, less" – the encounter between these two men enters a different register. Kenny showers and emerges wrapped in a blanket – "Kenny comes down wearing the blanket awkwardly, saved-from-shipwreck style" (166) – and while George swigs more and more Scotch, he asks Kenny more questions about his relationship with Lois and about, in short, his sex life. Kenny tells a story about how resistant Lois has been and how bad he feels trying to drag her to unsavory motels. He also talks about her refusal to consider marriage because he does not come from a Japanese family, as she does. Once he has told George this, he says that he should be going. But George tells him the buses won't be running at that hour, and he makes a proposal.

Very carefully, but indirectly, he offers Kenny free use of a bedroom in his house for Friday nights. "These nights, when I have supper with my friend, *I shall never, under any circumstances*, return here before midnight. Is that clear?" (172). And as he continues he spells this out even more: "All right! I have made a decision and now I've told you about it. Just as I might tell you I'd decided to water the garden on a certain day of the week. I have also told you a few facts about this house. You can make a note of them. Or you can forget them" (172). George is being as direct as he dare be in this situation, and Kenny understands him. But he is also embarrassed. To release the tension, George sends Kenny to get him another drink. "Is that an order, sir?" "You're damn right it is!"

After this encounter George enters a new phase. "George transformed: a formidable George ... An inquisitorial George, seated in judgment and perhaps to pass sentence. An oracular George" (173). "I suppose you've decided I'm a dirty old man?" he tells Kenny. And then he answers himself:

> "You needn't say anything," George tells Kenny (thus dealing with either possibility), "because I admit it – oh, hell, yes of course I admit it – I *am* a dirty old man. Ninety-nine percent of all old men are dirty. That is, if you want to talk in that language; if you insist on that kind of dreariness. I'm not protesting against what you choose to call me or don't. I'm protesting against an attitude – I'm only doing that for your sake not mine." (174)

It almost seems as if George is rambling, but this sudden shift to the question of language takes him into one of his most important pronouncements of all, as I quoted above: "Look – things are quite bad enough anyhow, nowadays – we're in quite enough of a mess, semantically and every other way – without getting ourselves entangled in these dreary categories" (174).

Given the sexually charged nature of the situation, George's history of loss, and Kenny's obvious fascination with George himself, and despite Kenny's attraction to Lois, George is talking about the categories of sexuality. George is claiming experience itself, the experience of these two men together in the middle of the night, as a means to defy attempts to label and categorize. George makes this even more explicit:

> Here am I. Here are you – in that damned blanket. Why don't you take it right off, for Christ's sake? What made me say that? I suppose you're going to misunderstand that, too? Well, if you do, I don't give a damn. The point is – here am I and here are you – and for once there's no one to disturb us. This may never happen again. I mean that literally! And the time is *desperately* short. All right, let's put the cards on the table. Why are you here in this room at this moment? *Because you want me to tell you something!* That's the true reason you came all the way across town tonight ... You came here this evening to *see me* – whether you realize it or not ... The point is, you came to ask me about something that really *is* important. So why be ashamed and deny it? You see, I know you through and through. I know *exactly* what you want. You want me to tell you *what I know*.

Oh, Kenneth, Kenneth, believe me – there's nothing I'd rather do! I want *like hell* to tell you. But I can't. I quite literally can't. Because, don't you see, *what I know is what I am?* And I can't tell you that. You have to find it out for yourself. I'm like a book you have to read. A book can't read itself to you. It doesn't even know what it's about. I don't know what I'm about. (175–6)

"Here am I and here are you … And the time is *desperately* short": this claim on the present moment as a precious moment that two men share, this insistence on the urgency of the moment: this is what George has to offer Kenny. Later he seems to equivocate and avoid direct statement, but what he is telling Kenny is absolutely direct. He is offering himself to Kenny in a way that would make it possible for the boy to think of this as the exploration of the older and more experienced man. Plato's *Symposium* is indirectly invoked once again – at least some of what is discussed there touches on this theme – even though the Platonic dialogue itself has been forgotten in a haze of alcohol. But just as Plato, in *Lysis* refuses to take the final step, in which the boy would recognize his interlocutor as the loving mentor he needs, so too George can only fascinate Kenny but he can never persuade him.

George goes on to flatter Kenny and to challenge him along the terms he has already established:

You could know what I'm about. You could. But you can't be bothered to. Look – you're the only boy I ever met on that campus I really believe could. That's what makes it so tragically futile. Instead of trying to know, you commit the inexcusable triviality of saying, "he's a dirty old man," and turning the evening, which might be the most precious and unforgettable of your young life, into a *flirtation!* You don't like that word, do you? But that's the word. It's the enormous tragedy of nowadays: flirtation. Flirtation instead of fucking, if you'll pardon my coarseness. All any of you ever do is flirt, and wear your blankets off one shoulder, and complain about motels. And miss the one thing that might really – and Kenneth, I do not say this casually – *transform your entire life.* (176–7)

"Flirtation instead of fucking": that puts a lot of George's ranting in perspective. But it doesn't undo the force of what he is saying. He places the immediate satisfaction of fucking in the context of a deeper knowledge. But in a sense, the attainment of that satisfaction is the deeper knowledge. And it almost seems that Kenny understands this, even as he flees.

George passes out and shortly after awakes to find a note from Kenny:

Thought maybe I'd better split, after all. I like to wander around at night. If those cops pick me up, I won't tell them where I've been – promise! Not even if they twist my arm!

That was great, this evening. Let's do it again, shall we? Or don't you believe in repeating things?

Couldn't find pajamas you already used, so took these clean ones from the drawer. Maybe you sleep raw? Didn't want to take the chance, though. Can't have you getting pneumonia, can we?

Thanks for everything,
Kenneth

Kenny seems to understand everything that has transpired, but in another way, he seems clueless. He's provocative, but still more in the realm of the flirtatious than anything more serious. "George sits on the bed reading this. Then with slight impatience, like a general who has just glanced through an unimportant dispatch, he lets the paper slip to the floor … Little teaser, his mind says, but without the least resentment. Just as well he didn't stay" (177–8). George likes Kenny, even though Kenny hasn't accepted his challenge this evening.

After he gets into bed, George begins to masturbate. He begins by imagining Kenny with one of the tennis players, but when George "enters," the Kenny he is imaging seems on the verge of giggles, so he substitutes the other tennis player, and as the two go at it, "George hovers above them watching; then he begins passing in and out of their writhing bodies. He is either. He is both at once. Ah – it is so good" (179–80). "You old idiot, George's mind says [after he comes]." But he is not ashamed of himself. Claude Summers says, "even the comic masturbation scene, so often in literature an emblem of loneliness and isolation, here symbolizes George's transformation from passive observer to active participant."[12] Active, to be sure, but removed at the same time: it is as if he stands outside of the very experience he records. He sees his life, that is, from a distance, and that distance is what creates comedy, even for George.

After this excitement, George falls asleep, and as Summers says, "he cedes the past to Charley and the future to Kenny, but clings to Now: 'It is Now that he must find another Jim. Now that he must love. Now that he must live….'"[13] And he dies. The death, as Summers notes, is "only suppositional," but it is posited clearly, and it releases George into something else: "if some part of the nonentity we called George has indeed been absent at this moment of terminal shock, away out there on the deep waters, then it will return to find itself homeless" (186).[14] But Isherwood

---

[12] Summers, " 'The Waters of the Pool,' " 212.
[13] See also Summers, " 'The Waters of the Pool,' " 212.
[14] Summers, " 'The Waters of the Pool,' " 212.

does not follow George into that other region. Instead he ends the novel with this image:

> For it can associate no longer with what lies here, unsnoring on the bed. This is now cousin to the garbage in the container on the back porch. But will have to be carted away and disposed of, before too long. (186)

This image of the material body, now dispossessed of George and seeming more like garbage, takes us far from the opening of the novel. But it is somehow less than tragic, this merely physical remainder. Love and friendship have no place in this final "garbage" image, but they have nonetheless shaped these desperate pages and they have given them more significance than other novels of the period have managed.

Isherwood understands this notion of queerness, and pushing George through his masturbation scene toward his death offers a vivid account of what Edelman calls "De-idealizing the metaphorics of meaning on which heteroreproduction takes its stand."[15] If Isherwood has done anything, it has been to "de-idealize the metaphorics of meaning." George nurtures a memory of Jim in the past, but then he forswears the past. He celebrates his own sexuality, even (or even more) when it offers him a simple outlet from the tensions of the day. In his enjoyment is embedded his death. Isherwood suggests that "deep down in one of the major branches of George's coronary artery, an unimaginatively gradual process began" (185) all those years ago when George "first set eyes" (185) on Jim at the Starboard Side.

George's death is a fulfillment of his devotion to living in the Now. It gives more meaning to the simple gestures of friendship in the novel. They define him now in a different way. Summers talks about George's "union with the universal consciousness," and that may well be something Isherwood has in mind.[16] But what he shows us is George's empty carcass. Still, the ending does not feel tragic. Death emerges as if it were a part of life.

This is in recognition of the truth of death: death as the end of all the desire that is articulated in the novel. What more resounding statement of the meaning of life could there be? That is where Isherwood takes us in the novel, and that is why it is as unsettling as it is. George is queer in these uncompromising terms, and he dies as he lives, at one with his limited physical desiring self. If friendship hovers here between life and death – a

---

[15] Edelman, *No Future*, 27.
[16] Summers, " 'The Waters of the Pool,' " 212.

lost ideal and shimmering possibility – this queer friendship takes its place as the answer to every question George has asked.

I said at the opening of this chapter that friendship pushes back. What I mean is that George's experiment of platonic friendship with a younger man becomes a moment of private masturbation that transforms the deep meaning of friendship into a quick release of sexual satisfaction. Friendship leaves George in this simple confrontation with himself. It almost undoes him: the "writhing bodies" are what move him, even as he laughs at himself as an old idiot at taking his pleasure. But this laugh, if it is a laugh, as he steps outside himself, marks this as a triumph of friendship after all. George dies in the knowledge that he has given Kenny something he would never otherwise have had.

This ending is less profound, perhaps, than the sudden discontinuance of talk at the end of Plato's *Lysis*. There we wish for more conversation in order to reach some kind of truth. But Isherwood has led us to his kind of truth: George's dead body lies there as a mode of confrontation. But the novel reminds us of how much life there is even in this remarkable last day. And that is a cause for celebration.

Works Cited

Ackerman, Susan. *When Heroes Love: The Ambiguity of Eros in the Stories of Gilgamesh and David.* New York: Columbia University Press, 2005.

Battestin, Martin C. "Introduction," in *Amelia.* Middletown: Wesleyan University Press, 1983. xv–lxi.

Battestin, Martin C., with Ruthe E. Battestin. *Henry Fielding: A Life.* New York: Routledge, 1989.

Bender, John. "Impersonal Violence: The Penetrating Gaze and the Field of Narration in *Caleb Williams,*" in *Critical Reconstructions: The Relationship of Fiction and Life,* ed. Robert M. Polhemus and Roger B. Hinkle. Stanford: Stanford University Press, 1994. 111–26.

Bray, Alan. *The Friend.* Chicago: University of Chicago Press, 2003.

"Homosexuality and the Signs of Male Friendship in Elizabethan England," *History Workshop Journal* 29 (Spring 1990): 1–19; reprinted in *Queering the Renaissance,* ed. Jonathan Goldberg. Durham, NC: Duke University Press, 1994. 40–61.

Bree, Linda. "Introduction," in *Amelia.* Peterborough, ONT: Broadview Press, 2010. 9–30.

Bristow, Joseph. *Effeminate England: Homoerotic Writing after 1885.* New York: Columbia University Press, 1995.

Brooks, Peter. *Reading for the Plot: Design and Intention in Narrative.* New York: Alfred A. Knopf, 1994. Reprinted Cambridge, MA: Harvard University Press, 2002.

Brown, Walter. *Walter Scott and the Historical Imagination.* London: Routledge & Kegan Paul, 1979. 6–30.

Buckton, Oliver S. "'The Reader Whom I Love': Homoerotic Secrets in *David Copperfield,*" *ELH* 64.1 (1997): 189–222.

Campbell, Jill. *Natural Masques: Gender and Identity in Fielding's Plays and Novels.* Stanford: Stanford University Press, 1995.

Cantrell, Pamela. "Writing the Picture: Fielding, Smollett, and Hogarthian Pictorialism," *Studies in Eighteenth-Century Culture* 24 (1995): 68–89.

Castle, Terry. *Masquerade and Civilization: The Carnivalesque in Eighteenth-Century English Culture and Fiction.* Stanford: Stanford University Press, 1987.

Chaterjee, Ranita, and Patrick M. Horan. "Teaching the Homosocial in Godwin, Hogg, and Wilde," in *Approaches to Teaching Gothic Fiction*, ed. Diane Long Hoeveler and Tamar Heller. New York: MLA, 2003. 127–32.

Cheyne, George. *The English Malady*, ed. Eric Carlson. Delmar: Scholar's Facsimiles and Reprints, 1976 [1733].

Childers, Joseph. " 'What do you play, boy?': Violence, Masculinity, and 'Beggaring your Neighbor' in *Great Expectations*." Unpublished manuscript.

Cicero. "De Amicitia," in Cicero, *De Senectute, De Amicitia, De Divinatione*, trans. William Armisted Falconer. Cambridge, MA: Harvard University Press, 1923. 103–211.

Cohen, William A. *Sex Scandal: The Private Parts of Victorian Fiction*. Durham, NC: Duke University Press, 1996.

Corber, Robert. "Representing the 'Unspeakable': William Godwin and the Politics of Homophobia," *Journal of the History of Sexuality* 1 (1990): 85–101.

Craft, Christopher. *Another Kind of Love: Male Homosexual Desire in English Discourse, 1850–1920*. Berkeley: University of California Press, 1994.

"'Descend, Touch, and Enter': Tennyson's Strange Manner of Address," in *Another Kind of Love, Male Homosexual Desire in English Discourse 1850–1920*. Berkeley: University of California Press, 1994. 44–70.

Cregan-Reid, Vybarr. "Bodies, Boundaries, and Queer Waters: Drowning and Prosopoeia in Later Dickens," *Critical Survey* 17.2 (2005): 20–33.

Daffron, Eric. "'Magnetical Sympathy': Strategies of Power and Resistance in Godwin's *Caleb Williams*," *Criticism* 37.2 (Spring 1995): 213–32.

D'Arcy, Julian Meldon. *Subversive Scott: The Waverley Novels and Scottish Nationalism*. Reykjavik: University of Iceland Press, 2005.

Das, Santanu. *Touch and Intimacy in First World War Literature*. New York: Cambridge University Press, 2005.

Davidson, James. *The Greeks and Greek Love: A Bold New Exploration of the Ancient World*. New York: Random House, 2007.

Day, Robert Adams. "Sex, Scatology, Smollett," in *Sexuality in Eighteenth-Century Britain*, ed. Paul-Gabriel Boucé. Manchester: Manchester University Press, 1982. 225–43.

Deleuze, Gilles, and Félix Guattari. *Anti Oedipus: Capitalism and Schizophrenia*, trans. Robert Hurley. New York: Penguin, 2009.

Dellamora, Richard. *Friendship's Bonds: Democracy and the Novel in Victorian England*. Philadelphia: University of Pennsylvania Press, 2004.

Derrida, Jacques. *The Politics of Friendship*, trans. George Collins. New York: Verso, 2005.

Dickens, Charles. *Great Expectations*. London: Penguin, 1996 [1860–1].

Dowling, Linda. *Hellenism and Homosexuality in Victorian Oxford*. Ithaca: Cornell University Press, 1994.

Edelman, Lee. *Homographisis: Essays in Gay Literary and Cultural Theory*. New York: Routledge, 1994.

No Future: Queer Theory and the Death Drive. Durham, NC: Duke University Press, 2004.

Ellis, Havelock. *Sexual Inversion*. 3rd ed. Philadelphia: F. A. Davis, 1931.

Felman, Shoshona. *The Literary Speech Act: Don Juan with J. L. Austin, or Seduction in Two Languages*, trans. Catherine Porter. Ithaca: Cornell University Press, 1983.

Ferris, Ina. *The Achievement of Literary Authority: Gender, History, and the Waverley Novels*. Ithaca: Cornell University Press, 1991.

Fielding, Henry. *Amelia*, ed. Martin C. Battestin. Middletown: Wesleyan University Press, 1983 [1751].

Forster, E. M. *The Longest Journey*, ed. Elizabeth Heine. London: Penguin, 2006 [1907].

Maurice. New York: Norton, 1993.

Maurice, ed. David Leavitt. London: Penguin, 2005 [1971].

Fothergill, Brian. *The Strawberry Hill Set: Horace Walpole and his Circle*. London: Faber, 1983.

Frankel, Nicholas. *The Picture of Dorian Gray: An Annotated, Uncensored Edition*. New York: Belknap Press, 2011.

Freccero, Carla. "Queer Spectrality: Haunting the Past," in *A Companion to Lesbian, Gay, Bisexual, Transgender, and Queer Studies*, ed. George E. Haggerty and Molly McGarry. Oxford: Blackwell, 2007. 194–213.

Furneaux, Holly. *Queer Dickens: Erotics, Families, Masculinities*. Oxford: Oxford University Press, 2009.

Gay Sunshine Interviews. Ed. Winston Leyland. San Francisco: Gay Sunshine Press, 1978.

Gilbert, Sandra M., and Susan Gubar. *The Madwoman in the Attic: The Woman Writer and the Nineteenth-Century Literary Imagination*. New Haven: Yale University Press, 1979.

Godwin, William. *Caleb Williams*, ed. Gary Handwerk and A. A. Markley. Peterborough, ONT: Broadview, 2000 [1794].

Gold, Jr., Alex. "It's Only Love: The Politics of Passion in Godwin's *Caleb Williams*," *Texas Studies in Language and Literature* 19 (1977): 135–60.

Goldberg, Jonathan. *Sodometries: Renaissance Texts, Modern Sexualities*. Palo Alto: Stanford University Press, 1992.

Gray, Erik. "Introduction," in *In Memoriam*. New York: Norton, 2004. xi–xxvii.

Gray, Thomas. "Elegy Written in a Country Churchyard," in *Poems by Mr. Gray: A New Edition*. London: J. Dodsley, 1768. 109–20.

Haggerty, George E. "Amelia's Nose; or, Sensibility and Its Symptoms," *The Eighteenth Century: Theory and Interpretation* 36 (1995): 139–56.

"Desire and Mourning: The Ideology of the Elegy," in *Ideology and Form*, ed. David Richter. Lubbock: Texas Tech University Press, 1999. 184–206.

Horace Walpole's Letters. Lewisburg: Bucknell University Press, 2011.

Men in Love: Masculinity and Sexuality in the Eighteenth Century. New York: Columbia University Press, 1999.

Unnatural Affections: Women and Fiction in the Later Eighteenth Century. Bloomington: Indiana University Press, 1998.

Hallam, Arthur. "Essay on Cicero." Quoted in Christopher Ricks, "*In Memoriam, 1850*," in *Tennyson*, 2nd ed. London and Berkeley: Macmillan and University of California Press, 1989. 201–18.

Halperin, David M. *How to do the History of Homosexuality*. Chicago: University of Chicago Press, 2002.

  One Hundred Years of Homosexuality and Other Essays on Greek Love. New York: Routledge, 1989.

Hammond, Dorothy, and Alta Jablow. "Gilgamesh and the Sundance Kid: The Myth of Male Friendship," in *The Making of Masculinities: The New Men's Studies*, ed. Harry Brod. Boston: Allen & Unwin, 1987. 241–58.

Handwerk, Gary. "Of Caleb's Guilt and Godwin's Truth: Ideology and Ethics in *Caleb Williams*," *ELH* 60 (1993): 939–60.

Heine, Elizabeth. "Editor's Introduction," in E. M. Forster, *The Longest Journey*, Vol. 2, Abinger edition. London: Edward Arnold, 1984. vii–lxv.

  "Afterword," in E. M. Forster, *The Longest Journey*. London: Penguin, 2006. 291–349.

Hodges, Devon. "*Frankenstein* and the Feminine Subversion of the Novel," *Tulsa Studies in Women's Literature* 2.2 (Fall 1983): 155–64.

Hook, Andrew. "Introduction," in *Waverley; Or Sixty Years Since*. London: Penguin, 1988. 9–27.

Hornback, Bert G. *Great Expectations: A Novel of Friendship*. Boston: Twayne, 1987.

Isherwood, Christopher. *A Single Man*. Minneapolis: Minnesota University Press, 2001 [1964].

Janes, Dominic. *Visions of Queer Martyrdom, from John Henry Newman to Derek Jarman*. Chicago: University of Chicago Press, 2015.

Jeffreys, Peter. *Eastern Questions: Hellenism and Orientalism in the Writings of E. M. Forster and C. P. Cavafy*. Greensboro: ELT Press, 2005.

Johnson, Barbara. "My Monster/ My Self," in *The Barbara Johnson Reader: The Surprise of Otherness*, ed. Melissa Fruerstein, Bill Johnson González, Lili Porten, and Keja Valens. Durham, NC: Duke University Press, 2014. 179–90.

Kaplan, Carola M. "Absent Father, Passive Son: The Dilemma of Rickie Elliot in *The Longest Journey*" in *E. M. Forster*, ed. Jeremy Tambling. New York: St. Martin's Press, 1995. 51–66.

Kiely, Robert. *The Romantic Novel in England*. Cambridge, MA: Harvard University Press, 1972.

King, Ross. "*Tristram Shandy* and the Wound of Language," in *Laurence Sterne's Tristram Shandy: A Casebook*, ed. Thomas Keymer. Oxford: Oxford University Press, 2006. 123–46.

King, Thomas. *The Gendering of Men, 1600–1750*. 2 vols. Madison: University of Wisconsin Press, 2004, 2008.

Kristeva, Julia. *Black Sun: Depression and Melancholia*, trans. Leon S. Roudiez. New York: Columbia University Press, 1989.

  Powers of Horror: An Essay on Abjection. New York: Columbia University Press, 1982.

Lamb, Charles. "Sterne's Use of Montaigne," *Clio* 32.1 (Winter 1980): 1–41.

Lamont, Claire. "Introduction," in Sir Walter Scott, *Waverley*. Oxford: Oxford University Press, 1998 [1986].

Lawler, Donald L. "Keys to the Upstairs Room: A Centennial Essay on Allegorical Performance in *Dorian Gray*," in *The Picture of Dorian Gray*, ed. Donald L. Lawler. New York: Norton, 1988. 431–57.

Lawlor, Claire. "Consuming Time: Narrative and Disease in *Tristram Shandy*," in *Laurence Sterne's* Tristram Shandy: *A Casebook*, ed. Thomas Keymer. Oxford: Oxford University Press, 2006. 147–67.

Leavitt, David. "Introduction," in E. M. Forster, *Maurice*. London: Penguin, 2005. xi–xxxvi.

Levy, Paul. *Moore: G. E. Moore and the Cambridge Apostles*. London: Weidenfeld & Nicolson, 1979.

London, Bette. "Mary Shelley, *Frankenstein*, and the Spectacle of Masculinity," *PMLA* 108.2 (March 1993): 253–65; reprinted in the Norton Critical Edition of *Frankenstein*, ed. Paul Hunter. New York: Norton, 2012. 391–403.

Lumsden, Alison. *Sir Walter Scott and the Limits of Language*. Edinburgh: Edinburgh University Press, 2010.

Markley, Robert. "Sentimentality as Performance: Shaftesbury, Sterne, and the Theatrics of Virtue," in *The New Eighteenth Century*, ed. Felicity Nussbaum and Laura Brown. New York: Routledge, 1987. 210–30.

McFarlane, Cameron. *The Sodomite in Fiction and Satire, 1660–1750*. New York: Columbia University Press, 1997.

McKenna, Neil. *Oscar Wilde: An Intimate Biography*. New York: Basic Books, 2011.

Mellor, Anne K. "Possessing Nature: The Female in *Frankenstein*," in the Norton Critical Edition of *Frankenstein*, ed. Paul Hunter. New York: Norton, 2012. 355–68.

Miller, Jacqueline T. "The Imperfect Tale: Articulation, Rhetoric, and Self in *Caleb Williams*," *Criticism* 20 (1978): 366–82.

Miracky, James. *Regenerating the Novel: Gender and Genre in Woolf, Lawrence, Forster, Sinclair, and Lawrence*. New York: Routledge, 2003.

Miyoshi, Misao. *The Divided Self: A Perspective on the Literature of the Victorians*. New York: New York University Press, 1969.

Moffat, Wendy. *A Great Unrecorded Life: A New Life of E. M. Forster*. London: Picador, 2011.

Montaigne, Michel de. "On Affectionate Relationships," in *The Complete Essays*, ed. and trans. M. A. Screech. London: Penguin, 2003. 205–27.

Moon, Michael. "Memorial Rags," in *Professions of Desire*, ed. George E. Haggerty and Bonnie Zimmerman. New York: MLA, 1995. 233–40.

Moore, G. E. *Principia Ethica*. Cambridge: Cambridge University Press, 2000 [1903].

Mowl, Timothy. *Horace Walpole: The Great Outsider*. London: John Murray, 1996.

Mullan, John. *Sentiment and Sociability: The Language of Feeling in the Eighteenth Century*. Oxford: Clarendon, 1988.

Nunokawa, Jeff. "*In Memoriam* and the Extinction of the Homosexual," *English Literary History* 58.2 (1991): 427–38.

Phillips, Jerry. "Narrative, Adventure, and Schizophrenia: From Smollett's *Roderick Random* to Melville's *Omoo*," *Journal of Narrative Theory* 25.2 (1995): 177–201.

Plato. *Phraedus. The Dialogues of Plato in Four Volumes*, trans. Benjamin Jowett. Oxford: Oxford University Press, 1892.

Plato: Complete Works, trans. Stanley Lombardo, ed. John M. Cooper. Indianapolis: Hackett, 1997.

Symposium, trans. Alexander Nehamas and Paul Woodruff. In *Plato: Complete Works*, ed. John M. Cooper. Indianapolis: Hackett, 1997. 457–505.

Potkay, Adam. "Liberty and Necessity in Fielding's *Amelia*," *The Eighteenth-Century Novel* 6–7 (2009): 335–58.

Rahman, Tariq. "Alienation and Homosexuality in E. M. Forster's *The Longest Journey*," *The Literary Half-Yearly* 27.1 (1986): 44–65.

Rajan, Tilottama. "Judging Justice: Godwin's Critique of Judgment in *Caleb Williams* and Other Novels," *The Eighteenth Century* 51 (2010): 341–62.

"Wollstonecraft and Godwin: Reading the Secrets of the Political Novel," *Studies in Romanticism* 27 (1988): 221–51.

Raschke, Deborah. "Breaking the Engagement with Philosophy: Re-envisioning Hetero/Homo Relations in *Maurice*," in *Queer Forster*, ed. Robert K. Martin and George Piggford. Chicago: University of Chicago Press, 1997. 151–65.

"Re-Envisioning the Platonic Ideal: Forster's *Passage to India and Maurice*," in *Modernism, Metaphysics, and Sexuality*. Selinsgrove: Susquehanna University Press, 2006. 102–27.

Regan, Tim. *Bloomsbury's Prophet: G. E. Moore and the Development of His Moral Philosophy*. Philadelphia: Temple University Press, 1986.

Ricks, Christopher. "*In Memoriam*, 1850," in *Tennyson*, 2nd ed. London and Berkeley: Macmillan and University of California Press, 1989. 201–18.

Rizzo, Betty. *Companions Without Vows: Relations Among Eighteenth-Century British Women*. Athens, GA: University of Georgia, 1994.

Rogers, Pat. "Introduction," in *Platonism and the English Imagination,* ed. Anna Baldwin and Sarah Hutton. Cambridge: Cambridge University Press, 1994. 181–5.

Ross, Ian Campbell. *Laurence Sterne: A Life*. Oxford: Oxford University Press, 2001.

Rousseau, G. S. "The Pursuit of Homosexuality in the Eighteenth Century: 'Utterly Confused Category' and/or Rich Repository?" *Eighteenth-Century Life* 9 (1985): 132–68.

Sabor, Peter. "*Amelia*," in *The Cambridge Companion to Henry Fielding*, ed. Claude Rawson. Cambridge: Cambridge University Press, 2007. 94–108.

Sacks, Peter M. *The English Elegy: Studies in the Genre from Spenser to Yeats*. Baltimore: Johns Hopkins University Press, 1985.

Schweitzer, Ivy. *Perfecting Friendship: Politics and Affiliation in Early American Literature*. Chapel Hill: University of North Carolina Press, 2006.

Scott, Sir Walter. *Waverley; Or Sixty Years Since*. London: Penguin, 1988 [1814].

Sedgwick, Eve Kosofsky. *Between Men: English Literature and Male Homosocial Desire*. New York: Columbia University Press, 1985.

Shaftesbury, Lord. *Characteristics of Men, Manners, Opinions, Times*, ed. Lawrence Klein. Cambridge: Cambridge University Press, 2001.

Shakespeare, William. *William Shakespeare: Complete Sonnets and Poems*. Oxford: Oxford University Press, 2002.

Shannon, Laurie. *Sovereign Amity: Figures of Friendship in Shakespearean Contexts*. Chicago: University of Chicago Press, 2002.

Shaw, W. David. *Elegy and Paradox: Testing the Conventions*. Baltimore: Johns Hopkins University Press, 1994.

Shelley, Mary. *Frankenstein, or The Modern Prometheus*. Oxford: Oxford University Press, 1980 [1819].

Introduction to the 1831 edition of *Frankenstein*, reprinted in the Norton Critical Edition of *Frankenstein*, ed. Paul Hunter. New York: Norton, 2012. 165–9.

Shelley, Percy Bysshe. *Epipsychidion*, in *Shelley's Poetry and Prose*, ed. Donald A. Reiman and Neil Fraisat. New York: Norton, 2002 [1821]. 390–407.

A Single Man. Directed by Tom Ford. 2009. Culver City, CA: Sony Pictures Studios, 2010. DVD.

Smith, Adam. *The Theory of Moral Sentiments*. New York: Augustus M. Kelley, 1966 [1759].

Smith, Ruth. "Love Between Men in Jennens' and Handel's *Saul*," in *Queer People: Negotations and Expressions of Homosexuality, 1700–1800*, ed. Chris Mounsey and Caroline Gonda. Lewisburg: Bucknell University Press, 2007. 226–45.

Smollett, Tobias. *The Adventures of Roderick Random*, ed. Paul-Gabriel Boucé. Oxford: Oxford University Press, 1981 [1748].

Staves, Susan. "Kind Words for the Fop," *Studies in English Literature* 22 (1982): 413–28.

Sterne, Laurence. *Tristram Shandy*. Ed. Melvyn New and Joan New. Gainesville: University Press of Florida, 1978.

A Sentimental Journey. New York: Oxford University Press, 2008.

Stockton, Kathryn. *The Queer Child: Or Growing Sideways in the Twentieth Century*. Durham, NC: Duke University Press, 2009.

Sullivan, Andrew. *Love Undetected: Notes on Friendship, Sex, and Survival*. New York: Vintage, 1999.

Summers, Claude J. *E. M. Forster*. New York: Macmillan, 1983.

"'The Waters of the Pool': Christopher Isherwood's *A Single Man*," in *Gay Fictions Wilde to Stonewall*. New York: Continuum, 1990. 195–214.

Symonds, John Addington. *The Memoirs of John Addington Symonds: The Secret Homosexual Life of a Leading Nineteenth-Century Man of Letters*, ed. Phyllis Grosskurth. Chicago: University of Chicago Press, 1986.

A Problem in Greek Ethics, Being an Inquiry into the Phenomenon of Sexual Inversion: Addressed Especially to Medical Psychologists and Jurists. London, 1901.

Tennyson, Alfred, Lord. *In Memoriam*, the Norton Critical Edition, ed. Erik Gray. New York: W. W. Norton & Company, 2004.

Thompson, James. "Surveillance in William Godwin's *Caleb Williams*," in *Gothic Fictions: Prohibition/Transgression*, ed. Kenneth Graham. New York: AMS Press, 1989. 173–98.

Trotter, David. "Introduction," in *Great Expectations*. London: Penguin, 1996. vii–xx.

Turley, Hans. *Rum, Sodomy, and the Lash: Piracy, Sexuality, and Masculine Identity*. New York: New York University Press, 2001.

Veeder, William. *Mary Shelley & Frankenstein: The Fate of Androgyny*. Chicago: University of Chicago Press, 1986.

Voogd, Peter J. de. "*Tristram Shandy* as Aesthetic Object," in *Laurence Sterne's Tristram Shandy: A Casebook*, ed. Thomas Keymer. Oxford: Oxford University Press, 2006. 108–19.

Wall, Kathleen. "Significant Form in *Jacob's Room*: Ekphrasis and the Elegy," *Texas Studies in Literature and Language* 44.3 (2002): 302–23. Reprinted in the Norton Critical Edition of *Jacob's Room*, ed. Suzanne Raitt. New York: Norton, 2007. 281–302.

Wallace, Miriam L. "Duplicitous Subjects and the Tyranny of Ideology: Godwin's *Things As They Are; or Caleb Williams* (1794) and Fenwick's *Secresy* (1795)," in *Revolutionary Subjects in the English "Jacobin Novel."* Lewisburg: Bucknell University Press, 2009. 36–60.

Welsh, Alexander. *The Hero of the Waverley Novels, with New Essays on Scott*. Princeton: Princeton University Press, 1992.

Wilde, Oscar. *The Picture of Dorian Gray*, the Norton Critical Edition, ed. Donald L. Lawler. New York: Norton, 1988.

Wilt, Judith. *Secret Leaves: The Novels of Sir Walter Scott*. Chicago: University of Chicago Press, 1985.

Wolf, Amy. "Bernard Mandeville, Henry Fielding's *Amelia,* and the Necessities of Plot," *The Eighteenth-Century Novel* 6–7 (2009): 73–102.

Woolf, Virginia. *Jacob's Room*. Oxford: Oxford University Press, 2008 [1922].

Zieger, Susan. "Dickens's Queer Children," *Literature Interpretation Theory* 20.1–2 (2009): 141–57.

Žižek, Slavoj. *The Sublime Object of Ideology*. New York: Verso, 1989.

Zwerdling, Alex. "*Jacob's Room:* Woolf's Satiric Elegy," *ELH* 48 (1981): 894–913. Reprinted in the Norton Critical Edition of *Jacob's Room*, ed. Suzanne Raitt. New York: Norton, 2007. 244–63.

Index